THE

REFERENCE

SHELF

THE SOVIET UNION

edited by JANET PODELL and
STEVEN ANZOVIN

THE REFERENCE SHELF

Volume 60 Number 2

THE H. W. WILSON COMPANY

New York   1988

THE REFERENCE SHELF

The books in this series contain reprints of articles, excerpts from books, and addresses on current issues and social trends in the United States and other countries. There are six separately bound numbers in each volume, all of which are generally published in the same calendar year. One number is a collection of recent speeches; each of the others is devoted to a single subject and gives background information and discussion from various points of view, concluding with a comprehensive bibliography. Books in the series may be purchased individually or on subscription.

Library of Congress Cataloging-in-Publication Data

Main entry under title:

The Soviet Union / edited by Janet Podell and Steven Anzovin.
     p.   cm. — (The Reference shelf ; v. 60, no. 2)
  Bibliography: p.
  Summary: Presents a compilation of reprinted articles discussing current issues and social trends in the Soviet Union, focusing on reforms initiated by Soviet leader Gorbachev and foreign policy decisions involving arms control agreements.
  ISBN 0-8242-0766-1
  1. Soviet Union—Politics and government—1982- 2. Soviet Union-
-Foreign relations—1975- 3. Gorbachev, Mikhail Sergeevich, 1931-
. 4. Soviet Union—Foreign relations—United States. 5. United States—Foreign relations—Soviet Union. [1. Soviet Union-
-Politics and government. 2. Gorbachev, Mikhail Sergeevich, 1931-
. 3. Soviet Union—Foreign relations—United States. 4. United States—Foreign relations—Soviet Union.]
  I. Podell, Janet. II. Anzovin, Steven.
  III. Series.
DK288.S66 1988
947.085'4—dc19   88-15061
                                                CIP
                                                  AC

Printed in the United States of America

CONTENTS

PREFACE

As a political entity, Russia traces its origins to the Scandinavian traders and raiders who established a state based in Kiev in the tenth century. The Soviet Union, however, is only sixty-six years old. During the first half of its existence it underwent civil war, famine, the deaths of 20 million people in World War II, the death of millions more in forced relocations, labor camps, and purges, and complete submission to a state terror establishment. The leaders who succeeded Josef Stalin in the postwar years, and the populations they ruled, were formed by these events.

Mikhail S. Gorbachev, who became general secretary of the Communist Party after the death of Konstantin Chernenko in 1985, is the first Soviet leader to come of age after the worst excesses of the Stalin years were over. The nation of which he became leader, though greatly feared in the West for its control of Eastern Europe and its subversion of progress toward democracy in developing countries, also suffered from a moribund economy and from the lack of creativity that plagues all rigid and repressive societies. According to Zhores A. Medvedev, Gorbachev's biographer, the postwar years have seen a decline in the standard of living in the USSR: " . . . [T]he food situation has deteriorated, the average diet has developed protein deficiencies, life expectancy began to decline after 1964 for all groups . . . , environmental pollution reached dangerous levels. . . . Crime, accidents, alcoholism, smoking, drug addiction, industrial accidents, and the population of the prison camps have all risen. The divorce rate has more than doubled, reaching 50 per cent in the European part of the Soviet Union. The Soviet Army is still the largest in the world and Soviet soldiers are dying in Afghanistan in a war which has been going on for longer than any war in the last two centuries of Russian history."

Gorbachev would not have come to power if he were not a dedicated Marxist-Leninist. It is to protect the Soviet system and prevent it from breaking down that he has set in motion a series of reforms that took the West (and, apparently, many Soviets as well) by surprise. This movement, called *perestroika* ("restructuring," the title of a bestselling book by Gorbachev), is described in detail in the first section of this anthology. In es-

5

sence, they require workers, bureaucrats, and everyone else to accept personal responsibility for their actions—a difficult task in a nation where all decisions are made by the state.

The aspect of perestroika that most intrigues the West is glasnost. This word, variously translated as "openness," "publicity," and "propaganda," derives from an archaic word for "voice"; what it means in practice is a selective loosening of the censorship that pervades Soviet society. The second section in this book explores the consequences of glasnost for the arts. It also examines a number of other factors with which Gorbachev and the Soviets must contend as they try to seek the right balance between Marxist doctrine and productivity.

The West, ever fearful of the USSR's intentions to remake the world in its own image, has greeted Gorbachev with a mixture of suspicion and relief. Americans, tired of the constant threat of nuclear war and of confrontations between the superpowers in every volatile region, would be pleased to find that Gorbachev is what the journalists and television cameras make him out to be, a reasonable, cosmopolitan, educated man, the opposite of the secretive, inscrutable Soviet leaders who preceded him. Yet Gorbachev, despite his attractive manner, is surely more enigmatic than they were, for he seems poised between two contradictory ideals. The third section of this volume presents a variety of views on how much we should trust Gorbachev, especially concerning arms control agreements. For, as the emigre professor Alexander Yanov remarks, "What is different about the current attempt [at reform] is that it takes place in the age of Chernobyl and Star Wars. For the first time in history the future of humanity may depend on the fate of reform in Russia."

The editors wish to thank the authors and publishers who kindly granted permission to reprint the material in this collection. Special thanks are due to Diane Podell of the B. Davis Schwartz Memorial Library, C. W. Post Center, Long Island University.

JANET PODELL

STEVEN ANZOVIN

April 1988

I. GORBACHEV'S GAMBLE

EDITOR'S INTRODUCTION

Over the four decades of the Cold War, the Soviet Union has taken its place alongside Nazi Germany in the minds of most Americans as an example of a terrifying political nightmare come to life. However troubling and intransigent the problems of America might be, there could be no comparison with the Soviet Union, an enormous prison of eight and a half million square miles whose entire population lived, ate, fought, thought, and died according to the wishes of a faceless bureaucracy. Worse, the Soviet Union appeared determined to inflict this identical misery on as many people as it could, through force, persuasion, or lies. The effort to contain this nightmare has dominated American foreign policy and heavily affected its domestic culture for generations. Liberating the Soviet people from their own system was considered to be a project attainable only through divine intervention.

Then, in March 1985, along came Mikhail S. Gorbachev, the new general secretary of the Communist Party, an agronomist, economist, and lawyer who had been rising through the party hierarchy since 1952. To the American public, which caught a good look at him when he came to Washington, D.C., for a summit meeting in the fall of 1987, he appeared to be remarkably youthful, energetic, and articulate. Still more surprising, he had proposed a series of economic and social reforms that had the potential to bring about substantial changes in the Soviet system. For this very reason, these reforms were likely to meet strong opposition from the party and from those Soviet people who fear a more open society. These reforms are described in Thomas A. Sancton's "Can He Bring It Off?," the first selection in this section, reprinted from *Time*.

Several questions have dominated the debate over Gorbachev by observers in the West. Do these reforms indicate a real willingness to restructure Soviet society in the direction of greater openness, or are they mainly cosmetic, designed to fool the West into complacency? If the reforms are legitimate, does Gorbachev have the power to impose them, and can he be removed if he goes too far? Whether he succeeds or fails, what will be the consequences for the West, and what should our stance be while we await developments?

These questions are taken up by the authors of the next three selections. Seweryn Bialer, in "Gorbachev's Move," reprinted from *Foreign Policy*, focuses on Gorbachev's efforts to modernize the economy. Dimitri K. Simes, in "Gorbachev: A New Foreign Policy?," taken from *Foreign Affairs*, examines the connection between these efforts and the USSR's relations with its client states and with the West. Both authors note the paradox that a modernized USSR, while possibly more democratic, might also be made more efficient in the pursuit of its ideological and geopolitical goals. As Bialer says, the changes have "great potential creativity and great potential destructiveness."

Vladimir Bukovsky, who spent 12 years as a political prisoner in the Soviet Union, explores another paradox in his article from *Commentary*, "Will Gorbachev Reform the Soviet Union?"—the fact that "reforms will have to be implemented through the same party apparatus whose power they inevitably serve to diminish." "If people are going to be promoted according to their talents and rewarded according to their performance," Bukovsky continues, "who will bother to join the party? And if people are not treated according to their merits, where is the reform?" In either case—whether Gorbachev chooses the party over the marketplace, or the marketplace over the party—Bukovsky predicts that the Soviet system, if given no material aid by the West, will implode within the next 20 years.

The final article, taken from Tass, presents Gorbachev's vision of Soviet history and his program of reform in his own words. It is an excerpt from a speech he delivered before 5,000 Soviet and foreign dignitaries on the 70th anniversary of the October Revolution, when the Bolsheviks seized power.

CAN HE BRING IT OFF?[1]

At first glance, Moscow this summer looks much as it has for decades: office workers queuing up at street-side ice cream stands, red-kerchiefed flocks of Young Pioneers fidgeting in the mile-long line outside Lenin's Tomb, old women sweeping court-yards with twig-bundle brooms, faded red signs proclaiming VICTORY TO COMMUNISM. But beneath the capital's seedy, socialist exterior there is an unaccustomed hum of excitement. Passersby pore over posted copies of Moscow *News*, marveling at articles on (gasp!) official corruption and incompetence. Once banned abstract paintings hang at an outdoor Sunday art fair. In public parks and private living rooms, families plan futures that many believe will be better, richer, freer than ever before. To the delight of many Soviet citizens—and the dismay of others—their country is in the midst of its most dramatic transformation since the days of Stalin.

Mikhail Gorbachev's calls for *glasnost* (openness),* *demokratizatsiya* (democratization) and *perestroika* (restructuring) have become the watchwords of a bold attempt to modernize his country's creaky economic machinery and revitalize a society stul-tified by 70 years of totalitarian rule. In televised addresses, speeches to the party faithful and flesh-pressing public appear-ances—often with his handsome wife Raisa—he has spread his gospel of modernization. Translating his words into action, he is streamlining the government bureaucracy, reshuffling the mili-tary, moving reform-minded allies into the party leadership and allowing multicandidate elections at the local level. He has loos-ened restrictions on small-scale free enterprise and introduced the profit principle in state-owned industries. His policy of open-ness has encouraged the press to speak out more freely and pro-duced an unprecedented thaw in the country's intellectual and cultural life. In the human-rights field, scores of political prison-ers have been freed and the rate of Jewish emigration has been

[1]Reprint of a magazine article by associate editor Thomas A. Sancton. *Time.* 130:30+. Jl. 27, '87. Copyright © 1987 Time Inc. All rights reserved. Reprinted by permission from TIME.

*In current Soviet parlance, the word's meaning is not so much openness as public airing or public disclosure.

increasing—to 3,092 for the first half of this year, up sharply
from last year's level but far below the peak of 51,320 in 1979.

For all his innovations, the Soviet leader has hardly, at 56, become a convert to Western-style democracy. He rose to power
through the Communist hierarchy and deeply believes in the tenets of Marx and Lenin. His goal is not to scrap that system but
to save it from permanent economic decline through a series of
bold, pragmatic measures. As he told a gathering of editors and
propagandists in Moscow on July 10: "We intend to make socialism stronger, not replace it with another system."

Gorbachev's rejuvenating crusade raises the question of
whether he can achieve durable change without provoking insurmountable opposition from party conservatives and fearful bureaucrats. After all, Nikita Khrushchev was swept from power 23
years ago for attempting reforms far less daring than Gorbachev's. More recently, when Deng Xiaoping's economic liberalization in China began to spill over into the political sphere, hardliners rose up and forced the ouster of reformist Communist
Party Chief Hu Yaobang early this year. Even if such internal party opposition does not stop Gorbachev, how far can he push
change without unleashing democratic forces that could ultimately destabilize Soviet society? Mindful of that danger, Gorbachev warned the editors and propagandists that openness "is not
an attempt to undermine socialism."

Gorbachev cleared a major hurdle at last month's Central
Committee plenum, when he won backing for a far-reaching new
law on state enterprises. The measure is intended to loosen the
stranglehold of the central planning bureaucracy by giving greater independence to factory and farm managers. Among other
provisions, it will require that local managers be elected by their
workers and that the country's 48,000 state enterprises fund new
and continuing operations from their own profits. Before the law
takes effect next January, it must be accompanied by a package
of enabling legislation dealing with such things as credit and finance, technological research and an overhaul of the state-controlled pricing system.

Gorbachev had in fact prepared eleven draft decrees along
those lines, but chose not to put them to a vote at the plenum.
Some Western analysts took this as a sign that he had yet to overcome resistance from conservatives among the Central Committee's 307 members, 60% of whom are holdovers from the

Brezhnev era. Gorbachev is widely expected to seek a purge of such foot draggers at a national party conference that he has scheduled for June 1988. Nonetheless, the plenum left little doubt about his political strength, which was underscored by the naming of three of his supporters to the ruling Politburo. The new appointments meant that Gorbachev allies now occupy at least half of the 14 seats on the expanded Politburo.

Gorbachev had demonstrated his clout four weeks before the plenum by taking swift action against the military in the wake of West German Pilot Mathias Rust's spectacular landing just outside Red Square. When the Hamburg teenager's single-engine Cessna penetrated some 400 miles of Soviet airspace with impunity, Gorbachev immediately sacked Defense Minister Sergei Sokolov and Air Defense Chief Alexander Koldunov. In addition to giving the country an object lesson in the personal accountability of those in power—and demonstrating the military's subservience to the political leadership—Gorbachev seized the occasion to place a reform-minded ally, General of the Army Dmitri Yazov, 63, in the Defense Minister's job.

In the past month, and especially in the wake of the Central Committee session, Gorbachev has moved decisively in the direction of what he calls radical reform. Before the plenum, some Western analysts suspected that *perestroika* was largely a rhetorical exercise backed by a set of diluted half-measures. But Gorbachev's latest proposals, along with recent declarations by some of his key economic advisers, point to more far-reaching structural changes. Economist Abel Aganbegyan, for example, has advocated letting prices rise to market levels. At present, government subsidies on such items as food, clothing and shelter run to $114 billion a year, straining the government budget and encouraging shortages and inefficiency. Aganbegyan has also raised the possibility of closing "thousands" of unprofitable enterprises.

Similarly radical solutions were outlined by Economist Nikolai Shmelev in the June issue of *Novy Mir* (New World), a literary monthly. Lambasting inept managers for "their feudal ideology," he warned that "economics has laws that are just as terrible to violate as the laws of the atomic reactor in Chernobyl." Shmelev called for the introduction of free-market mechanisms even if that meant tolerating unemployment—a concept virtually unheard of in the Soviet Union. Gorbachev later praised the article for painting a "picture close to what in fact exists," but he stressed his commitment to full employment.

Gorbachev must realize, however, that any meaningful reform of pricing and central planning will inevitably cause some inflation and unemployment. Another consequence of his proposals would be an increase in pay incentives, thus risking the creation of rich and poor in a society that has long been, for the most part, egalitarian in pay though not in perquisites. Perhaps a greater danger is that incentives may undermine the very ideological underpinnings of Communism and thus prove unworkable. Nonetheless, Gorbachev appears to be serious about that reform. As he said in his plenum speech last month, "It is particularly important that the actual pay of every worker be closely linked to his personal contribution to the end result, and that no limit be set." The Soviet leader also applied the profit principle to agriculture, calling for a sharp increase in small-scale private farming to supplement the inadequate output of the collective farms. In a departure from traditional Soviet thinking, he declared that "competition is central to activating the motive forces of socialism."

In these and other ways, the General Secretary has hurled new challenges at a nation that was temperamentally and ideologically unprepared for change. It is not surprising, therefore, that his policies have met with resistance from an entrenched party and government bureaucracy that is wary of losing its prerogatives. As Gorbachev put it in an interview with the Italian Communist Party daily *L'Unità* last May, "It is a question of old approaches, the inertia of old habits and of fear of novelty and responsibility for specific deeds. We are also being hampered by encrusted bureaucratic layers."

This opposition has no identifiable organization, leadership or platform. It includes an amorphous mass of party officials, civil servants and managers whose administrative foot dragging can stall or ultimately sabotage the reforms. Gorbachev has tightened his control over the Politburo, the party's supreme body, but he still faces formidable opposition from this large, inchoate group.

Even if he enjoyed unanimous support, Gorbachev would need a rare combination of skill and luck to solve the awesome economic problems that have been accumulating for a half-century. Stalin's legacy of centralized planning, collectivized agriculture and reliance on heavy industry, while effective at first in building up the Communist economy, ultimately produced a rigid and inefficient system. Having grown dramatically during the 1930s, the Soviet economy was sputtering along at an anemic average rate of 2% by the mid-'80s—lower than any other industrialized country except Britain. Agricultural output rose less than 1% a year between 1971 and 1979 because of a combination of bad weather and bad management. Industrial production has been chronically hampered by supply bottlenecks, absenteeism and equipment failures. Most Soviet industrial goods remain far below worldwide standards in quality and design. A recent article in a Moscow newspaper noted that 40% of the 28,056 fires reported in the city last year were caused by faulty television sets. In a 1986 speech, Gorbachev cited the example of a TV factory in Kuybyshev that turned out 49,000 defective sets. Said he: "We cannot put up with such things."

Shoddy TV sets are typical of the Soviet consumer's woes. Moscow's elephantine planning bureaucracy, which fixes production targets for more than 70,000 items and sets some 200,000 prices each year, has traditionally stinted the production of consumer goods and favored the military, heavy industry and, with impressive results, the space program. Soviet shoppers have long been subjected to recurring shortages of such essentials as shoes, matches, fruits and vegetables. This summer there have even been shortages of those most common of Soviet staples, potatoes and onions. Some 20% of the country's urban population still lives in communal apartments, where several families must share a kitchen and a bathroom. Alcoholism and a decline in the quality of health care contributed to an alarming jump in the Soviet death rate, from 6.9 per 1,000 in 1964 to 10.3 in 1980 (the figure was 8.7 for the U.S. in 1980).

By the time Gorbachev came to power, the Soviet system was desperately in need of change, and the new General Secretary was determined to bring it about. As soon as he took office, Gorbachev began preaching *perestroika*, exhorting his fellow citizens to work harder, ordering a crackdown on alcoholism and vowing to "rap inefficient economic executives over the knuckles." Meanwhile, he launched his *glasnost* campaign in a bid to win the support of the intelligentsia.

Suddenly Soviet television began broadcasting frank discussions of social and economic problems. Press articles appeared on such subjects as drug abuse and juvenile delinquency. The picture magazine *Ogonyok* and the multilanguage weekly Moscow

News started printing hard-hitting stories about corrupt officials, inefficient factories and alienated youth. *Ogonyok*, for example, has published such long-banned writers as Vladimir Nabokov and Osip Mandelstam. Moscow *News* has exposed police harassment of a journalist seeking to document shoddy construction of a power plant. Just how daring the press became is illustrated by a joke making the rounds in Moscow. A pensioner calls a friend and exclaims, "Did you see that incredible article in *Pravda* today?" "No, tell me about it," says the friend. "Sorry," the pensioner replies, "not on the phone."

Meanwhile, what is by Soviet standards a spectacular thaw has got under way in the cultural domain. During the past year more than a dozen previously banned movies have been screened before fascinated audiences. On the stage, plays like Mikhail Shatrov's *Dictatorship of Conscience* examine past failures of Communism. Anatoli Rybakov's *Children of the Arbat*, a novel that chronicles the murderous Stalinist purges of the 1930s, appeared in a literary journal after going unpublished for two decades. Last month a group of ex–political prisoners and dissident writers applied for permission to publish their own magazine, aptly titled *Glasnost*. The government has so far given no official answer, but the first issue, in the form of typed carbon copies, has been allowed to circulate freely.

By providing more journalistic and cultural freedom, Gorbachev has been able to produce an immediate, highly visible burst of reform at relatively little cost. A more difficult task will be introducing more *demokratizatsiya* into the political system, though here too the Soviets have taken some tentative first steps. Late last month, for the first time since the early days of Soviet power, voters in 5% of the country's roughly 52,000 districts were allowed to choose from party-appointed electoral lists with more candidates on the ballot than positions to be filled. The Supreme Soviet, the country's nominal parliament, voted to permit popular referendums on regional political and social issues and to allow citizens the right of judicial appeal against certain decisions by Communist Party officials.

For all his cultural and political innovations, Gorbachev's greatest challenge remains the economy. He has vowed to double economic output by the year 2000, though his policies have not yet begun to produce measurable results. Some critics say the reforms proposed so far involve more tinkering than reconstruction. Still, Gorbachev has launched an impressive array of initiatives to get the economy moving while preparing the way for more structural changes.

He has created a system of factory inspectors who can reject substandard products. Discouraged by the industrial ministries' reluctance to introduce new technology, he has formed conglomerates that combine both research and production facilities. The new high-tech factories, most of them run by the Academy of Sciences instead of the ministries, will be allowed to keep part of any profits they earn. In addition, the Academy of the National Economy is functioning as a management training institute, with seminars and case-study courses similar to those at top U.S. business schools.

Several hundred of the 48,000 state-owned firms have already been put on a self-financing basis and have elected their own plant managers. Some 20 ministries and more than 70 large firms have been allowed to buy and sell products abroad without going through the bureaucratic bottleneck of the Foreign Trade Ministry. Part of the hard currency these firms earn from such transactions may be used to buy badly needed foreign equipment and technology. A similar strategy seems to be behind a new law permitting joint ventures with foreign companies. Under regulations adopted last January, a Western firm may hold up to a 49% interest in a venture with a Soviet company.

Gorbachev has also encouraged economic innovation in agriculture and the woefully inadequate service sector. In Moscow and Leningrad, collective farms are beginning to sell produce through their own outlets as well as through the state stores. A parallel development is the appearance of private-enterprise restaurants set up in competition with state-owned eateries. Another flirtation with free enterprise is the new "individual-labor" law that took effect last May. It legalizes a kind of small-scale service business that may be run by an individual or family. Owners of private automobiles, for example, are now allowed to use their cars as taxis during their time off from regular state jobs, and skilled workers like carpenters and plumbers can legally take on private work. The government last week reported that 137,000 of these individual enterprises have been registered nationwide. For all its liberal trappings, however, the law seems aimed less at increasing consumer services than at bringing under state control—and thus taxation—a flourishing underground economy that is clearly essential to the day-to-day functioning of society.

The major obstacle to the spread of private enterprise, says Duke University Economist Thomas Naylor, "is not ideology but rather the lack of familiarity with market mechanisms." That shortcoming was illustrated recently by the baffled reaction of a shopkeeper in a state-owned Moscow clothing store when asked her views on the new private companies. Suppose someone wanted to produce shoes privately, she said. "Where would they get the leather or the rubber?" Such materials have always been distributed to state-run enterprises by Gossnab, the government's main supply agency. There is not yet a procedure under which a private shoemaker can purchase leather from a private tanner. Nor are there many credit institutions that would lend an individual producer money to start a business, much less provide the sort of venture capital that fuels entrepreneurship in the West. Work is currently under way to set up such structures.

The long-range effects of Gorbachev's policies are difficult to gauge. In 1986 the aggregate national income, roughly equivalent to the gross national product, increased by an impressive 4.1% (vs. 2.5% in the U.S.). Western experts attributed the rise to higher Soviet oil exports and the best grain harvest since 1958. Those are mostly short-term factors that do not reflect the fundamental changes the economy requires. With the current grain crop off to a bad start because of severe winter weather, this year's growth figure is likely to be lower.

Sustained economic improvement will be impossible unless Gorbachev can energize the apathetic Soviet masses. He has alienated many workers by demanding more discipline, harder work and better-quality output without giving them immediate benefits in return. His anti-alcohol drive has deprived the populace of a favorite pastime. "It's a vicious circle," says Marshall Goldman, a Soviet expert at Harvard University. "For workers to produce more, Gorbachev needs to offer them more consumer goods and services. Yet in order to be able to offer them more goods and services, he needs more productive workers."

Indeed, ordinary Soviet citizens appear to be generally supportive but widely skeptical of his reforms. When Sociologist Vilen Ivanov polled workers in a large plumbing-equipment factory, 62% complained that so far *perestroika* meant only more work. Conversations with workers bear out such ambivalence.

"You cannot imagine how much inertia there is," says Boris, a sullen, red-faced young man who works in an aging Moscow metallurgical plant. "There are no changes at all in our factory, except that we get less money now. As soon as we became self-financing, our bonuses dropped because we weren't getting big subsidies from the state anymore. There may be reforms going on somewhere out there, but they certainly aren't here."

A Ukrainian driver similarly wrote to the Central Committee last May: "We all vote yes, yes, yes for *perestroika*, but something is lacking. The desire burns inside, but when it comes out into the open it is all smoke and no fire." A woman living in a suburban Moscow housing block voices apprehension over the idea of price reform. "Whenever meat is available," she says, "the price is too high. If they raise the rent on this apartment, we will not be able to afford it. The authorities cannot raise prices because the people would have even less." Some older Soviet citizens express strong reservations about changes that they feel are compromising their Communist ideals. "I don't want life to turn into a race for rubles," says a 63-year-old educational administrator. "How can they call that Communism? This democratization smells like capitalism to me."

The new economic measures appear to have more enthusiastic backing among white-collar workers. "We've just become self-sufficient and have been promised pay increases," says a tall, well-dressed woman who works for a shoe-repair shop. "We'll be expected to do more for our money, of course, but we're all for that. I'm saving for the first time in my life." A middle-aged administrator in a Moscow carpet factory agrees that there has been visible change under Gorbachev. "People think what they're doing is more worthwhile," he says. "Russians were never given the chance to use their traditional wisdom because they were always being told what to do by bureaucrats. Now we are self-sufficient, and we feel more responsible about our work."

Whatever workers and bureaucrats may think, Gorbachev's *glasnost* has been greeted with an almost giddy euphoria by the intelligentsia. Says Yegor Yakovlev, editor of the innovative Moscow *News*: "We are hurrying, as if walking on hot coals. We want to show, print and stage all the things that were buried for decades as quickly as possible. We want to do it overnight."

That excitement is understandable. Gorbachev's reform campaign represents potentially the most wrenching transformation

in the lives of Soviet citizens since World War II. But can he succeed? Many Western experts are doubtful. Predicts former U.S.
Ambassador to Moscow Arthur Hartman: "Russian history will
prove stronger than the modernizers. Real reform means distribution of power away from the center, away from the party. I
don't think those guys will accept that voluntarily." Some students of Soviet history, noting that periods of reform have
typically alternated with periods of reaction, suggest that Gorbachev's policies may proceed for a while and then be followed by
a retrenchment, as his party and bureaucratic opponents organize to stymie them. Yet the Soviet leader has two things going
for him: a lack of alternatives to his leadership and his image
among the intelligentsia as the last best hope for reform.

Gorbachev may represent the West's last chance, at least in
this century, of better integrating the Soviet Union into the
world economy. There it would come under pressure to behave
like a Western country, competing for capital and markets, lower-
ing the barriers to foreign investment and even making its currency convertible. "The present seems to be an unusually
promising time for doing business with the Soviet Union," says
Peter Reddaway, director of the Washington-based Kennan Institute for Advanced Russian Studies. A senior U.S. diplomat in
Moscow agrees, saying that Gorbachev "may be for real, in the
sense that he's tackling the fundamentals."

The scope of Gorbachev's reforms and the vigor with which
they are being pursued indicate that they are not merely a Potem-
kin village of minor improvements designed for foreign consumption. Standing before the Central Committee last month,
Gorbachev irrevocably put his political future on the line in favor
of principles that sound like those the West has always champi-
oned: economic freedom, individual rights and private initiative.

These concepts do not mean the same in the Soviet Union as
in the West, and their application will certainly remain limited by
Western standards. There is cause for concern that an economically rejuvenated Soviet Union would be an even more dangerous
military rival than it is now. Yet if *glasnost*, *demokratizatsiya* and
perestroika result in less repressiveness and more economic security, and if that helps make the U.S.S.R. a better global citizen and
the world a safer place—some very big ifs—then the West too
may benefit from Gorbachev's reforms.

GORBACHEV'S MOVE[2]

A giant experiment has started in the Soviet Union—with years to go if Mikhail Gorbachev survives politically but with enormous global consequences whether he succeeds or fails. Both Western observers and the Soviet political public view his experiment as an attempt at economic reform. But to reverse the process of economic stagnation and modernize the Soviet economy, much more is needed than the reform of Soviet economic organization and policies. A dynamic and technologically advanced economy will require significant changes in almost all fields of endeavor. Yet the social and political order over which Gorbachev presides remains deeply Soviet in oppressiveness, centralization, bureaucratic domination, public apathy, and social inertia. More and more, the new Communist party general secretary appears to understand that success demands fundamental political and cultural change reaching to the very ideas that rule the country.

In the economic field itself the measures Gorbachev has announced thus far have been directed more at improving human performance than at promoting structural change. This distinction is critical, since the lack of such change imposes harsh limits on human performance. While limiting structural change, Gorbachev is seeking reform in two areas that may promise greater short-term improvements for the average citizen than one would expect. The first area concerns agricultural production and marketing. Agriculture already contains a significant private sector. Given the opportunity, this sector can grow quickly and deliver needed goods. By expanding private plots of land, encouraging private activities, and creating so-called family brigades on collective land, Gorbachev is determined to provide such opportunities. These steps are meant to stimulate peasants to produce more and waste less in return for a guarantee that they will enjoy the fruits of their labor. Marketing of farmers' produce is to be improved by expanding cooperative enterprises tying the farmers to urban markets.

[2]Reprint of an article by Seweryn Bialer, Ruggler Professor of Political Science and director of the Research Institute on International Change at Columbia University. *Foreign Policy.* pp. 59–87. Fall '87. Copyright © 1987 by the Carnegie Endowment for International Peace.

The potential for expanding private enterprise in the service sector also is significant. Private entrepreneurial initiative for profit may quickly produce visible expansion and improvements in this most neglected of Soviet economic sectors. If unshackled from bureaucratic restrictions, private restaurants, grocery markets, repair shops, and small production units of basic consumer goods also could make a difference for the urban dweller. Such activities, whether in agricultural production and marketing or in services, will be called cooperatives to cover with the proper ideological language what will in fact be private entrepreneurship.

In manufacturing, mining, and construction—the heart of Soviet economic power where the success of modernization finally will be decided—the chances for improvement are much less certain. The June 1987 plenum of the Soviet Communist party's Central Committee adopted by far the most important reforms in this area. Gorbachev defined his proposals to the plenum as a plan of fundamental reconstruction of the management of the economy. They mark a clear radicalization of his vision.

The new steps move beyond the changes introduced by the general secretary in the last two years. The new system seeks to replace administrative methods of management and planning with economic instruments. In theory, the new steps abolish central planning; assign to the management of an enterprise or a firm sweeping prerogatives and independence; institute a new system of quality control, price formation, and encouragement of competition; and increase the role of money, credit, and profit in economic activity. The intention is to restructure dramatically the inherited Stalinist system of centralized planning, administrative control, and bureaucratic interference in economic decision making. Transition from the existing system to the one proposed will require, just in its initial form, at least one to two years.

Yet despite the sweep of Gorbachev's program, it is doubtful that the new system can fulfill the promise of a radical improvement in capital and labor productivity, the quality of goods, and the rate of industrial growth. For at the crucial interface of price formation, quality control, and competition, it is not the market forces that will lead but administrative structures new and old. The various committees, commissions, boards, and offices will perform the role that in other, economically more successful, societies domestic markets and international competition provide.

In the decentralized environment envisaged by Gorbachev, these bureaucratic organizations may act more rationally and efficiently, but they will not eradicate the basic irrationality of the existing economic model—artificial costs, prices, and profits divorced from the quantity and quality of labor and capital employed.

Still, the proposed reform remains of great importance. It creates the organizational and psychological preconditions for a series of reforms to come later. Some of these reforms may be announced as early as the 19th party conference in June 1988, but most likely their introduction will be spread over several years. These reforms will phase, directly and indirectly, the market mechanism into price formation, quality control, and competition. Indeed, the reform announced at the June 1987 plenum makes sense only if it is treated as the preparatory stage during which the state will assign a greater and eventually maybe even central importance to market forces in Soviet economic life. It cannot be known for certain if this is Gorbachev's intention. But from press discussions and from the evolution of Gorbachev's economic thinking, this conclusion seems justified.

The most startling developments of Gorbachev's more than two years in office are not in the economy, however, but in the political and cultural areas. Already they have created turmoil with immense potential. Whether in the end it will be creative or destructive is not yet certain. These measures could change profoundly the nature of the system Gorbachev inherited unless he is forced to reverse them. In one of the world's most secretive countries, talk now is of openness. In a society that throughout its history has not known a single day of democratic order, the leadership preaches democratization and grass-roots participation. A state that has put a premium on homogeneity is shifting toward innovation and individuality. Authorities for whom the truth was once "self-evident" now promote clashing views. While stressing patriotism, they no longer equate it with the cult of the military. They are retreating from the goal of the secular utopia regularly invoked to explain societal imperfections. And they are starting to take account of the past to avoid repeating it.

Why is this exciting and, in the final analysis, dangerous experimentation taking place? It would stretch the imagination to believe that Gorbachev and his associates now accept the intrinsic value of democracy as the West understands it—genuine grass-roots political participation, openness and governmental accountability, a free press, diversity, and the unimpeded clash of ideas. A more realistic view is that for Soviet leaders the new course, with its different values, has primarily functional importance. Gorbachev and his colleagues have become "democrats" because they have concluded that this course is required as a precondition for and a part of modernization.

Thus Gorbachev realizes that the Soviet Union's systemic crisis is not primarily economic but social and political—even moral, ethical, and existential. Economic backwardness and decline are symptoms of a deeper malaise. The new course attempts to attack the crisis at its source—the alienation of the Soviet people from their government. The depth of the crisis apparently has convinced Gorbachev that economic reform must be more fundamental than he initially thought. To be effective, he needs more time. The new course clears the way for economic reform by building social, political, and cultural foundations. Gorbachev recognizes that the consolidation of power necessary to force reform demands personnel changes from top to bottom. His new course seeks to mobilize party leaders of his choice as well as the educated levels of the population, especially the creative intelligentsia, both to promote modernization and to neutralize its enemies.

Gorbachev's Vision of Reform

Gorbachev's reluctance to express publicly a coherent, integrated vision of what he is working to realize is striking. The words *novoye myshlenye* (new way of thinking), *uskorenye* (acceleration), *obnovlenye* (renewal), *perestroika* (restructuring), and *glasnost* (openness) resist clear definition. Gorbachev's approach avoids the rhetorical inflation associated with "socialism" and "communism." It also underlines the pragmatic character of the reform effort, which is directed toward shaping the political, social, cultural, and psychological conditions that in the long run may create an environment more conducive to better overall performance by administrators, managers, and workers. The point of departure is based not on theory but on common sense.

Of course, one may speculate that Gorbachev envisions a new society and economy that bold reforms will liberate from the shackles of Stalinism, but that he dares not unveil his vision until his power is more firmly consolidated. Or, it can be argued, the process of learning from practice will lead him to such a vision. However this may turn out, the important issue is the extent of support Gorbachev can mobilize with respect to his existing goals and his knowledge of how to accomplish such reforms. Time and again in discussions with Soviet officials and economists, one finds a clear and realistic recognition of existing ills. They also are fairly clear about what they want to achieve—the socioeconomic end product of present and future Soviet reforms. Where one encounters confusion and indecision, however, is on the question of how the Soviet Union gets from here to there. Gorbachev and his associates do not seem sure how this qualitative jump, which will be as much political as economic, can be accomplished. Gorbachev has shown himself to be a talented politician and an improviser. He is learning on the job, so to speak. There is nothing unusual in this state of affairs. After all, he has set a course outside of his and his country's experience.

If Soviet leaders themselves are reluctant to generalize, Western observers must hazard their own analysis of the processes at work behind the exhilarating language and implementation of reform. The emerging Soviet concept of "democracy" is the place to start. What Gorbachev says and does suggests that the Soviet Union may be developing something that could be called "inverted democracy." In capitalist democracies the most visible focus of democratic institutions and behavior exists at the macrosocietal level. The microsocietal units, especially those concerned with economic life, are in most cases nondemocratic in intent, structure, and behavior. Corporations, enterprises, and trade unions are, to some degree, authoritarian.

Gorbachev's "democratic" vision appears to be the reverse of patterns in the West. It envisages elements of a grass-roots democracy at the microsocietal level—election of a director by the workers in an enterprise, real elections of members of the local soviets by citizens, and maybe even genuine election of local trade union leaders. It would include making microindustrial management accountable to the workers, making local officials accountable to their constituencies, and probably genuine election of leaders in primary party organizations.

At the macroinstitutional level, however, Gorbachev's initiatives do not call for democratic patterns of behavior in either state or party institutions now or in the foreseeable future. Already the Soviet constitution and the party statutes present an impressive array of prescribed "democratic" procedures, but the words are without substance. (Indeed, one of the most democratic Soviet constitutions was adopted in 1936 at the height of Joseph Stalin's Great Purge.) Even were the All-Union 19th Party Conference scheduled for 1988 to succeed in adopting the rumored compulsory retirement age of 65 for high-level officials or perhaps the less likely limitation on tenure in high-level party and state positions, these steps could scarcely be defined as "macrodemocracy." Turning over one-third of Central Committee members at party congresses would no doubt improve the functioning of the party-state but would do little to democratize it.

Gorbachev seems quite conscious of the unusual nature of the democracy he is trying to launch. He has said often that the Soviet Union will become a unique international model deserving of emulation. But on the basis of experience with earlier efforts to install this sort of inverted democracy—such as Yugoslavia— Gorbachev's concept seems to have little chance of success. It simply will add new elections, such as for plant managers, to the large number of elections already taking place. For the Soviet Union already may have more elections than any other country in the world. Even if low-level elections evolve from meaningless plebiscites for a preselected candidate into meaningful choices, it will not promote macrodemocracy or serve as its substitute.

These efforts of Gorbachev represent a utopian strain in his thinking and are likely to prove futile for at least two reasons. First, historically, modernization does not require and is not associated with microinstitutional democracy. Rather, the reverse is true. The vertical line of organizational authority and the need for technological discipline and steep stratification of responsibilities and rewards all contribute decisively to the authoritarian nature of modern economic institutions. Second, Western sociology has, with only a few exceptions, well established the validity of the "iron law of oligarchy" in formal organization. American governmental bureaucracies, cooperative movements, trade unions, and even religious associations have shown that microinstitutions soon become authoritarian and oligarchic even if their origin may be genuinely democratic. If this is true under a macrodemocratic order like that found in the United States, how much more likely will it be in an authoritarian Soviet Union, especially in light of Soviet and Russian traditions?

Two related aspects of Gorbachev's new direction are worth stressing: the rise of relatively autonomous social units and the evolution of the Soviet bureaucracy. From Alexis de Tocqueville to Antonio Gramsci, social scientists have been concerned with relations between state and society, and particularly with what they have defined as "civil society." This concept describes the significant degree of autonomy that such social units as community organizations and professional associations attain as they achieve freedom from direct state supervision and control. Totalitarianism is the extreme example of the eradication of all vestiges of civil society. Populist capitalist democracy of the variety found in America is the best-known example of the other extreme, where elements of civil society are widespread, encouraged, and even dominant.

Gorbachev's program for the Soviet Union's future seems to assume the creation and cultivation of selected elements of civil society, which has never existed in Soviet or even in much of Russian history. If Gorbachev is serious about abolishing cultural censorship and allowing a significant degree of freedom for investigative reporting, grass-roots participation in community life, worker influence on enterprise management, and free elections in the party's primary organizations, he will create elements of a civil society in the Soviet Union. The political logic behind such steps also may be connected with Gorbachev's vision of modernity but is more directly related to the nature of the present Soviet bureaucracy and his plans to transform it.

From ancient empires to modern times, it has been possible to characterize bureaucracies as ruler-dependent, corporatist (that is, centered on their own collective interests), or client-oriented. From Stalin's rise to power after V. I. Lenin's death in 1924 to the beginning of Gorbachev's rule, Soviet bureaucratic organizations have gone through two basic changes.

Under Stalin's personal dictatorship they became more ruler-dependent than those of any other modern state, including pre-war Nazi Germany. Within physical limits, they were entirely dominated by Stalin and his chief subordinates. Access to Stalin, direct or indirect, constituted the main political recourse in bureaucratic conflicts. Then Soviet leader Nikita Khrushchev's abolition of mass terror in the 1950s, particularly within the elites, eroded the ruler-dependent nature of Soviet bureaucracies. When Khrushchev, during his last two years in office, attempted to build a power base independent from the bureaucracies, and particularly from the party bureaucracy that had secured his power, an alliance of leaders of all major bureaucracies displayed the first significant sign of independence by ousting him without serious difficulty in 1964. The rule of Leonid Brezhnev, Khrushchev's successor, signified the final and far-reaching transformation of the bureaucracies into corporatist-oriented bodies presided over by an oligarchy within which the interests of every principal bureaucracy were amply represented. The corporatist model, involving the ability to escape control from above and pressure from below, was only reinforced by the prolonged interregnum that developed under Brezhnev and lasted until Gorbachev assumed office.

A significant element of the political logic behind Gorbachev's new direction is his desire to break the corporatist orientation of the Soviet bureaucracies in order to make some of them client-oriented and all of them leader-oriented. If this view is correct, he has set himself a truly major task, one that defeated Khrushchev and that, if attainable at all, will require major strengthening of the instruments and methods of control. It also may require further changes for which Gorbachev may not be ready.

To understand the nature of the corporatist bureaucracy facing Gorbachev, it may be instructive to look at some of its important characteristics during the Brezhnev era. Most visible was the unprecedented security of office, which became virtually a life-long sinecure. And, in a majority of cases, when bureaucratic leaders retired or died, they were replaced by aged principal deputies already well placed in the bureaucratic hierarchy. The bureaucracies thus developed into vertical factions or horizontal regional political machines of great cohesiveness where formal lines of authority were reinforced by informal arrangements that stressed personal loyalty to the bureaucratic leader.

Under Brezhnev, the political leadership had only superficial control of the bureaucracies. Many of the individuals or institutions allegedly in control actually were co-opted by the bureaucracies. *Paradnost*, a false rendering of the state of affairs in a given bureaucracy's sector, flourished. The flow of information to the top, outrageously manipulated and misleading, forced the bureaucratic leaders each year to produce bigger lies to cover up those of the year before. Officials of lower units provided false documentation to buttress rosy reports sent to their superiors. This reporting pattern created a system of criminal mutual interdependence and protection from the top to the bottom of every bureaucracy.

Such destructive bureaucratic behavior was assisted by the policy of official secrecy, whose range the bureaucracies themselves pushed to extend. A pervasive campaign of lies kept both the leaders and the populace misinformed. The bureaucracies were at the same time highhanded and ignorant of the citizenry's thoughts and needs.

Gorbachev wants to abolish just this type of bureaucracy at the intermediate level and to transform it at other levels. Ironically, Gorbachev the anti-Stalinist wishes to and must achieve mastery of the bureaucracies to some extent as Stalin achieved it earlier. But the methods that Gorbachev can and wishes to use are quite different from those available to Stalin.

Gorbachev's most obvious and important method in the transitional period has been wide-ranging replacement of personnel. This process commenced from the moment Gorbachev assumed power, and it shows signs of accelerating. Moreover, in a growing number of cases Gorbachev's purge has not simply cleared the way for leading deputies well plugged into the existing bureaucratic machine to receive a promotion. By choosing outside candidates, Gorbachev increases the likelihood of securing the loyalty of new appointees. One example of his new approach took place in May 1987 when Gorbachev by-passed all available marshals and senior generals to elevate General Dmitri Yazov to the post of minister of defense. Gorbachev's power in the highest decision-making body, the Politburo, and the highest executive body, the Secretariat of the Central Committee, is now consolidated beyond challenge with the co-optation of three party secretaries, Aleksandr Yakovlev, Nikolai Slyunkov, and Viktor Nikonov, to full membership in the Politburo at the June 1987 plenum. Gorbachev probably aims to achieve a similar conquest of the second echelon of leadership—the Central Committee of the Communist party—at the 19th party conference in 1988.

Purges may work for Gorbachev in the short run, but without eventual structural changes they may prove ineffective. Every bureaucracy has a built-in tendency to become corporatist. The new appointees will exploit this tendency to build their own machines. How to make the bureaucracies more leader- and client-oriented through the short-term instrument of purges itself is a difficult question. Success will require a viable system of incentives and disincentives for government officials. Gorbachev therefore has started to develop tools, such as *glasnost*, with whose help he hopes to control more effectively the vast Soviet bureaucracies. He will have to move much further to break the corporatist spirit that is fueling hard resistance to his reform, or at least to keep it within manageable limits.

The relative autonomy of the media, and particularly the encouragement of investigative reporting, will serve Gorbachev's anticorporatist campaign. So will the growing freedom of the intelligentsia in the cultural field. Gorbachev is using this autonomy and freedom as a mechanism to control the bureaucracies and to help mobilize support for his program. Courageous writers, directors, journalists, and artists continually are testing the permissible limits, which therefore are still expanding. But to ensure reconstruction's success and to keep the conservative bureaucracies on the defensive, Gorbachev may have to continue broadening the autonomy and freedoms to the point of totally abolishing preventive censorship, which will need to be institutionalized in new laws and legal codes.

Grass-roots organization of communal affairs, increased participation of the working people in the lives of their microeconomic units, and greater attention to complaints about local leaders' abuse of power and privileges are intended and could serve as restraints on the bureaucracies. Yet as these reforms now are carried out, and despite encouragement from the general secretary, they resemble guerrilla warfare against entrenched interests, or marginally effective hit-and-run raids against established political machines. So long as the macropolitical order of the Soviet Union remains the same, this picture may not change.

The strength and staying power of the Soviet bureaucracies rest on their vertical structure, which makes each separate organizational unit a link in a long hierarchical chain. Gorbachev cannot be successful if such tight centralization is permitted to survive. His reforms, which achieved their most far-reaching expression in the edicts of the June 1987 plenum but which have only just started, intend to alter the centralized bureaucratic structure in three basic ways. First, they will abolish or reduce drastically the intermediate levels of the bureaucratic hierarchies. This step will disengage the links that now tie together the policymaking organizations—the chief ministerial bureaucracies—from those more directly engaged in policy implementation—the economic associations, firms, and enterprises. Second, the reform will restrict dramatically the controlling prerogatives of the top organizations with regard to the lower-level units. Principally, the role of the Gosplan, the state economic planning giant, in shaping day-to-day planning and in controlling implementation at this level of detail will be curbed. Third, they will expand significantly the operational rights and independence of lower-echelon units and establish relations among them based on contractual agreements rather than bureaucratic directive.

Even if Gorbachev's decentralizing efforts are consistent and forceful, in all probability large segments of the bureaucratic hierarchies will remain untouched. Certainly the secret police, the armed forces, including the military-industrial sector, and the professional party bureaucracy, or apparat, are unlikely to be affected.

Moreover, it is doubtful that the reforms will have a lasting effect as formulated even in the administrative and economic areas, where Gorbachev's effort to break up the supercentralization and to change the political orientation of the bureaucratic hierarchies is most pronounced. Political and economic forces are drawn into a vacuum. If there is a need for them, new administrative units and organizations will assume the policymaking and controlling functions of those organizations that were abolished or reduced in importance. Or, more likely, the old organizations will regain their old power.

To break up the powerful bureaucratic hierarchies that now play a central role in resisting his reforms, Gorbachev must find a mechanism capable of carrying out the functions performed by these bureaucracies. In the economic field this substitute is clear—free-market forces. Gorbachev stresses in almost every major speech the absolute necessity of supplanting "administrative methods by economic mechanisms and instruments." Yet even in the latest version of reform—the far-reaching decentralization of Soviet planning and management adopted by the June 1987 plenum—market mechanisms only supplement, not supplant, administrative leadership. Gorbachev probably intends to enlarge the role of authentic market forces in the future through a series of steps. Until he does, however, the general secretary, besieged by the powerful bureaucracy under him, can win skirmishes or even battles but never the war.

In the political field, a free-market substitute for the central role of administrative forces is not realistic in the eyes of Gorbachev and his new leadership core. Nonetheless, they are considering measures that would be a major step forward in a Soviet context. They are contemplating innovative procedures and policies to temper the arbitrary character of Soviet power. The political leadership recognizes that the society over which it rules has changed greatly in the last two decades. People in their twenties and thirties, who constitute the majority of the Soviet urban population, have developed economic and cultural expectations far beyond those of their parents. The Soviet Union today has the world's largest professional class. Isolation of this group from knowledge of the outside world is a thing of the past. "Democratization" and "openness" are a necessity in Gorbachev's struggle not only to discipline the bureaucracy but also to close the growing gap between the regime and the most active and talented part of the citizenry, who were progressively alienated by the stagnant, oligarchic decade of Brezhnev's rule.

Reforming the Apparat

In the conflict between Gorbachev's leadership and Soviet bureaucracies there is one aspect of the new approach about which a Western observer must admit a lack of clarity. What is the role of the Communist party in Gorbachev's scheme of things? The mass party, with its estimated 18 million members and candidate members and 400,000 primary organizations, displays the same malaise that besets the entire Soviet society. Rather than serving as an effective instrument to mobilize the population for Gorbachev's program, the party itself needs to be mobilized. The apparat, in particular, presents a real problem for Gorbachev. Stalin and Khrushchev realized their rise to power through control over the party apparat. The party apparat was the foundation on which Brezhnev's power rested, and it also served as arbiter in interbureaucratic conflicts. But the same symptoms of stagnation, corruption, and decay evident elsewhere were found in the apparat when Gorbachev assumed the top office. Apparently the general secretary had these conditions in mind when he began to speak about the crisis in the party itself.

The party apparat outside Moscow does not constitute a power base for Gorbachev. It is more a part of his problem than a solution. Its middle and lower levels are filled with conservative figures for whom the general secretary's ideological innovations, such as support for private enterprise in agriculture and services, hold no appeal. But the roots of Gorbachev's problem with the party bureaucracy go deeper. They concern his own uncertainty about the role that the apparat is supposed to play in the "new" Soviet Union and the apparat's fear of the extent to which its power will be curtailed by Gorbachev's reforms.

In the post-Stalin era, the party apparat, though relatively small (about 200,000 strong), undoubtedly has been the most powerful bureaucracy. The apparat was set up as an organization parallel to all other bureaucratic hierarchies, present in all geographic and administrative areas down to the county level but highly centralized and with its own separate chain of command. Each set of activities for which a state bureaucracy is responsible is duplicated by a supervisory unit within the apparat. The scope of the duplicating organization and supervisory role of the party bureaucracy is all-inclusive and involves the administrative, economic, cultural, and even the police and military bureaucracies.

The functions performed by the party bureaucracy are therefore numerous and varied, but their specific mix and focus have differed from one period of Soviet history to another. The initial role of the apparat was to check on the political loyalty of the leading bureaucratic personnel. A closely related function was to control the appointments, promotions, demotions, dismissals, and transfers of "responsible personnel" in state bureaucracies— that is, to supervise the *nomenklatura*. Another central role of the apparat involved mass mobilization. The organization of mass campaigns, the enforcement of emergency procedures, and the unrelenting pressure on the state bureaucracies to meet the leadership's goals, constituted a major raison d'être of the party bureaucracy. Another function was to provide horizontal coordination at all levels of state management that otherwise would be caught in the maze of Soviet bureaucratic politics. The apparat could arbitrate among competing bureaucratic interests. It also served as the unquestioned guardian of ideological purity, whatever its specific nature at any point in Soviet development. Finally, and immensely important, the party bureaucracy played a unique role in policy decision making by determining the national agenda.

What will be the party's role if Gorbachev succeeds in his extraordinary effort to break with the ruling orthodoxy? The speeches of leaders, discussion in the press, and talks with Soviet officials, experts, journalists, and individuals on the system's margin provide clues. The different impact the reform has had on the central party apparat in Moscow and on the local apparats in the provinces and the republics needs to be stressed at the outset. The role of the Moscow-based apparat in conceptualizing and developing new policies has been greatly strengthened. The apparat of the Central Committee Secretariat in Moscow has received talented new cadres and serves Gorbachev as a personal political general staff of great importance in planning and supervising the reforms. The situation of the party apparats outside Moscow seems to be quite different. Every successful step to reformulate cultural policies, to introduce largely self-regulating forces into the economy, and especially to free the media from their traditional restraints, weakens their ideological and political power.

Brezhnev's rule created for the apparatchiks the best of all possible worlds. Their power was immense and both their legal and their illegal rewards were unrestrained while their responsibilities and accountability were limited. Those apparatchiks of Gorbachev's own generation probably hoped to enjoy, at least for a while, this ideal situation once they began to advance after Brezhnev's death. Instead, the extent of their power is now uncertain, their privileges remain under scrutiny, and their responsibilities multiply in the service of ideas that they are unwilling or unable to absorb. Meanwhile, the degree of accountability is higher than ever.

Gorbachev's strength within the leading party institutions may already be beyond challenge. The party conference of June 1988 probably will consolidate his position in the Central Committee as well. But the loyalty to Gorbachev of the primary Soviet bureaucratic hierarchy, the party apparat, is still in question. Moreover, Gorbachev himself seems uncertain what the apparat's function under new circumstances should be. His speeches and actions make clear only what the role of the apparat should not be: The party should not impede openness and democratization, nor should it discourage private enterprise in agriculture and services, economic decentralization, and movement toward economic mechanisms in planning and management.

In Moscow, and perhaps in a few other large metropolitan areas, well-established political leaders appointed by Gorbachev are not afraid to shoulder responsibility and deal with conflicts that inevitably develop in an era of greater freedom for the media. In the country as a whole, however, timidity and restraint are the rule rather than the exception. It is perfectly clear that at the local level, party organs, often working with local bureaucratic interests, are busy trying to prevent the "disease" of *glasnost* from taking hold.

What Gorbachev is asking of the local party bureaucracy is not so much that it encourage *glasnost* as that it tolerate it and defend the local intelligentsia, so easily intimidated, against the inevitable interference of and opposition from the county, city, province, or republic power structure. But this is asking the local party bureaucracy to act against its own interests as it has traditionally understood them. Gorbachev's call for democratization at the local level, for example, requires the party bureaucrats to abdicate full control over appointments. Free elections imply such a loss of control. *Glasnost* requires that they abandon the prerogative of being keepers of the ideological truth and end their role as power brokers who decide who should be criticized and when and how. However, he is not at the same time compensating the apparat by assigning it new power functions.

In the economic area Gorbachev is asking the local party bureaucracy not so much to help as not to interfere with the spontaneous expansion of private, profit-motivated activities. But the idea of legally sanctioned private initiative is alien to local party officials. It goes against their upbringing and sense of values. So do the spontaneous formation and expansion of private enterprises, which will remain outside their control. The most important uncertainty for the apparat in Gorbachev's reform plans does not concern ideology or marginal private enterprises but rather the very core of the apparat's power position and function—its relation to the economy, planning, and management.

There is another, even more critical, challenge to the party apparat's power. From the time of collectivization to the present the apparat's role in Soviet agriculture has always been central. The rural-county party committee ruled the collective and state farms. Gorbachev's agricultural reforms shift dramatically the nature of economic activity of collective farms and the trend of the post-Stalin decades, which channeled continuous or even increased power to the rural-county party apparats.

Now the focus of economic activities within collective farms is becoming the small contractual brigades that often consist of one family to whom land, necessary implements, livestock, and even credit eventually will be provided routinely. Collective-farm resources are to be exploited effectively by relying on peasants' profit motives, not on minute supervision and exhortation from administrators. Control over machines, implements, and livestock is to be largely decentralized. Administrative personnel are to be reduced and accounting procedures simplified. The tax in kind on the brigades and peasants' private production will be standardized by allowing the brigades to retain their surpluses. Surpluses can be marketed through special cooperatives, such as partnerships of private entrepreneurs.

Gorbachev's policies for agriculture, if consistent and successful, will undercut thoroughly the power base of the rural party apparats; for what the collective farms require is not political mobilization—the apparats' strong suit—but maximization of the profit motive, which the peasant can best judge. The rural apparatchiks must be conscious that Gorbachev is appealing to their sense of party loyalty to help him implement what, to them, is a self-destructive reform.

In the post-Stalin past the party bureaucracy was opposed to being too closely involved in industrial management and therefore held directly responsible for its failures and shortcomings. In 1963 Khrushchev, in his last "harebrained scheme," as the Central Committee subsequently called it, bifurcated the party apparat into agricultural and industrial sectors. He met fierce resistance that led ultimately to his downfall and subsequently to Brezhnev's rescinding the split because the apparat saw its role as political—that is, policy-setting and supervisory. It did not want to be directly responsible for management, which was the objective of Khrushchev's reorganization. At the same time the party bureaucracy, precisely because of its political prerogative, found it natural to intervene at will in matters of industrial management within its jurisdiction. Especially in the later years of Brezhnev's rule, the party's bureaucratic role in industrial management amounted to possessing major rights without responsibility.

If Gorbachev's reform of planning and industrial management is carried out, the party's bureaucratic role will be increasingly ambiguous and will decline in importance. Gorbachev's industrial reform calls for an expanded role for managers of industrial associations and enterprises and a steep decline in the role of economic and administrative bureaucracies in day-to-day supervision of managers' activities. Gorbachev's plan does not envisage an increase in the direct responsibility of the apparat, which, however, would still expect to guide industry's transition to the new methods of planning and management. And Gorbachev is dead set against the apparat's routine interference in the operation of the reformed industrial establishment. Gorbachev criticizes such interference and control as "petty tutelage." A Western rendering of Gorbachev's motto of industrial reform would be, "Business should be primarily the responsibility of businessmen." It may have been a sign of the times when, out of fifty attendees at a special meeting with Gorbachev prior to the June 1987 plenum, no more than five first provincial party secretaries were present, while most in attendance were economic managers.

Gorbachev's plans for the local party apparat leave more limited administrative tasks and a narrowed political role. It will supervise the local administrative organs, mobilize party activists to support directly Gorbachev's reforms and to work harder, and concentrate on such internal party affairs as political campaigns, party education, and propaganda. The party bureaucracy probably will continue to supervise and make relevant decisions about the *nomenklatura*. But two qualifiers are in order. First, the bulk of such decisions on leading central and local personnel will remain the prerogative of the Central Committee Secretariat in Moscow and its apparat. On such questions the local party bureaucracy will play only an advisory role. One has the impression that administrative and managerial decentralization will be accompanied by an enlargement of the central apparat's role. Second, evaluations of economic personnel who remain within the local apparat's jurisdiction will depend increasingly on more objective economic measures of their performance and less on the arbitrariness and favoritism of the local apparatchiks.

Remembering Khrushchev

Of course, the "new order" for Gorbachev's relations with the Soviet bureaucratic hierarchies will come to pass only if he continues to deepen his reforms. The bureaucratic hierarchies' passive and active resistance to Gorbachev's plans will not suddenly cease; the stakes in the struggle are too high. They concern items valued highly—power, privileges, and security. But for Gorbachev the stakes are even higher—not only his own political survival but the Soviet Union's future as well.

Every major Soviet leader's relationship to the bureaucratic hierarchies was central to his concept of Soviet power and to his program. In his *State and Revolution* (1917) Lenin theorized about a society without hierarchical structure and bureaucracies. In the last months of his life he was despairing at the visible growth of Soviet bureaucracies but offered unrealistic and weak prescriptions for avoiding their domination. Stalin went on to create the modern Soviet bureaucratic party-state. But physically and psychologically he crushed what he had created, establishing through terror personal dominance over all action and thought. Khrushchev, by ending terror, fulfilled the mandate of the Soviet political elite that brought him to power and provided conditions favorable to the independent growth of bureaucracies. He elevated the party apparat to a dominant role and became a beneficiary of its support. In the absence of terror, however, he was unable, despite his efforts, to achieve sufficient independence from his bureaucratic power base and was ousted by a unified front of the top bureaucratic officials. By reversing Khrushchev's organizational and policy experimentations Brezhnev fulfilled the mandate of the Soviet political elite after Khrushchev's fall. As the head of an oligarchic leadership he entered into a conservative compact with the major bureaucratic hierarchies to secure stability, professional autonomy, and privilege. At the point where Khrushchev failed, Gorbachev is now beginning. His key battles for power in service of innovation therefore lie ahead of him; behind him is the memory of Khrushchev's fate.

The new leadership had embraced most reform measures primarily for practical or instrumental reasons. In other words, Gorbachev and his supporters have adopted them not because they think the reforms are intrinsically right but because the measures are necessary to promote a particular purpose of the leadership in its struggle to modernize the Soviet Union. Yet already to a certain degree, and with increasing chances if the new direction continues, these values may become more than instrumental. Under the immense shock of the worldwide technological revolution, in which the Soviet Union is lagging further and further behind, the new leadership is trying to revise its outdated concept of modernity and the paths to it. The Soviet Union's approach toward modernization has been very traditional and has been associated mainly with Soviet industrialization—that is, with the first industrial revolution, in which all leading countries developed heavy industry, such as factories, railways, and mines. Under the pressure of reality, Soviet leaders and experts are moving away from this outdated understanding, recognizing that modernity today is very different from this past model. It requires changed attitudes as much as it does high technology.

When the Bolsheviks first took power in 1917, Lenin declared that "socialism equals electrification plus Soviet power." Gorbachev has not developed an integrated view of what socialism now equals. But it is becoming clear that its components cannot be electrification—the symbol of the first industrial revolution—plus Soviet power, if this means power as either Stalin or Brezhnev conceived it. The perception is growing in ruling circles, as it has been evolving in scientific and expert circles since the 1970s, that Lenin's equation needs new variables not only on the technological side but also on the sociopolitical side if "socialism" is to become a powerful, viable entity in the world. But the Soviet elite also understands that the task is enormous. The Soviet Union faces not one but two technological and economic revolutions: the revolution of mass consumption (the second industrial revolution) and the revolution of mass information and communication (the third industrial revolution). Because of overall backwardness, the changed nature of Soviet society, and the ambitious goals of the new leadership, however, the Soviets do not enjoy the luxury of undergoing these revolutions sequentially. The Soviet Union must attempt to go through both revolutions at the same time.

The revolution of mass consumption rests on the production of durable consumer goods, the industrialization of agriculture, the availability to the population of a high-quality diet, a major expansion of services, and the rapid development of the industrial and consumption infrastructure. The revolution of mass consumption started in the Soviet Union in the late 1960s, primarily in the large metropolitan areas. Overall, however, the Soviet Union has entered only the initial stages of this revolution and remains at a level comparable to that of the less developed industrial democracies, like Italy during the 1950s. Development has been and remains highly uneven. The Soviet Union already has the capacity to produce durable consumer goods en masse, but the goods produced are of low quality and limited variety. Moreover, their prices relative to income remain extremely high. In the agricultural sector, progress remains slow: With about 30 percent of annual labor force work hours being expended in the agricultural sector, as compared with 3–8 percent in the industrial democracies, one can hardly speak about the industrialization of Soviet agriculture. The labor effort in the rural sector notwithstanding, the quality of the popular diet remains relatively low. Meanwhile, the secondary manufacture and marketing of agricultural products continue to be primitive and undependable.

Likewise, consumer and industrial services in the Soviet Union make up only about one-tenth of the share of gross national product (GNP) typically devoted to these sectors in industrial democracies. The lack of services is filled partly by a second, illegal economy. But it, too, is undependable, and the high prices it commands benefit only a minority.

The level and scope of the Soviet infrastructure—roads, the telephone network, storage facilities, transport, refrigeration, packing, and other factors—are simply pitiful. Long neglect has led to enormous waste (as much as 20 percent of each grain harvest), has hampered the total productivity of labor, and has made possible only rudimentary marketing. In fact, to this day there is no national market for perishable goods. The weak infrastructure constitutes a significant bottleneck in the economy. Not surprisingly, the consumption revolution has experienced a slowing down of growth and even stagnation since the mid-1970s, remaining far short of plan.

For a variety of reasons the new leadership cannot afford to neglect the goals of the consumer revolution any longer. It is not certain whether a real revolution of rising expectations has engulfed the country and undermined the earlier docility of its population. What is certain is that expectations of all classes, but particularly the middle class and the skilled workers in major industrial centers, have risen sharply, and their patience may be running short. The sociopolitical impact of their expectations may be particularly significant because it is partly the result of a classic pattern—improvement followed by slowdown and stagnation. The speedy resumption of the consumer revolution has become pivotal to the regime's sociopolitical stability, party officials say privately.

Accommodating growth in consumption also has become necessary to raise dramatically the productivity of labor and capital and to shift from extensive to intensive growth. Labor productivity and product quality will not increase significantly if workers, engineers, managers, and peasants are denied significant incentives designed to reward their labor, even if new technology is spread more widely than before. For monetary incentives to be effective, however, they have to be backed in the marketplace by sufficient quantities of high-quality and reasonably priced goods and services. The sovereignty of the consumer has to penetrate the Soviet economic system for the first time.

As the new leaders assess the internal situation, therefore, they recognize the need to accelerate the consumption revolution in order to preserve sociopolitical stability, to halt the people's far-reaching alienation from the regime, and to raise the productivity of labor and capital. As the leaders weigh the Soviet international position and aspirations, they recognize the need to commence the information and communication revolution—the third industrial revolution. Here their plight is compounded because the mass consumption revolution is a precondition of the rapid advancements sweeping adversary countries in the information and communication fields.

The communication and information revolution flows from the explosive growth of electronics with miniaturized components; from automation and remote control of the production process; from higher productivity of services performed by white-collar workers; from the creation and flourishing of what the management expert Peter Drucker calls knowledge technologies, knowledge industries, and knowledge economies; and from an exponential growth of information transmitted to and between societies. The impact of the communication and information revolution is so profoundly fraught with such discontinuities that it is common practice to identify countries caught in this whirlwind of change as "postindustrial societies."

Not much has to be written about the Soviet Union's own third industrial revolution. Some progress may be observed in the military sector and to some degree in the hard sciences, such as theoretical and nuclear physics. The decisive characteristic of this transformation in other countries, however, is its move beyond select industries and laboratories into the economy as a whole. The Soviet Union will not be able to start this revolution if its efforts are concentrated, as they were in the past, on a few political and economic priorities.

The Soviet Union is totally unprepared for the burst of progress along the entire range of its economic activities that will be required to modernize. The existing political, economic, and cultural system runs contrary to the fluid attributes that energize postindustrial societies. It imposes constraints that have to be destroyed. Soviet society, particularly its highly educated strata, must be unshackled. Those characteristics of the Soviet polity, economy, and culture that stand as gigantic obstacles to the third revolution have been discussed often. Among others are the stifling Soviet penchant for secrecy, the extreme compartmentalization of knowledge and information flows, the lack of venture capital and entrepreneurship outside of the second economy, the staggering underdevelopment of the communication infrastructure, the cultural illiteracy toward modern technology, and the submersion of individuality in a collectivist mentality.

It appears that Gorbachev and his loyalists do understand the new meaning and substance of the term "modernity." They seem to have grasped the truth that the economic and technological prerequisites of reform require political, social, cultural, and psychological changes. Gorbachev and his aides and experts say as much in their speeches and articles. In practice, the new policies, or the "new way of thinking," express a growth in this understanding. It is becoming clear that the new direction is not simply tactical but also strategic. The new approach is meant to be not a transitional thaw but a long-range strategy to transform the Soviet superstructure. In this sense the attempted changes may expand from their primarily functional nature to attain a normative significance for the new Kremlin leadership.

Links with the Global Economy

One central phenomenon of the third industrial revolution is the rapid growth in global interdependence, first in the economic sphere, later in science and culture. The evidence is not sufficient to suggest that this process is understood fully by the new leaders. But they are well aware of the insufficiency of Karl Marx's and Lenin's concepts. Marx spoke of an international market; Lenin spoke about exporting capital and international cartels, key aspects of an international economy. Today the world is experiencing a growing multidimensional interdependence across national economies.

The idea of a global economy is especially troublesome for Soviet leaders. Its consequences for individual industrial countries are even more difficult to understand. After the initial phase of its industrialization in the 1930s, the Soviet Union developed under Stalin in a state of virtual autarky. Although Stalin's successors rejected such extreme economic isolation, the Soviet economy, particularly in light of its immense size, has played a minimal role in the global arena. The structure of Soviet exports, with the stress on oil, timber, and gold, resembles that of an underdeveloped country. Soviet trade (exports and imports) as a percentage of the GNP is so much lower than that of any industrial country as to be insignificant globally.

Quite a few communist leaders, past and present, have tried to form links with the global economy in order to facilitate modernization plans. Poland under Edward Gierek in the 1970s and China under Deng Xiaoping adopted such a strategy. It is clear that the new Soviet leaders want to expand international economic contracts through credit, joint ventures, and trade. However, they do not seem to put decisive stress on expanded contacts in their modernization program. In this and other respects, their program differs from Poland's ultimately unsuccessful program. It does not anticipate high-technology capital imports as a substitute for reform. Rather, imports will serve as one of the supporting pillars of reform. It does not envisage either capital imports or joint ventures as a substitute for domestically generated technological progress. If this turns out to be the real attitude of Soviet leaders, it will indicate that, in one respect, their understanding of technological progress is accurate. Both during the late stages of the second industrial revolution and throughout the third, the globalization of national economies has been accompanied by an additional characteristic: Technological progress in industrial countries has depended principally not on imports but on self-generated technological growth.

Globalization of national economies introduces common standards of modernity. To reach those standards, however, let alone to reach the cutting edge of modern technology, requires technological advances that are self-generated at the national level; these are impossible without adjustments in patterns of economic, social, and cultural behavior. To be successful, a state must open its national economy to the global circulation of theoretical and applied science, managerial methods and skills, and capital. Gorbachev's economic reforms move in the right direction by opening up more of the Soviet economy and Soviet science to global influences. The proposed steps are still mainly on paper, however. They are so far clearly inadequate and hardly developed as a broad plan for the future. Most important, even if developed they remain largely useless unless domestic structural reforms are adopted that channel the self-interest of the managerial strata toward technological progress. The creation of such liberalized economic conditions ultimately will not transform the Soviet Union into a new Japan, but they are the minimum prerequisites for arresting the yawning Soviet gap with capitalist states. Whether the political prerequisites of Soviet power will ultimately permit the transformations that can open the path to modernity is an open question.

Modernity also carries with it a number of propositions about the way in which the society can be stratified by class, status, and power. There seem to be some irreducible components of societal stratification associated with modernization. Common sense, if nothing else, would argue that two such components are that people in general should be rewarded on the quality and complexity of their work and that people in business, in the main, should be the ones who handle business.

If the second component was never adopted in the Soviet Union, the first was elevated to a doctrinal canon of the socialist society. According to Marx, socialism constitutes an early phase of communism in which individuals contribute to society according to their abilities and are rewarded according to their work. In practice, however, this canon was employed more as an exception than a rule. The reality of Soviet society's stratification is highly dysfunctional to the process of modernization. This truth is recognized not only in the West but also in the Soviet Union, and not only by sociologists and economists but by the new Soviet leaders as well.

The Soviet stratification system is characterized by the worst possible combination of features if the goal is a modern economy. It is highly elitist in its direct equation of political power and economic rewards, a sure road to alienation of the powerless. It is distinctively egalitarian in the loose relation between the quality and complexity of work performed and the real economic rewards offered, which leads to widespread lack of interest in sustained effort at the work place. The economic stratification between the powerful and the powerless peaked during Stalin's rule and probably declined under Brezhnev, although the powerful have continued to benefit from thievery and corruption. Nevertheless, for those employed in the "national economy"—including state and cooperative enterprises—concentration of wealth in the top classes has leveled off, and income disparities are low compared with those in other countries at a similar stage of development.

The immense political distance between those in and out of power, the lopsided relationship between political power and economic gain—including the high probability that the political elite's offspring will succeed—and the limited relationship between quality of work and economic reward would be a deadly combination for any country determined to modernize. Soviet leaders increasingly take note of the contradiction between their stratification system and their chief goals. Economic laws already promulgated on labor quality and economic incentives are directed at improving the situation. Other policies seek to make increasing economic stratification more palatable by strengthening normative factors such as grass-roots participation.

Yet shifting toward a stratification system that assists rather than impedes modernization will prove very difficult economically. The Soviets are in a Catch-22. To improve economic incentives and increase pay scales, the productivity and quality of available goods must also improve. This is likely, however, only when material incentives improve. The transition to a more functional economic stratification is extremely difficult. Gorbachev has attempted to fill this transitional void partly with calls to patriotism and exhortations to work hard and stay sober.

Perhaps no less difficult than the economic connotations of a shift in stratification are the sociopolitical ones. They may even become explosive. In the post-Stalin period the party entered into an unwritten compact with the Soviet working class: "They pretend they pay us, and we pretend we work," was the Soviet worker's description of the state of affairs. This was much more than a joking remark. Thus the party and the government raised minimum wages; increased average wages; accomplished a small but steady growth in the living standard; kept the differential between workers' wages and managers' salaries low, even reducing them; and, crucially, provided the workers with almost foolproof job security. Those in power started to treat the rural peasant as a citizen. In addition, they expended enormous subsidies on high-priority commodities, such as bread, lard, and potatoes, and services, such as rents and transportation, to keep prices low in the Soviet version of a welfare state. In return, they received from the workers docility, low expectations and aspirations, and participation in the farce of the propaganda double talk. The compact became somewhat frayed at the edges, however, when, in the mid-1970s, the economy experienced a new stagnation with noticeable decline of quality in the welfare state—for example, a crisis in medical services.

It is this tacit agreement, along with similar "equilibrium contracts" that workers have maintained in practice with managers and administrators, that Gorbachev seems determined to break and indeed must break if he wants his modernization plans to become more than slogans. Such a policy has great potential for modernization but also major political risks. These will be greatest during the transition from the old social contract to a new one, when the benefits of the new are yet to arrive and the advantages of the old are daily reduced.

At each stage of its development the Soviet system has faced potential dangers from a different social stratum. Stalin brutally destroyed, perhaps beyond revival, the Russian peasant class. After Stalin the enormous expansion of the professional, educated stratum, in conditions of the abolition of mass terror, created for the regime a new danger—dissidence and cultural opposition. But the opposition proved to be narrowly based and relatively easy to isolate and decimate through the coercive police state. The new intelligentsia made up of professionals was more or less coopted by means of threats and the bribe of limited professional autonomy. Today the main danger to the Soviet system may emanate from the industrial working class, which is being disrupted by the dismantling of the old social contract—a process already begun.

It is the perception of these dangers, not simply personal ambition for power and privilege, that threatens the system with destabilization and drives the substantial resistance to Gorbachev's plans. Meanwhile, Gorbachev displays a growing understanding of the paths necessary for modernizing the Soviet Union. He may be developing a more cohesive, more integrated program of development than he now discloses. He has shown thus far an unflagging determination to pursue his primary goal of modernization by all available means. By doing so he is entering a zone of danger. Factors of great potential creativity and great potential destructiveness are now emerging in one of the few countries that can determine the geopolitics of the planet.

GORBACHEV: A NEW FOREIGN POLICY?[3]

Since Mikhail Gorbachev became general secretary of the Communist Party on March 11, 1985, the conduct of Soviet foreign policy has improved. A skillful public relations effort has become an important component of Moscow's diplomacy, but the substance of the U.S.S.R.'s international behavior has also changed considerably. Gorbachev himself increasingly talks about the need for "a new approach" in addressing the problems of the world. At the 27th Party Congress in February 1986 he said:

It is not only in internal affairs that the turning point has been reached. It characterizes external affairs as well. The changes in contemporary world development are so profound and significant that they require a re-thinking and comprehensive analysis of all factors involved. The situation of nuclear deterrence demands the development of new approaches, methods and forms of relations between different social systems, states and regions. (*Pravda*, Feb. 26, 1986)

In a speech in Vladivostok in July, Gorbachev was even bolder, claiming that "the current stage in the development of civilization . . . is dictating the need for an urgent, radical break with many of the conventional approaches to foreign policy, a break with the traditions of political thinking." (*Pravda*, July 29, 1986)

Rhetoric, of course, comes cheap. But the foreign policy changes under Gorbachev have gone beyond words. He reshuffled the national security leadership, bringing younger and less doctrinaire officials to key positions and giving himself more personal control over decision-making. The new team quickly distin-

[3]Reprint of an article by Dimitri K. Simes, senior associate at the Carnegie Endowment for International Peace. Reprinted by permission of FOREIGN AFFAIRS, No. 3, 1987. Copyright © 1987 by the Council on Foreign Relations, Inc.

guished itself not only in launching Gorbachev's "charm offensive" but also by introducing a wide variety of foreign policy initiatives ranging from arms control proposals to overtures to China.

It is still far from certain how far, how fast and even in what direction Gorbachev intends to proceed. After less than two years on the job he needs more time to consolidate his authority. Until he became Yuri Andropov's de facto deputy after Brezhnev's death in November 1982, Gorbachev had little exposure to international affairs. His education as the chief architect of Soviet foreign policy is far from complete, and he himself probably cannot anticipate fully how his on-the-job learning will shape his attitudes toward the world.

If his record since assuming the leadership is any guide, Gorbachev is not inclined to depart from the fundamentals of Soviet strategy. Rather, the general secretary creatively uses a refreshing tactical flexibility in the pursuit of traditional Soviet objectives. These objectives include maintaining control over Eastern Europe; preventing whenever possible the emergence of unfriendly governments on the Soviet periphery; sponsoring Third World clients; aggressively seeking to undermine and/or replace U.S. geopolitical influence; and developing a military capability sufficient both to assure the U.S.S.R.'s ability to deal with any conceivable coalition of enemies and to project force on a global scale.

To respond properly to Gorbachev, the United States must distinguish between a newly pragmatic, vigorous and relatively sophisticated Soviet policy and a policy that would be truly more benign. America should welcome a more effective Soviet foreign policy only to the extent that it simultaneously becomes more moderate. Otherwise the United States and the West as a whole may find themselves mesmerized by an impressive Kremlin performance, forgetting that its final act is supposed to be their own demise.

II

The current Soviet domestic environment favors innovation in foreign policy as long as it does not abandon basic interests, ambitions and modes of behavior. Gorbachev frequently argues that the Soviet preoccupation with the modernization of its economy and society assures the peaceful nature of the U.S.S.R.'s global strategy: This is probably true to the extent that a period of international calm would help the Kremlin devote more resources to economic development. A new détente would also help Moscow obtain Western credits and technology.

But Soviet foreign policy is never dictated by economics. If anything, Gorbachev's difficulties in quickly improving the Soviet economy make it all the more important for him to demonstrate momentum in foreign policy. This momentum must be achieved without giving an impression of weakness or overeagerness. No conceivable economic benefits would be accepted by either the elite or the majority of the Soviet people as adequate compensation for the abandonment of the much cherished dream of Soviet imperial greatness.

This is not to suggest that the Politburo would block Gorbachev if he scaled down Soviet global ambitions; but his image as a formidable leader would be compromised. This image is crucial if the general secretary is to push through much needed but highly controversial economic reforms. On the one hand, as the writings of former Chief of the General Staff Nikolai Ogarkov suggest, the military and defense industrialists do appreciate that economic reform may be the only means to maintaining Soviet geopolitical competitiveness. But any Soviet leader might find his credibility among the powerful national security elite badly damaged if change at home were to become coupled with a perceived softness abroad. Nothing about Gorbachev or his career indicates that he is likely to take such chances.

The modest improvement in the Soviet economy in 1986 relieves pressure on Gorbachev to reduce the economic costs of acting as a global empire. Regardless of the eventual outcome of the general secretary's reforms, he is starting from such a low economic base that several reasonably successful years probably could result from just introducing a more competent management, reducing corruption and improving work discipline. In the long run, however, nothing short of systemic change will suffice for the Soviet Union to remain a great modern power. Meanwhile there is little fear in the Kremlin that economic difficulties will force the Soviet Union to abandon its basic security interests and responsibilities.

Nor is there any apparent political pressure on Gorbachev to reduce Soviet international assertiveness. The general secretary's campaign for *glasnost* (openness) has certainly prompted criticism of all kinds of abuses and inefficiencies. But the campaign does not reflect an across-the-board liberalization. Rather, *glasnost* is used by Gorbachev as a political tool to expose those individuals and practices that stand in the way of his reforms. The general secretary wants to run a tight ship. Questioning his own actions does not seem to be part of *glasnost*. Accordingly, while the Soviet media discuss in depth how to improve the economy and even society as a whole, foreign policy remains off limits to any meaningful debate.

Andrei Sakharov's return to Moscow from exile in Gorki changes little in this respect. True, he was given an opportunity to appear on American television, where he called for an expeditious Soviet withdrawal from Afghanistan and for decoupling the Strategic Defense Initiative (SDI) from other areas of arms control. But to put this in perspective, the Sakharov release took place just days after another well-known dissident, Anatoly Marchenko, died in a prison hospital after a long hunger strike he had begun to protest his mistreatment. Taking into account Sakharov's poor health and his well-known mistrust of doctors in Gorki, it was only prudent for Gorbachev to take measures so that the Kremlin would not be blamed for Sakharov's de facto murder. Although the Nobel Peace Prize–winning nuclear physicist was released unconditionally, months earlier he had sent a letter to the general secretary hinting that once back in Moscow he would prefer to focus on research rather than politics. Sakharov's skepticism toward SDI promised political advantages to Moscow. Also, interestingly, the announcement of his return was made on the very same day the Soviet government issued a statement declaring an end to its unilateral moratorium on nuclear testing.

Other well-known dissidents like Anatoly Shcharansky and Yuri Orlov were, in effect, exchanged for spies. Several others were released at the request of prestigious American visitors such as Occidental Petroleum Chairman Armand Hammer and then Senator Gary Hart (D-Colo.). Gorbachev should get credit both for being broad-minded in handling these hardship cases and for the skill with which he has exploited them to improve the Soviet image abroad. Nevertheless, Soviet repression has continued essentially unabated. Jewish emigration figures for 1986—914—are the second lowest for any year since 1969. Dissidents of all stripes continue to be arrested and persecuted. Soviet citizens are warned against contacts with foreigners. More generally, the scope of *glasnost* does not include the KGB. Activities of the security services today, unlike under Khrushchev, are not subject to critical scrutiny from outside the agency.

For the first time since Khrushchev, the Soviet media have openly criticized the KGB. The possibility that *glasnost* may extend to the secret police is interesting and encouraging. Still, the incident exposed by *Pravda* was not about mistreatment of a dissident. Rather, it involved a provincial KGB chief in the Ukrainian city of Voroshilovgrad who illegally ordered the arrest of a local journalist. Worse, according to *Pravda*, the KGB officer attempted to implicate the newspaper's own correspondent, whose investigative reporting had angered the provincial hierarchy. In short, KGB officers in Voroshilovgrad had challenged the Central Committee's principal media institution in Moscow, and by implication Gorbachev's *glasnost* campaign. Their punishment and public humiliation is an impressive demonstration of the general secretary's personal authority. Whether it is also a sign that the KGB will no longer be able to escape public scrutiny remains to be seen.

The new leadership is less insecure about exposing Soviet citizens to opposing viewpoints. For the first time in the U.S.S.R.'s history, Western officials, scholars and journalists are invited to appear on Soviet television, where some of them question Moscow's arms control initiatives and occasionally go so far as to condemn the invasion of Afghanistan. Yet their Soviet colleagues, as in the past, do not go beyond explaining the party line with varying degrees of sophistication.

It may very well be that Gorbachev is unleashing forces he will have difficulty controlling. Intellectuals who today are delighted to have an opportunity to expose the sins of the past may develop a taste for independence and eventually become a problem for the regime. Nationalists in ethnic republics—as the recent riots in Alma-Ata have demonstrated—have an even greater potential for challenging the central authority. Whether such challenges indeed take place and how Gorbachev would respond to them—by cracking down once again or by allowing a degree of genuine pluralism—are matters of conjecture.

III

Most Soviet people are intensely patriotic and cherish the Soviet great power image. Gorbachev's own devotion to Soviet greatness is not in doubt. On the contrary, he has often emphasized that one of the principal reasons behind his call for far-reaching economic reform is the need to maintain and enhance the Soviet role in international affairs.

In this connection, however, there is evidence that not everyone in the Soviet Union is comfortable with Gorbachev's arms control concessions. In a speech to a group of workers in Togliatti in April 1986 the general secretary himself referred to "numerous letters" to the Communist Party Central Committee from those worried that "under the cover of peaceful talk and fruitless negotiations the West will make a leap forward in armaments," catching the U.S.S.R. unprepared. The Soviet leader sounded somewhat defensive when he provided assurances that "this will not happen." (*Pravda*, Apr. 9, 1986)

But even if some Politburo members are uneasy about Gorbachev's arms control proposals, they will not rush to mount an attack against him. The tremendous power associated with the general secretary's post should not be underestimated. He is much more than the first among equals. Once elected by the Politburo, the general secretary becomes both the chief executive of "U.S.S.R., Inc.," and the high priest of Soviet Communist orthodoxy. His speeches are treated as official party documents, almost as holy texts. And he is built up as a symbolic figure whose stature is linked to the very legitimacy of the system.

Unlike the pope, however, the general secretary may be ousted. But that has happened only twice in Soviet history. Georgi Malenkov, demoted in 1953, had never enjoyed full authority as Stalin's successor. Khrushchev's dismissal in 1964 occurred only after he had managed to push through his "harebrained" schemes and, more importantly, had conducted constant assaults on the privileges of elites throughout the Soviet establishment. After Khrushchev every Soviet leader, despite physical infirmities (and in Brezhnev's case even outright senility), was allowed to die on the job. Andropov was able to exercise considerable authority even from a hospital bed. Konstantin Chernenko, whose health also rapidly deteriorated, made his imprint by slowing down reforms at home and adopting a less confrontational posture vis-à-vis the United States.

As for Gorbachev, there is a certain similarity between his position and Ronald Reagan's political mandate of 1980. Both men came to power after several failed administrations. Both benefited from an intense desire by their respective bodies politic to have finally a successful government. And both were propelled to power largely by a widespread belief that the ways of the past were no longer acceptable.

Yet the differences are obvious. The Politburo has the right to ask for a general secretary's resignation, but under ordinary circumstances this right is more apparent than real. Like members of a corporate board, individual Politburo members serve at the pleasure of the general secretary. Grossly unskilled chiefs can be brought down by a coalition, but as long as a general secretary plays his cards carefully, does not fail too dramatically and does not challenge the interests of the elite too drastically, his position is secure. The last thing other Politburo members would want to do is expose themselves as his premature critics or opponents. Gorbachev is not yet a dictator. But he has both the mandate and the temperamental predisposition to act as a decisive chief executive.

This is particularly true in foreign policy, where the elite have fewer vested interests and there are fewer opportunities for sabotage. Western observers who speculate about hard-line challenges to Gorbachev too often uncritically project into the Kremlin's national security formulation the widely publicized bureaucratic procrastination, ineptness and corruption that frustrate economic reforms. But in foreign policy the institutions are much smaller, the degree of centralization much greater and the general secretary's control over both decision-making and policy implementation much stronger.

In contrast to Brezhnev, who allowed an essentially cabinet-type government, run by key party and state agencies, to retain considerable autonomy, Gorbachev has quickly moved to consolidate his hold. In the area of national security, the general secretary, instead of delegating authority to several senior officials, has built around himself an impressive team of associates. All of them had qualifications for their new positions. But none were sufficiently entrenched politically to risk deviating from Gorbachev's instructions.

The new minister of foreign affairs, Eduard Shevardnadze, was an unusual choice. He made his entire career in the republic of Georgia, as a Communist Youth League functionary, a party official, minister of internal affairs—in effect the chief of police—and finally the party leader. Despite a lack of foreign policy expertise, Shevardnadze apparently had several important qualifications. He reportedly had been friendly with Gorbachev since the late 1950s. He had established a reputation in Georgia as an efficient, no-nonsense, but also open-minded, administrator. After 30 years of Andrei Gromyko's iron rule, the Foreign Ministry needed a fresh approach. Moreover, although tough and decisive, Shevardnadze was known for his jovial, open personality, which was bound to contrast favorably with Gromyko's dour manner. As long as he was not expected to act as a foreign policy mastermind, the new foreign minister was an imaginative choice for the job.

With Gromyko's departure, the Foreign Ministry ceased being the center of gravity of the Soviet national security formulation. That role shifted to the Central Committee Secretariat, which is personally directed by Gorbachev. Two new secretaries appointed at the 27th Party Congress became the general secretary's principal foreign policy lieutenants. One, former Ambassador to Washington Anatoly Dobrynin, took over the International Department. That office, which in the past dealt primarily with non-ruling communist parties and so-called national liberation movements, was given new responsibilities and personnel to focus on East-West affairs, specifically arms control.

The other, Aleksander Yakovlev, a former ambassador to Canada and before that a career party official, joined the Secretariat to coordinate all Soviet propaganda activities, internal as well as international. Anatoly Chernyaev, previously one of five International Department deputy chiefs, was made Gorbachev's key foreign policy aide, replacing the venerable Andrei Aleksandrov-Agentov, who had performed this function under Brezhnev and his successors since 1964. Chernyaev, like his predecessor, is less a high-powered conceptualizer than a competent assistant, who keeps the general secretary well briefed and exposed to a variety of opinions. Among others contributing viewpoints are the directors of two leading Moscow international think tanks—the Institute on the United States and Canada and the Institute of World Economy and International Relations—Georgi Arbatov and Yevgeny Primakov, respectively. While Arbatov occasionally was consulted by Soviet leaders before the Gorbachev era, only recently has his and Primakov's participation in the leadership councils been put on a regular footing.

The absence of a military man in the Politburo concentrates even more power in Gorbachev's hands. The minister of defense, Marshal Sergei Sokolov, 75, was appointed during the last months of Chernenko's tenure after the death of Dmitri Ustinov. From the beginning he has appeared to be little more than a caretaker. His status as merely a candidate (non-voting) Politburo member may say more about his personal situation than about any intent to downgrade the military's political role. Yet the absence of a forceful military voice on the Politburo obviously enhances Gorbachev's authority. The chief of the general staff, Marshal Sergei Akhromeyev, who accompanied the general secretary to the Reykjavik summit, impressed members of the U.S. delegation as a competent officer. But particularly in anticipation of a succession at the Defense Ministry, neither he nor his colleagues are likely to resist Gorbachev's wishes.

The character of this new national security team is telling. Most of the new appointees are definite improvements over their predecessors. All of Gorbachev's hand-picked lieutenants have already had long and largely successful careers, and none were recruited from outside the narrow party-government institutional framework. None were ever known to dissent from Soviet policy. While younger (although not always so young—Dobrynin, Yakovlev and Chernyaev are all in their mid-sixties), more vigorous and creative, Gorbachev's top foreign policy appointees as a team are more suited to adjust the Soviet foreign policy course than to change it drastically.

IV

The concept of a bipolar world remains central to Soviet thinking. Gorbachev's address to the 27th Party Congress was notable for its unprecedented preoccupation with East-West relations and particularly the relationship with the United States. The general secretary's aides in Reykjavik revealed that he is personally involved in all major decisions on relations with America. No other country, including China, receives anything approaching the same level of attention from the Soviet leader.

Both Dobrynin and Yakovlev, as noted, are experienced America watchers. Dobrynin's deputy, Georgi Kornienko, used to work for him at the Soviet embassy in the United States. So too did Yuli Vorontsov, one of the two first deputy ministers of foreign affairs, who was Dobrynin's deputy chief of mission for many years. The other deputy is Anatoly Kovalev, who, like Chernyaev, is an expert on Western Europe. Never before has Soviet foreign policy formulation been so dominated by officials with backgrounds in Western, and especially American, affairs.

Why does the United States occupy such a central place in Gorbachev's world outlook? The new Soviet leader is a patriot and a pragmatist. He has little of Khrushchev's romantic enthusiasm for Third World revolutionaries. And unlike Brezhnev, he does not run foreign policy by inertia. Gorbachev defines his own priorities and pursues them with dogged determination. From his perspective, it is the United States that represents the greatest threat to the security and prosperity of the Soviet Union. It is also the United States that remains the toughest obstacle to the expansion of Soviet global power. But the existence of the American giant offers Moscow attractive opportunities to play the role of the only other superpower benefactor for any nation disenchanted with Washington. Because the United States has a unique place in Soviet political thinking, agreements with it—particularly agreements that codify Soviet equality—contribute to Gorbachev's standing inside the U.S.S.R.

Soviet preoccupation with the United States does not mean neglect of other international interests: the general secretary has made new moves to improve ties with a variety of nations. Yet he has always made clear that while relations with other countries would be built on their own merits, it is with America that the issue of mutual survival would have to be worked out.

Soviet analysts themselves reject the notion that the U.S.S.R. could benefit from lesser concentration on the United States. For example, American Sovietologist Jerry Hough recently wrote an article published in *Literaturnaya Gazeta* in which he suggested that "the most realistic way to improve the Soviet-American relationship is to pursue a policy of a relative neglect of the United States," because otherwise Moscow's concessions would lead only to "the arrogance of power" on the part of the Reagan Administration. A leading Soviet commentator, Fedor Burlatsky, voiced a strong objection. In a rejoinder, Burlatsky argued that the relationship with the United States was too important to be put on the back burner for even a relatively short time. (*Literaturnaya Gazeta*, Aug. 27, 1986)

Continuity in Soviet foreign policy has also been evident with respect to Eastern Europe, where Gorbachev has combined flexibility and firmness. At the Soviet party congress, Gorbachev stated that disagreements among communist parties should not be overly "dramatized." In a departure from the Kremlin's previous insistence that deviations from the Soviet model of development and differences with Soviet foreign policy positions were unacceptable, the general secretary acknowledged that "identical views on all issues without an exception are probably impossible." Gorbachev's statement was interpreted by East European leaders as an official blessing to do things their own way. Simultaneously, Gorbachev instituted regular consultations with Warsaw Pact leaders on such international developments as the Geneva and Reykjavik summits. And East European officials were pleased that instead of always being summoned to Moscow, as was customary under Brezhnev, they now were frequently briefed in their own capitals.

Gorbachev's sensitivity to East European concerns has its limits. He has actively discouraged Eastern bloc countries from becoming dependent upon economic cooperation with the West. Instead they have been strongly urged to integrate further with the Soviet and other East European economies. All broadminded talk aside, the practical side of Gorbachev's policy has been to force unenthusiastic client states to accept a plan for the merger of Soviet and East European enterprises on terms beneficial to the U.S.S.R.

The Brezhnev Doctrine is very much a part of Gorbachev's policy. Speaking at the Polish party congress in June 1986, the Soviet leader issued a stern warning to those seeking genuine independence from Moscow:

. . . socialism now manifests itself as an international reality, as an alliance of states closely linked by political, economic, cultural and defense interests. To threaten the socialist system, to try to undermine it from the outside and wrench a country away from the socialist community means to encroach not only on the will of the people, but also on the entire postwar arrangement, and, in the final analysis, on peace. (*Pravda,* July 1, 1986)

Gorbachev's approaches toward China reveal a certain flexibility, but he is not promising to give away anything important. In his Moscow party congress address he unequivocally described China as being a socialist state. He also noted an improvement in Sino-Soviet relations and declared that "the reserves of cooperation between the U.S.S.R. and China are enormous." Even more significant was what Gorbachev did not say; his speech carefully avoided explicit or even implicit criticism of Chinese policies.

The effort to rebuild bridges to China was initiated during the last months of Brezhnev's rule. Speaking in the Central Asian city of Tashkent on March 22, 1982, he expressed strong interest in normalizing relations with Beijing. He offered a symbolic ideological concession by calling China a socialist country for the first time in years. Andropov and Chernenko made similar gestures during their brief tenures.

But it was Gorbachev who made rapprochement with China a diplomatic priority. Much has been accomplished already: the Sino-Soviet border has been generally quiet; trade is increasing; cultural exchanges have resumed; and some Soviet specialists have returned to China. But relaxation still has not led to true accommodation. Both powers share a desire to stabilize the relationship but neither appears to want to re-create the close alliance of the early 1950s. The Soviets speak rather positively about changes introduced by Deng Xiaoping. But behind a facade of curiosity and even grudging admiration there is a noticeable concern that successful modernization in China might change the balance of power to the detriment of the Soviet Union.

Gorbachev offered several inducements to Beijing in his Vladivostok speech. He disclosed that "the question of withdrawing a considerable number of Soviet troops from Mongolia is being examined." He made an apparent concession on the Amur River boundary dispute by accepting a demarcation along the middle of the main channel. Earlier, however, at the Moscow party congress, Gorbachev had emphasized that rapprochement with China would be "on the basis of principle and equality and not at the expense of third countries." The meaning was clear: the Kremlin would not meet China's demands for a Soviet withdrawal from Afghanistan and an end to its support of the Vietnamese occupation of Cambodia. Deng Xiaoping's offer, after the Vladivostok speech, to meet with Gorbachev if the Soviets disassociated themselves from the Vietnamese occupation did not receive a positive response.

Nor has the new Soviet leadership been willing to forgo its assertiveness in the Third World. At the 27th Party Congress Gorbachev acknowledged that the process of change in the Third World "has encountered considerable difficulties." In his view:

Through political maneuvering, promises and bribes, military threats and blackmail, and not infrequently through direct intervention in the internal affairs of liberated nations, capitalism to a large degree has managed to save previously established relations of economic dependence. On this basis, imperialism has succeeded in creating and fine-tuning the most sophisticated system of neocolonial exploitation, in tying up closer to itself a significant number of liberated states.

There has not been such pessimism in Soviet official speeches since Khrushchev announced an alliance with the Third World at the 20th Party Congress in 1956.

But Westerners who saw Gorbachev's realistic assessment as a sign that Soviet involvement in the Third World would be scaled down to save resources and improve relations with the United States have been disabused of such hopes. Setbacks in the Third World only motivated Gorbachev to try harder to uphold already existent Soviet commitments and more generally to keep the U.S.S.R. as a credible global power. A sense of overextension may have limited Moscow's willingness to accept costly new responsibilities, but it has not led Moscow to reduce its support for friends and clients, particularly those directly or indirectly challenged by the United States. New realism has not been translated into greater moderation.

In Nicaragua, Angola and Afghanistan, the Soviet Union made considerable new investments to support its embattled allies. Sophisticated weapons worth hundreds of millions of dollars were delivered to the Sandinistas and to the government of Angola. In Afghanistan, where the Soviets are reported to spend about $3 billion a year, there was an increase in the number of ground and air incursions into and artillery bombardments of Pakistan. A token withdrawal of Soviet troops from Afghanistan completed in November, by all indications, was no more than a public relations gesture.

The replacement of Babrak Karmal with secret police chief Najibullah in May 1986 as the Afghan Communist Party leader brought new sophistication to Kabul's policy. The new leadership did make some new approaches to tribal and religious leaders, and on January 1 Kabul proposed a cease-fire. Nevertheless, both the Soviet and Afghan governments made abundantly clear that their version of a "just settlement" of the war would keep the communist regime firmly in control. The "national reconciliation" in Afghanistan advocated by Gorbachev presupposes that Kabul will moderate some of its practices and even include some opposition elements in the government. But these elements are offered no more than token participation. In return, the United States, China, Pakistan and Iran are requested to stop all support of the rebels. And despite his professed desire to remove Soviet troops from Afghanistan, Gorbachev assured the visiting Najibullah that the Soviet Union "will not abandon our southern neighbor in trouble." (*Pravda*, Dec. 18, 1986) This does not sound like a formula for genuine power-sharing.

In the Middle East the Soviet Union sent new weapons, including long-range SA-5 missiles and advanced MiG-25 fighters, to Libya and Syria. Moscow denounced the U.S. raid on Libya in April as "state terrorism." Realistically, the Soviets could do nothing to prevent the American attack. They had neither the naval and air power nor, presumably, the desire to risk a direct military confrontation with the United States in the Mediterranean just to protect Muammar al-Qaddafi. In any case, they apparently provided no early warning to the Libyans.

Still, in evaluating the Soviet response to the raid, it is fair to say that for Libya the glass was half full rather than half empty. The Politburo canceled a scheduled May visit to the United States by Foreign Minister Shevardnadze, who was supposed to confer with Secretary of State George Shultz about arrangements for a U.S.-Soviet summit. To put this step into perspective, one should remember that Brezhnev did not cancel President Nixon's trip to the Soviet Union in May 1972 following the American bombing of Hanoi and mining of Haiphong harbor. Shevardnadze's cancellation could be partly explained by the Kremlin's uncertainty whether another summit with Ronald Reagan could accomplish much. But North Vietnam in 1972 was a much closer and important ally than Libya in 1986, and Qaddafi's endorsement of international terrorism was implicitly criticized even by Gorbachev himself. (*Pravda*, May 29, 1986) Beyond diplomatic retaliation and verbal denunciations of "the barbarian attack," the U.S.S.R. agreed to make an additional contribution to Libyan defenses. Qaddafi's deputy, Major Abd al-Salam Jalloud, went to Moscow in late May and, in addition to meeting with Gorbachev, had extensive negotiations with a high-powered Soviet delegation headed by Soviet Premier Nikolai Ryzhkov, with Marshal Sokolov as a member. Upon his return to Tripoli Jalloud reported that the Kremlin promised to deliver new military aid.

Moscow also made additional commitments to Syria. After the U.S. raid Gorbachev personally assured visiting Syrian Vice President Abd al-Hakim Khaddam that Moscow would assist in "the strengthening of [Syrian] defense capability." (*Pravda*, May 30, 1986) When Britain broke diplomatic relations with Damascus over Syrian involvement in an attempt to blow up an El Al airliner in London, the Soviet Union accused Prime Minister Margaret Thatcher's government of following the instructions of "American reactionary circles and Zionists."

The Soviets also made new approaches to Japan and even to Israel. In both cases they went far enough to create an impression of movement but not far enough for any specific accomplishment. It had been ten years since a Soviet foreign minister had visited Tokyo, and the Japanese welcomed the fact that Shevardnadze's arrival in January 1986 restored a higher level of diplomatic dialogue. Still, like Gromyko before him, Shevardnadze refused to incorporate a specific reference to the contested northern islands in the joint communiqué. Similarly, discussions in Helsinki in August 1986 with the Israelis regarding the establishment of consular links collapsed over the Soviet refusal to discuss Jewish emigration.

All in all, Soviet geopolitical maneuvering under Gorbachev has demonstrated a new sense of purpose, a new realism and a new creativity. What it has not demonstrated is any kind of turn inward, any evidence that Gorbachev and his colleagues are scaling down Soviet global ambitions in order to concentrate on domestic economic modernization. Nor has the Soviet Union shown any hesitation to use force to accomplish its objectives or, for that matter, any reluctance to support governments charged with terrorism. Gorbachev's advisers publicly argue about "the need not to view conflict situations only through the prism of Soviet-American relations." However, the Soviet approach to world politics continues to be based on a familiar mind-set that views relations with the United States as a zero-sum game, in which any gain for Washington is automatically a loss for Moscow and, conversely, any American setback is a plus for the U.S.S.R.

The essence of Gorbachev's attitude to international affairs was summed up in his report to the party congress: "Continuity in foreign policy has nothing in common with the simple repetition of the past, especially as far as approaches to accumulated problems are concerned. . . . What is required is firmness in de-

fending principles and positions coupled with tactical flexibility. . . . " And it is precisely in tactical flexibility, rather than in
a strategic reappraisal of Soviet international interests, that
Gorbachev has already made a major impact on the conduct of
Soviet foreign policy.

V

Where Gorbachev truly differs from his predecessors is in his
handling of arms control. He has made a number of dramatic new
proposals for which he received public credit, even from Ronald
Reagan. It is first and foremost the general secretary's approach
to arms control that leads two seasoned American analysts to argue that "his foreign-policy perspectives differ significantly from
those of his predecessors and could reshape the ways in which the
Kremlin deals with the outside world." (F. Stephen Larrabee and
Allen Lynch, "Gorbachev: The Road to Reykjavik," *Foreign
Policy*, Winter 1986-87, p. 3)

A dynamic and imaginative arms control diplomacy has
helped Gorbachev to determine, to a large degree, the focus of
the East-West dialogue. For the Soviet Union to project a benign
image, establishing arms control as the number-one international
issue makes inherent sense. It turns attention away from events
that otherwise could cause the Soviet Union considerable embarrassment. Gorbachev boldly used the Chernobyl nuclear plant disaster to make a case for his arms control program. The scandal
over the arrest of *U.S. News & World Report* correspondent Nicholas Daniloff damaged the general secretary's reputation in the
United States. The Reykjavik summit, proposed by the Soviet
leader, helped to erase the memory of the Daniloff entrapment
and to revive the image of Gorbachev the arms controller.

On this issue—arms control—Gorbachev could safely occupy
the high moral ground. Whenever the Soviet Union finds itself
on the defensive because of internal repression, the Kremlin
makes a case that it is the true champion of the most important
among all human rights—the right to survival. The tendency in
the West to equate arms control with peace allows Gorbachev to
make a favorable impression without sacrificing Soviet global aspirations or changing domestic practices.

If arms control talks end in a stalemate, the Kremlin is posi-
tioned to blame America and appeal to Western public opinion

to put pressure on the American Administration. Since there is no audience on the other side that the United States could hope to engage on its behalf, the arms control public relations contest must be played exclusively on Western turf. Consequently, even a draw is advantageous to the Kremlin. Gorbachev has perfected this use of disarmament diplomacy as a political weapon. But he also has offered enough substance to suggest that the professed Soviet interest in reaching an agreement is not just propaganda.

There has been an interesting evolution in the Soviet attitude toward nuclear weapons. Until the mid-1970s Soviet military doctrine argued that nuclear war, while inherently undesirable, would result in a Soviet victory. Accustomed to a position of nuclear inferiority, the Soviets charged the United States with all kinds of sinister designs to exploit the American edge. As the Soviet strategic forces grew, Moscow portrayed them as a symbol of the Soviet Union's parity with the United States, in effect a symbol of Soviet superpower status.

Gradually, however, first civilian and then military analysts in the Soviet Union began saying openly that nuclear war was unwinnable, would not bring victory to the U.S.S.R., but would destroy human civilization. The general recognition that in terms of nuclear capabilities the Soviet Union was, at a minimum, second to none has reduced Moscow's need to remind the world of its strategic might. In fact, such bragging had proved counterproductive, providing ammunition to Soviet critics in the West.

In the early 1980s some leading Soviet strategists, including Marshal Ogarkov, issued thinly camouflaged warnings regarding the limited military and political utility of acquiring more and more nuclear weapons. They emphasized that new types of conventional arms had the potential of accomplishing the same goals without creating unacceptable collateral damage. Yet the priority given to nuclear matters was retarding the Soviet effort to compete with the United States in these other increasingly crucial areas of military technology. Other Soviet experts pointed out that nuclear weapons had not helped the Americans in Vietnam or intimidated U.S. opponents elsewhere; privately they were willing to concede that the Soviet Union faced an identical problem.

The Soviet Union is less dependent on nuclear weapons than the United States. The U.S.S.R. enjoys a margin of conventional superiority on the entire periphery of its empire. No Soviet clients, in contrast to America's NATO allies, feel that the Soviet nuclear umbrella is the key to their security. Furthermore, the growing Soviet non-nuclear force projection capabilities make nuclear weapons less indispensable for Moscow's global military role.

Because the Kremlin is deadly serious about the political utility of military power, and precisely because the Soviet force posture is determined largely by the professional military, there is an emerging consensus in Moscow about de-emphasizing the nuclear component of the Soviet arsenal as long as it can be done without giving an advantage to other nuclear nations. Arms control gives the Soviet Union a chance to accomplish exactly that.

There are also economic and technological considerations. The Soviet Union can afford its current level of spending on strategic forces, which constitutes eight to ten percent of the military budget. Any conceivable arms reductions would allow little savings; paradoxically, they may initially require some additional expenditure if the Soviets are forced to accept as the price of a deal the restructuring of their forces, which would require a move from heavy land-based missiles to a greater emphasis on missile-carrying submarines and bombers armed with cruise missiles—two categories in which the U.S.S.R. lags behind the United States.

But in a longer-term perspective, the Soviet Union is not interested in unrestricted competition with America in creating new types of weapons. An intensified technological arms race would occupy thousands of Soviet scientists and engineers whose work is vital for economic modernization. Moscow's concern is magnified by a fear that after all the resources invested in nuclear forces, it may find itself confronted with some completely new and unexpected technological threat. That is the main reason, as Gorbachev explained in his post-summit press conference in Reykjavik, for the Soviet concern over the U.S. Strategic Defense Initiative.

On the one hand, Gorbachev defiantly declared that the Soviet Union "is not frightened by SDI" and will be able to find an effective "asymmetrical" response to it "without having to sacrifice much," but the Soviet leader complained that "through SDI one can come into new types of weapons." (*Pravda*, Oct. 13, 1986)

From the Soviet standpoint it does not help that the United States may be better prepared for a race in new military technologies. In his party congress address Gorbachev admitted that "the current stage of the general crisis of capitalism" does not preclude "the mastering of new scientific-technological directions," even to the extent of achieving "social revenge, the recapture of previously lost positions." Anything arms control can do to address this danger by killing, or at least retarding, SDI would be a major accomplishment for the Politburo.

Finally, the Soviet system puts a premium on planning and predictability. Soviet leaders do appreciate the value of arms control in exchanging information, providing mutual reassurances and avoiding the need to think about each other's strategic programs in terms of worst-case scenarios.

The 1986 Soviet arms control offensive started on January 15 with the unveiling of a major new negotiating package. The proposal was typical of Gorbachev's approach: it included new ideas and was presented with dramatic flair. Only three hours after Gorbachev's letter to Reagan outlining his proposals was delivered to Secretary of State Shultz, the general secretary's detailed statement about the initiative was read on Soviet television and distributed by Tass.

Much of the package was pure public relations. Gorbachev proposed a complete elimination of nuclear weapons by the end of the century. Almost equally unrealistic was an appeal to begin by 1990 the elimination of nuclear missiles and battlefield weapons by all nuclear powers. Taking Soviet conventional preponderance into account, the negative reactions of the French, British and Chinese were easy to predict. The first stage of the nuclear disarmament plan, to reduce all U.S. and Soviet strategic arms by 50 percent, had already been proposed by the Soviets and rejected by the Reagan Administration. The proposal failed to satisfy the U.S. concern with heavy Soviet intercontinental ballistic missiles, yet precluded deployment of the U.S. MX missiles as well as the Trident II submarine. Finally, in the Soviet package, SDI research had to be confined to a restrictively defined "laboratory."

Real Soviet concessions consisted of an extension of a unilateral nuclear test ban moratorium, a willingness to allow on-site inspection, acceptance of the old U.S. zero-option for intermediate-range missiles in Europe (but no willingness to scrap missiles in Asia) and an agreement that British and French nuclear forces would not have to be included in the reductions as long as London and Paris guaranteed that they would not be expanded or modernized. But probably most encouraging was Gorbachev's apparent willingness not to demand U.S. abandonment of SDI as a precondition for progress on all other arms control issues.

Gorbachev also committed himself to a summit with President Reagan in Washington, but only if there could be movement on an intermediate-range nuclear forces (INF) agreement and a nuclear test ban. This commitment was delivered both publicly and through private diplomatic channels, including via intermediaries such as Senator Edward Kennedy (D-Mass.) and former President Richard Nixon. It was on this basis that the Reagan Administration finally accepted the Gorbachev request to hold a preparatory summit in Reykjavik. Washington assumed—now it is clear, far too casually—that Gorbachev wanted the encounter because he needed assurances that he would not leave the United States empty-handed after his visit. Apparently the Administration believed there had been enough progress on INF that some agreement could be completed in Reykjavik.

Instead of pursuing a limited agreement, Gorbachev confronted President Reagan with another comprehensive nuclear arms control package. In this case, all American and Soviet medium-range missiles would be banned in Europe. French and British nuclear arsenals would not have to be frozen. Moreover, Soviet missiles in Asia would be limited to 100 warheads, and Washington would be entitled to deploy the same number in the continental United States. Soviet short-range missiles in Europe would be frozen and negotiations regarding their "further fate" would begin. The 50-percent reduction in strategic weapons was revived, to be achieved in five years. But all of these concessions were at a price: the United States had to agree to limit SDI research beyond even the narrow interpretation of the 1972 Anti-Ballistic Missile Treaty for a period of ten years. Not only components but also elements of SDI systems could not be tested in space. After ten years the ABM treaty would still be in effect. Acceptance of the Soviet demand would amount to barring most SDI-related research efforts. The whole program could be considerably retarded if not stopped altogether.

What was the rationale for returning to the previous Soviet all-or-nothing position? Did Gorbachev expect President Reagan to surrender his SDI dream? Was it a calculated step to make major concessions to Western Europe while presenting SDI, and accordingly the Reagan Administration, as the only stumbling block to an arms deal of "historic proportion"? Or is it possible that Gorbachev has a gambler's streak which overcame his prudent judgment, that the Soviet leader misinterpreted Reagan's interest in his ideas and gave away too much to be able to settle at the end with a modest agreement on INF and a test ban?

There are no definite answers. But there was a real difference in both tone and substance between the Soviet leader's initial assessment at his Reykjavik press conference and his two subsequent television addresses in Moscow on October 14 and October 22. With each appearance Gorbachev sounded increasingly disappointed and bitter. At the press conference he stated that it would be a mistake "to say that the encounter produced no results" and claimed that the summit in Washington was "closer." His first television appearance in Moscow combined a sharper attack on the U.S. performance in Reykjavik with an assertion that "the meeting was useful." The fact that the third address on the same topic had to be delivered so soon after the first two suggests that something went wrong. Gorbachev indeed has acknowledged that what has happened since Reykjavik was "totally different" from original Soviet hopes.

Gorbachev's initial cautious optimism was based on two misconceptions. First, the Soviet leader failed to understand that there was more to the differences between the two sides' positions in Reykjavik than just SDI. Reagan's peculiar negotiating style and his emphasis on the big picture at the expense of crucial details obscured major areas of disagreement on strategic offensive weapons cuts. U.S. efforts to interpret the President's words, contrary to Gorbachev's own perception, evidently touched a sensitive nerve. The Soviet leader sounded particularly angry over the American insistence that all Mr. Reagan had promised was to eliminate ballistic missiles rather than all strategic arms.

Second, Gorbachev's press conference suggested a strong expectation that the public in the United States and particularly Western Europe would pressure the Reagan Administration to accommodate Moscow on SDI. Instead, the Kremlin discovered that the President was able to rally American opinion around his refusal to yield on SDI research. Even more shocking to the Soviets was the advice of key West European governments to deemphasize those elements of the agreement in Reykjavik that Gorbachev has highlighted: a complete elimination of strategic ballistic missiles and the elimination of all intermediate-range missiles from Europe. The Soviet leadership finally had to see that the risky improvisation at Reykjavik, while in many respects embarrassing and potentially damaging to Washington, also had set back Gorbachev's arms control agenda.

VI

As frustrated as the Kremlin was with the Reagan Administration, it recognized that an overreaction might backfire. In a furious personal attack on the President published in *Pravda*, Georgi Arbatov nonetheless stated that the Politburo was not going to be "provoked." (*Pravda*, Nov. 21, 1986) Arbatov and other Soviet commentators were still saying that there was no alternative to negotiating with the Reagan Administration. Privately some Soviets were sending messages suggesting that a way might be found to decouple SDI again from INF and the test ban. They hinted that if that happened, preparations for a full-scale Washington summit could be put back on track.

The Iran/contra scandal, following the Democratic takeover of the Senate, was bound to raise the question in Moscow whether the President had become a lame duck. It is unlikely that the Soviets will try to exploit the President's moment of weakness by engaging in risky adventures. Gorbachev's advisers caution that the politically injured U.S. President may even welcome a Soviet challenge to divert attention from his domestic problems. But, conversely, the Soviets hesitate to do anything that may help the President; that obviously precludes an arms deal, at least temporarily. The Soviet leadership knows that the time to reach an agreement with Reagan is running out and, other factors being equal, it would prefer to accomplish whatever is possible with one president who can realistically deliver. Still, before genuine bargaining resumes, Gorbachev will have to conclude that the worst is over for President Reagan.

It is clear that any agreement that might be reached in the near term, while possibly beneficial politically, is not going to lead to significant changes in the military balance. Arms control can make some useful, if modest, contribution to managing nuclear competition, and failure to practice arms control seriously is probably detrimental to the West's ability to sustain a coherent policy toward the Soviet Union. It helps both superpowers to avoid deploying systems that neither really wants but may be compelled to proceed with in the absence of an agreement. The ABM treaty is a perfect example. It theoretically allows both sides to block the emergence of particularly destabilizing new weapons, although on this score the record is rather discouraging. Most importantly, arms control serves as useful political and psychological shock absorbers on the bumpy road of the nuclear race. Without it a worst-case mentality would inevitably flourish on both sides. Both the political stability of the U.S.-Soviet relationship and rational military planning would be jeopardized.

Nevertheless, arms control successes will be useful only as long as their limited impact on the East-West competition is evaluated realistically. The roots of the superpower rivalry are not in the nuclear arms buildup. Rather, the buildup itself is a reflection of basic conflicts of interests and values between the two systems of alliances. Accordingly, Gorbachev will have to show much more than his "new" arms control thinking to be accepted as genuine good news to the West.

What would really make the difference for America and its allies is if Moscow were to come to terms with its reduced ideological and cultural appeal, its technological backwardness as well as limited economic resources, and if it abandoned as a practical foreign policy objective the aspiration of being a global equal of—to say nothing of being superior to—the United States. Unless and until the Kremlin at least begins moving in this direction or, alternatively, succeeds in making the Soviet model attractive to the rest of the world, it will have to continue its unique reliance on force and coercion as foreign policy tools. It would be even more meaningful if the Soviet Union concluded that its security does not require an iron grip over Eastern Europe.

Speculating whether Gorbachev is interested in, or capable of, such a historic change in Soviet policy is an exercise in futility. What he has done up to this point may be either a case of tactical modification or a prelude to strategic reassessment. Gorbachev may not be quite sure himself. The United States does not know enough about his circumstances and does not have the adequate leverage and talent for foreign policy fine-tuning to influence the Soviet leadership's deliberations.

Following America's own interests is a more appropriate course during this time of Soviet transition. Identifying these interests clearly and coolly should be the first order of the day. And that requires a recognition that the Soviet domestic renaissance is not necessarily a blessing to the West.

Throughout Russian history the modernizers rather than the conservatives have pursued the most ambitious international strategies. Peter the Great, Catherine the Great, Alexanders I and II proved to be overall more assertive and menacing to Russia's neighbors than such conservative tsars as Nicholas I and Alexander III. The realization that things had to be changed at home was to a large extent caused by failures abroad. And to make Russia more powerful and competitive was traditionally one of the main rationales for reforms. Domestic renovation was usually accompanied by a new spirit of popular self-confidence and patriotism that could be mobilized by the rulers to support foreign exploits.

Khrushchev's de-Stalinization campaign is a case in point. During Khrushchev's time the Soviet Union underwent a far-reaching internal liberalization. Soviet foreign policy—as rapprochement with Yugoslavia and arrangements with Finland and particularly Austria would testify—became more flexible and imaginative. But it also became more vigorous and ambitious. It was Khrushchev who ordered the crushing of the Hungarian rebellion, built the Berlin Wall and deployed Soviet missiles on Cuba. It was he who presided over the missile buildup and the aggressive effort to organize an "anti-imperialist coalition" with Third World Nations that transformed the U.S.S.R. into a truly global power.

There are both moral and geopolitical arguments for why the United States may benefit from a reformed Soviet Union. A pluralistic democracy would not only make Soviet society more humane but would also probably force it to devote resources and energy to internal problems at the expense of global assertiveness. But what if the impact of Gorbachev's "revolution" from above were limited to having the enlightened and determined autocrat adjust the Soviet regime to modernity? A new dynamism and efficiency on the part of an adversary is also a legitimate cause for concern. There are more unknowns that ever in the U.S.-Soviet relationship. Both new opportunities and new dangers abound. Americans must approach them with an open mind but without wishful thinking and excessive sentimentality.

WILL GORBACHEV REFORM THE SOVIET UNION?[4]

The current "crisis" of the Soviet system about which everybody has been talking must seem very strange to an outside observer: there are no starving crowds or dead bodies along the roads, no riots or clashes with the police, virtually nothing to show or hide on the evening news. Of course, Soviet economic performance is appalling: GNP growth has declined almost to zero; and a 30-percent decrease in oil production has been aggravated even further by the recent drop in the price of oil. To this, add obsolete industrial equipment, chronically ill agriculture, and nearly catastrophic environmental problems, and the resulting picture will seem frightening enough. Yet within the Soviet system, only a fundamental challenge to the principles upon which the regime is built can be seen as a true crisis, and then that challenge can only be taken with full seriousness if it is described in the terminology of Marxism-Leninism.

Such a description is precisely what has been given by Professor Tatyana Zaslavskaya in her famous "Novosibirsk Document." This influential scholar (the new Soviet leader Mikhail Gorbachev himself uses many of her definitions in his speeches) sees the cause of Soviet economic problems in

the lagging of the system of production relations, and hence of the mechanism of state management of the economy which is its reflection, behind the level of development of the productive forces.

Lest anyone wonder about the actual meaning of her definition, Professor Zaslavskaya quotes a classic Marxist formula describing what actually happens in a time of contradiction between "productive forces" and "the system of production relations":

There ensues either a period of acute socioeconomic and political cataclysms within the given formation, which modify and readjust production relations to the new mode of production, or there comes an epoch of a general crisis of the given social formation and of its downfall caused by a social revolution.

Nor, she adds, is a socialist society miraculously exempt from this general rule:

[4]Reprint of a magazine article by the writer Vladimir Bukovsky. Reprinted from *Commentary*, 82:19+, S. '86, by permission; all rights reserved. Copyright © 1986 by the American Jewish Committee.

Attempts at improving production relations, bringing them into greater correspondence with the new demand of productive forces, . . . cannot run their course without conflict.

The Soviet people, then, should brace for a new spell of class struggle in their classless society (or a struggle of "interest groups," as Professor Zaslavskaya tactfully calls them), because a

radical reorganization of economic management essentially affects the interests of many social groups, to some of which it promises improvements, but to others a deterioration in their position.

And no class (or "interest group") in history has been known to give up its position without a struggle.

Not surprisingly, Professor Zaslavskaya becomes vague and inconsistent, even evasive, when she defines the "social group" whose interests are antagonistic to the goal of social progress, and whose position, therefore, must "deteriorate" in the forthcoming class struggle. She talks about an "intermediate link of the management" which has acquired more rights and responsibilities than those on the top and at the bottom. She alludes to some bureaucrats at the top who do not want to have more responsibilities requiring better professional qualifications than they possess. She also mentions some officials who "occupy comfortable positions with high incomes and vaguely defined responsibilities." And she describes a general tendency within the Soviet system to reward those who are more docile instead of those who are more gifted and efficient.

However, these generalized descriptions of personality types and tendencies cannot serve as a substitute for a clear definition of a social group (with common economic interests and a certain place in the system of production relations, as required for Marxist analysis). She comes very close to naming this mysterious group when she says that the "central element in the system of production relations is the dominant form of ownership of the means of production"—a classic Marxist formula. But if she went a bit further and actually named the culprit, she would no longer be an influential Soviet scholar but a dissident, because every schoolboy in the Soviet Union knows that under socialism the means of production belong to the Communist party apparatus, acting on behalf of the "proletariat."

This is exactly the group (or "New Class," as Milovan Djilas called it long ago) which occupies the cushiest positions with high incomes and vaguely defined responsibilities, which rewards the docile instead of the gifted, and whose interests are opposed to a radical reorganization of economic management. When Professor Zaslavskaya speaks about the need to shift from "administrative methods to economic means of management," when Gorbachev, echoing her, emphasizes the need to give more "independence and rights" to enterprises, and when he, finally, says that "It is impossible to achieve any tangible results in any sphere of activity as long as a party official substitutes for a manager," one has little doubt as to whose interests will be affected by this "reorganization."

The emerging dilemma is truly paradoxical: if the party retains its control over the economy, socialism will be endangered and will finally collapse; if, however, the party loses its control over the economy (and, therefore, its control over Soviet society), what Gorbachev calls "the position of socialism in the modern world" will collapse just as surely.

In short, the implacable logic of Marxist-Leninist analysis predicts the inevitable demise of socialism. Here indeed is a fundamental crisis of the entire system.

That system grew out of the compromise between revolutionary ideology and reality that the Communists were forced to make from the very beginning.

According to Lenin's own theory, the state was supposed to "die out" under socialism. Yet so long as the Communist state was encircled by powerful capitalist enemies, its power had to grow in order to survive and to promote revolution throughout the world. The Soviet state emerged out of this contradiction, according to the laws of dialectics.

The new system of government was proclaimed to be a "dictatorship of the proletarians," which in practical terms meant a dictatorship of the "advance-guard of the proletarians"—the Communist party—ruling on behalf of the proletarians. At that time, the proletarians—industrial workers and poor peasants—constituted barely 10 percent of the population, while the party members constituted about 10 percent of the proletarians. Leaving aside the scope of terror needed for such a tiny minority to rule dictatorially, "partocracy" was the only possible way to resolve the new regime's fundamental contradiction.

Thus, behind the backs of everyone and every governmental institution, there developed a party "shadow government"—the

Central Committee of the CPSU and its respective Departments—overseeing and directing every aspect of work in accordance with ideological requirements. Today, after nearly seventy years, this network of party cells penetrates every institution, from top to bottom, in order to guarantee that each party directive will be carried out to the letter.

The Foreign Ministry of the USSR, like a foreign ministry in any normal state, is preoccupied with its professional duties of maintaining relations, promoting trade, negotiating agreements, and in general advancing the national interests of the Soviet state. But at the same time, the International Department of the Central Committee is promoting world revolution and making sure that the interests of Communist ideology are given priority over any considerations of diplomacy.

The Ministry of Education is concerned with preparing qualified specialists in every sphere of activity, but its counterparts in the Central Committee are concerned with making a good builder of Communism out of every student. And the Central Committee's task is given priority when it comes to promotions and appointments, as well as to the content of educational programs.

The Ministry of Defense is responsible for the security of the country, and for training good soldiers and officers. But a corresponding Department of the Central Committee, acting through a Chief Political Directorate of the Army, makes sure that these soldiers are good *Soviet* soldiers, the liberators of humanity from the chains of capitalism.

The Ministry of Culture is charged with promoting art, literature, and entertainment. But being subordinate to the Department of Propaganda of the Central Committee, its main concern is effective propaganda on behalf of the official ideology. Accordingly, it becomes a ministry of political censorship, weeding out the "wrong" tendencies and promoting the "right" ones.

The intelligence service has the job of collecting military and strategic information about potential enemies, but disinformation, organization of mass movements, "liberation movements," international terrorism, drug smuggling, etc.—in short, organization of any activity which might destabilize, confuse, or scare other countries into submission—is even more important.

The double structure—established in every sphere of life and on all levels: national, district, regional, local, with vertical and horizontal subordination—is a perfect instrument of control and an ideal system for maintaining socialism at home and spreading it abroad. For the Soviet state is not a state in the traditional meaning of the word; it is the material and operational base of the world socialist revolution. Internally, it maintains a regime of occupation; externally, a state of permanent ideological war. Each needs and feeds the other.

Of course, the double structure of the Soviet state did not appear overnight, but evolved during the civil war and the subsequent struggle within the party. Initially, party control over the governmental apparatus was introduced because most of the specialists were former "class enemies" and could not be trusted. Even in the Red Army during the civil war, former czarist officers had to be conscripted by the Communists to lead the troops. Since they had to fight against their former colleagues and friends in the White Army, instances of "treason" were quite likely. Therefore, political commissars were appointed to each unit to watch over the officers.

The same was true in other areas, such as education or industry, where old czarist teachers and engineers were equally mistrusted as "class enemies." The party was small (some estimates show 115,000 members on January 1, 1918; 250,000 in March 1919), and consisted of mostly uneducated people (even by 1927 only 1 percent had graduated from universities, 8 percent had graduated from elementary school, while over 25 percent were registered as "self-educated," and 2 percent were completely illiterate). For a party of proletarians, this was as it should be.

To say that is not to make a joke, but to point to a very serious contradiction which was never resolved by the leadership. On the one hand, a party of proletarians ruling on behalf of the working class must have in its ranks a clear majority of workers. And indeed, demand for real proletarians was so great that only complete imbeciles were left in the factories or on the farms where they started. On the other hand, this practice, continuing almost until the present day, created an ill-educated and incompetent party bureaucracy.

As far as the "specialists" were concerned, in due course most were replaced by the new "Soviet specialists," often members of the party. Thus, in the army only 4,500 former czarist officers out of 50,000 were still serving by 1930. The number of party "specialists" in the governmental apparatus increased from 5 percent in 1923 to 20 percent in 1927. But the practice of party control through political commissars persisted, creating conflicts between the more competent specialist and his party controllers, who were usually less competent but more influential.

The considerable resentment thus accumulated acquired a new dimension after Lenin's death in 1924 and became an essential part of the internal struggle in the party under the new General Secretary, Stalin.

Stalin had to build his personal authority in a tough competition with "old revolutionaries," who even in 1927 constituted three-quarters of the leadership, while being only 1.4 percent of the total membership. By combining promotion of new members with purges of old, and by increasing the power of the party apparatus, Stalin consolidated his position. This meant an even more complete double structure. In 1925, the apparatus constituted only 2.5 percent of the membership; by 1939, it was 10 percent. After the mass terror of the 1930's, the party could not be challenged by anybody. Its power became enormous, its privileges huge. Total membership was 1,589,000 and at least half of them were no longer proletarians. Thus, the formation of a double structure was completed by the end of the 1930's, with its innermost core—the party apparatus—reaching its maximal power.

This new class of bosses, of professional leaders, and of organizers was and has remained the very embodiment of revolutionary ideology, its priests and caretakers. For without the ideology, they are nothing but a bunch of careerists and cynical parasites. As long as ideology reigns, however, they are omnipotent. There is no law, human or natural, which they cannot cancel: "Our task," declared one of them, "is not to study the economy. But to change it. We are not bound by any law. There are no such fortresses which Bolsheviks could not storm."

After Stalin's death, the appalling state of the Soviet economy and its centralized inflexibility forced Khrushchev to attempt a reorganization. Basically, he tried to subordinate the party to the economy, so to speak, by giving priority to economic factors over ideological ones. To no avail. The people he shifted and shuffled were the same old party bureaucrats, and bureaucracy only multiplied as a result of all his desperate efforts to loosen central control of the economy.

Khrushchev was pensioned off as a "voluntarist" who rocked the boat too much, but the problem refused to depart with him. His successors, Kosygin and Brezhnev, divided the functions of state and party leadership between them. Kosygin represented the interests of the government (and, therefore, the need for reforms), while Brezhnev embodied the interests of the party apparatus. However, it soon became clear which of these two sets of interests was the more important. Kosygin's reforms turned out to be modest: all he achieved was to insist that state-run enterprises should be self-sufficient and should bring profits instead of losses. Even this simple economic wisdom was never fully accepted. Kosygin's reforms were largely watered down by his colleagues from the party apparatus and then quietly sabotaged by the middle management of the bureaucracy.

Still, Kosygin's efforts were not entirely in vain: his campaign for reforms generated debates within the Soviet hierarchy, and a barely noticeable split into two trends: "managers" and "ideologists" (the actual terms they used). Certainly, there was no questioning by the managers of Communist ideology or its ultimate goals. Rather, the argument was over how to achieve these goals better and more efficiently. According to Marx, said the managers, economic relations are the essence of history, a material force which moves society, and we are Marxists, are we not? Indeed, we are, replied the ideologists, but Lenin wrote that the "idea which comes to possess the masses becomes a material force," and we are Leninists, are we not?

As this debate proceeded, a number of interesting new industrial experiments were carried out, and these were written up ecstatically in the Soviet newspapers of the 1960's. But this early euphoria evaporated as it became evident that the experiments illustrated all too clearly the superiority of capitalist over socialist methods. Although these capitalist methods would undoubtedly foster more rapid economic growth, the state would no longer maintain its control over economic life. More importantly, party control of the economy would be rendered both superfluous and impossible. As between economic growth and party control, the choice fell on the latter. And with good reason.

There are currently 18 million party members, roughly 6.5 percent of the population, or about 10 percent of its adult part. The ruling elite, the *nomenklatura*, is estimated at between 3 and 5 million, families included. It is impossible to determine how many of them are "ideologists," but whatever they believe in, they stand to lose a great deal, perhaps even everything, from a real diminution of party control. Because it is to the party, not to their skills or talents, that they owe their positions, they would have no chance of remaining on the same level in any other socio-political system (if, indeed, there is such a level of power and privilege under any other system). Besides, many might be held responsible for crimes and corruptions committed in the service of the regime, if this regime were ever to change dramatically (as has happened in China).

For these reasons, the partocrats prefer a longer course of economic decline, a slower way of death, should the worst become inevitable. Dangerous as such a continuous decline of the Soviet economy is, it would mean only a *gradual* defeat of the socialist forces, with the ultimate catastrophe postponed for perhaps fifteen to twenty years. By contrast, radical economic reforms mean for the partocrats an immediate ouster and a loss of status, and without even any guarantee that the cause of socialism can thereby be saved.

On the other hand, the "managers" apparently think that they do not stand to lose anything, except their ideological chains. Being competent specialists, better educated, and more confident, they believe they will remain on the same level (or even higher) in a more competitive society. The top echelon of "managers" in the *nomenklatura* probably hope to become the sole masters of the country once the partocrats are removed.

Somebody has already said of this new class of managers or "meritocrats" that they are "the gravediggers of Communism." In the long run, perhaps, they may turn out to be just that. But let us have no illusions: these "reformers" are no more eager than the old partocrats to bury Communism. Being specialists, they are willing to run the risk of reforms in order to save the socialist cause. Being younger, they do not want to preside over the downfall of their regime. It is less clear, however, how much they understand of the system's limitations on the one hand or the possible consequences of needed reforms on the other.

And Gorbachev? Is he one of them, as many seem to believe? We do not really know, but assuming that he is, he will find himself basically in the same situation Khrushchev did twenty years ago. His reforms will have to be implemented through the same party apparatus whose power they inevitably serve to diminish. And since the General Secretary has no other instrument of control over the country, by reducing the power of the party apparatus he will be reducing his own as well.

During Andropov's brief reign, according to some accounts, "hundreds of persons who held real power either in Moscow or in the provinces were removed. Thousands of middle-echelon officials were replaced or shifted to other duties." The purge continues, but even if Gorbachev places like-minded people in every position of influence in the country, he is bound to discover what Napoleon discovered when he appointed his brother to be the "king" of a conquered country: the brother became a real king in due course, and acted accordingly. Khrushchev made a similar discovery: it was the very people he himself had chosen and promoted who removed him when they felt he had gone too far.

This structural constraint alone makes far-reaching reforms quite impossible. Yet if they do not reach far enough, they will not work. The time when the government could govern, leaving the party to conduct propaganda, is long past. Once revolutionary enthusiasm died, the party had to rely on its exclusive right to promote and to dismiss, to enrich and to impoverish any individual in the country. Now, if people are going to be promoted according to their talents and rewarded according to their performance, who will bother to join the party? And if people are not treated according to their merits, where is the reform?

So far Gorbachev has not unveiled his plan of reorganization. We can only guess its main features from the hints he has dropped in his early speeches. Amid invigorating appeals for better discipline, he emphasizes once again Kosygin's principle of "self-sufficiency," which must be introduced this time "in reality," and he threatens, like Khrushchev, to eliminate many bureaucratic governmental institutions. His constant theme is the need to give more rights and independence to enterprises, to simplify central planning, and to institute a "revolutionary shift" to the latest technology. Thus far the program looks like a fairly minimal adjustment within the system.

But Gorbachev's other ideas are bound to be more controversial. For example, his remedy for agriculture is believed to be the "family-based productive link system" (*zveno*) which was tested in experiments of the 1960's with spectacular results but was rejected as an attempt to restore capitalism. The question remains whether Gorbachev will actually try to pursue such ideas.

Two variables will largely determine the answer: first, the behavior of the West; second, the behavior of the Soviet population.

If the West, repeating the mistake it made in the 1970's version of détente, provides assistance on a great scale, then the Soviet regime can get away with minimal reforms for another decade before coming to its next major crisis. In other words, the scale of reform will be inversely proportional to the scale of Western economic assistance.

Moreover, if the West goes on protecting and perpetuating the external Soviet empire by recognizing Soviet client-states and providing them with economic help (Central Europe, Mozambique, Angola, and, perhaps soon, Vietnam), then the economic burden of empire will continue to be reduced and the risk of its collapse will be diminished, thus slowing down the drive for more radical changes in the Soviet economy. If, however, the West dissociates itself from these regimes, and instead supports resistance movements, then the pressure to improve the performance of the Soviet economy will increase dramatically. Equally, any slowdown in military competition, or any sweeping arms-control or arms-reduction agreements, will only serve to reduce the need for reforms.

As for the second variable, the possible response of the Soviet people, the question is how far reform must go in order to evoke their enthusiasm. How big must the new incentives be in order to increase productivity to the required level?

One must remember that at least three generations have grown up under the present system, watching the slow destruction of their country, culture, and fellow countrymen. There is hardly a family which has not experienced repression at some point or other. For three generations these people have been obliged to listen to and to repeat the obvious lies of official propaganda and to be cheerful at the same time because it is antisocial not to be cheerful in a socialist paradise. This contradiction between reality and propaganda alone is sufficient to produce profound psychological damage, to say nothing of the ever-present fear, suspicion, and misery.

The current condition of the Soviet people is not simply one of disillusionment, apathy, or resignation. It is a biological exhaustion, a fatigue of human material. The signs of this are high infant mortality, low birthrate (below replacement level among the Russians and some other nationalities), life expectancy of about sixty, and an exceptionally high percentage of children born physically and mentally handicapped (about 6–7 percent by the end of the 1970's, and projected to be 15 percent by the end of the 1990's). The latter is partly due to massive environmental pollution, but it is mainly a product of alcoholism.

Contrary to popular belief, the current epidemic of alcoholism has little to do with traditional Russian drinking habits. Thus a pre-revolutionary Russian encyclopedia indicates that in 1905 about 50 percent of men and 95 percent of women were total abstainers. (For comparison, per-capita consumption was much smaller than in the United States today.) A document smuggled out of the Soviet Union in 1985 shows an enormous increase in alcohol consumption. It asserts that, in 1979, only 0.6 percent of men and 2.4 percent of women were abstainers, and only 5 percent of young people under age eighteen. In 1983, according to this document, there were 40 million "medically certified alcoholics" in the Soviet Union, and the number was estimated as growing to 80 million by the year 2000, which would be 65 percent of the working population.

In addition to these signs of degeneration, there is widespread dissent. This should not be understood in narrowly political terms; it is broader and deeper than that. Professor Zaslavskaya explains it in the "Novosibirsk Document" as follows:

Even with the most rigid regimentation of behavior in the economic sphere, the population is always left with a certain choice of reactions to the governmental restrictions, which it does not necessarily . . . accept. Hence a possibility of overt and covert conflicts between the interests of the groups and of the society. When the established norms and rules affect the vital interests of certain groups of the population, . . . the latter often find a way to shirk the restrictions and to satisfy their demands. When the state takes more strict measures to curb undesirable types of activities, the population responds by finding more subtle patterns of behavior, which will secure satisfaction of its demands in the new conditions, etc. Thus, reciprocally oriented behavior and interactions, of the state on the one hand, . . . and of socioeconomic groups, on the other, represent an important part of the social mechanism of economic development.

Needless to say, the same kind of implicit "dialogue" occurs between the regime and society in all spheres of life, not just in economic relations. In the latter sphere this "dialogue" has led to the development of a black market of many semi-legal activities, and of corruption and theft of public property. In other spheres, it has led to cultural, nationalist, and political dissent.

The black market is everywhere. A general shortage of consumer goods and food, of services and materials, has made it necessary for the people to develop their own system of distribution. The government has tried to fight it tooth and nail (since the early 1960's, a wide variety of these activities is punishable by death), but the system has continued to grow into a huge and intricate network of underground business and industry. Quite often even the party bosses, top governmental executives, and the police have become involved or have been bribed to cover up this activity. Few have been caught.

One can only guess what effect corruption on this scale is having on the top echelon of power. As far as the general population is concerned, however, the effect has clearly been profound. If nothing else, people have become less dependent on official favors and state distribution, while becoming more and more cash-oriented.

To sum up, nearly seventy years of ruthless and unscrupulous Communist rule have destroyed the trust which may have existed originally between the Soviet rulers and the people. The people can hardly expect significant improvements as a result of any within-the-system reforms because the very idea of this system has outlived itself. But even if the system is dismantled, it could take a couple of generations before the people recover completely. Collectivized farmers have to learn how to be peasants, "proletarians" have to learn how to be workers, surviving craftsmen have to teach their skills to new generations.

Surely, Gorbachev cannot count on the millions of "medically certified alcoholics" to sober up suddenly and to become Stakhanovites, even if he pays them five times the present level of wages. If they were capable of sobering up, they would already have joined one or another of the semi-legal businesses existing in the country. Whatever Gorbachev's reforms are going to be, then, they must appeal to those who are interested in working and earning, which means that they must compete in incentives and rewards with the black market.

It is of some interest to note what Gorbachev wants to do with the economy; it is far more interesting to see what the economy will do with Gorbachev as he learns what Lenin discovered sixty-five years before him: that the "marketplace is stronger" than socialism. The best guess is that Gorbachev will choose socialism—

which is to say the rule of the party—over the marketplace. Thus he has only three options: He could introduce no changes, and then philosophically watch over the slow disintegration of the empire, the loss of superpower status, and the final collapse of the system, perhaps within fifteen or twenty years. Second, he could adopt a Chinese-type version of Lenin's New Economic Policy (NEP), only to see himself swept away by rising inflation, unemployment, industrial unrest, and disintegration of the party system—and with no real hope of avoiding the final collapse. Third, he could follow the example of Brezhnev in getting the West to bail him out with enough aid and trade to postpone the day of reckoning for several more decades.

In the final analysis, then, it is the West that must choose between the death of Communism in the 20th century and its survival into the 21st.

ON SOVIET HISTORY[5]

It is 70 years since the unforgettable days of October 1917, those legendary days that started the count of the new epoch of social progress, of the real history of humankind.

The October Revolution is truly the shining hour of humanity, its radiant dawn. The October Revolution is a revolution of the people and for the people, for every individual, for his emancipation and development.

Seventy years is not a long time in world civilization's ascent over the centuries, but history has known no other period like it for the scale of achievements that our country has attained since the victory of the October Revolution.

There is no greater honor than to be pioneers, devoting one's strength, energy, knowledge, and ability to the triumph of the October Revolution's ideals and goals. The jubilee is a moment of pride, pride in what has been achieved. Arduous trials fell to our lot, and we withstood them honorably. We did not simply

[5]Excerpted from a transcript of a speech delivered by Mikhail Gorbachev, general secretary of the Communist Party of the Soviet Union, on November 2, 1987 in Moscow, and distributed by the Soviet press agency Tass.

withstand them, but wrested the country out of its state of dislocation and backwardness, and made it a mighty power, transforming life and changing man's inner world beyond recognition.

I

The past—its heroism and drama—cannot fail to thrill our
contemporaries. Our history is one, and it is irreversible. Whatever emotions it may evoke, it is our history, and we cherish it.

Today we turn to those October days that shook the world.
We look for and find in them both a dependable spiritual buttress
and instructive lessons. We see again and again that the socialist
option of the October Revolution has been correct. . . .

The 1917 Revolution

The year 1917 absorbed the energy of the people's struggle
for self-sustained development and independence, of the progressive national movements, and the peasant risings and wars against
serfdom abounding in our history.

It embodied the spirited search of the 18th-century enlight-
eners, the heroes and martyrs of the Decembrist movement, the
splendid champions of revolutionary democracy, and the moral
dedication of the eminent men of our culture.

Crucial for the future of our country was the time when at the
dawn of the 20th century, Vladimir Ilyich Lenin put himself at
the head of a close-knit group of comrades and set out to organize
a proletarian party of the new type in Russia. It was this great party of Lenin that roused the nation, its best and most devoted
forces, for an assault on the old world.

The cornerstone in the success of the October Revolution was
laid by the first Russian revolution of 1905–1907. This includes
the bitter lessons of the Ninth of January, the desperate heroism
witnessed on the Moscow barricades in December, the exploits of
thousands of known and unknown freedom fighters, and the
birth of the first workers' Soviets, the prototypes of Soviet power.

The victory of the October Revolution was also rooted in the
gains of the February 1917 revolution, the first victorious people's revolution in the imperialist epoch. Lenin stressed that following the victory in February the revolution went forward with
incredible speed. Its leading characters were the workers and

peasants wearing soldiers' greatcoats. The spring of 1917 showed all the muscle of the people's movement.

There also surfaced its limitations, the contradictions in the revolutionary consciousness of that stage, the power of historical inertia, with the result that for a time the exploiter classes departing from the scene took advantage of the fruits of the people's victory.

The February Revolution provided October with its main weapon—power organized in revived soviets. The February Revolution had been the first experience of tangible democracy, of political education of the masses through practice—an experience acquired in the intricate conditions of a diarchy. . . .

And how sensitively Lenin kept his finger on the pulse of the revolution, how brilliantly he determined the beginning of a new revival of the soviets; they were acquiring a truly popular essence in the process of struggle, which enabled them to become the organs of a victorious armed uprising, and then also the political form of worker-peasant power. . . .

Like Marx and Engels, Lenin was convinced that the defense force of the revolution would be a people's militia. But the concrete conditions prompted a different solution. The Civil War and the intervention from outside, imposed on the people, called for a new approach. A worker-peasant Red Army was formed by Lenin's decree.

It was an army of a new type which covered itself with undying glory in the Civil War and in repulsing the foreign intervention.

Those years brought severe trials for the newly established Soviet Republic. It had to settle the elementary and crucial question of whether socialism would or would not be. The party mobilized the people to defend the socialist motherland, the gains of the October Revolution. Hungry, ill-clad and unshod, the poorly armed Red Army crushed a well-trained and well-armed counter-revolutionary host which was being generously supplied by imperialists of East and West.

The fiery dividing line of the Civil War ran right across the country, across every family, wreaking havoc with the habitual way of life, with the psychology and fate of people. The will of the nation, the striving of millions towards a new life, won out in this deadly clash.

The country did everything it could to help the newly established army; it lived and acted by Lenin's slogan: "Everything For Victory."

We will never forget the exploits of those legendary heroes—gallant sailors and cavalrymen, men and commanders of the young Red Army, and the red partisans.

They had safeguarded the revolution: Everlasting glory is their due! . . .

The 1920s

The early 20's were highlighted by a spectacular surge of popular initiative and creativity. They were a truly revolutionary laboratory of social innovation, of search for the optimum forms of the workers' alliance with the working peasantry, and the shaping of a mechanism for attaining the whole spectrum of the working people's interests.

From organizing production and consumption by methods of War Communism necessitated by war and dislocation, the party went over to more flexible, economically justified, "regular" instruments of influencing the social reality.

The measures of the New Economic Policy were directed to building socialism's material foundation.

These days, we turn ever more often to the last works of Lenin, to Lenin's New Economic Policy, and strive to extract from it all the valuable elements that we require today.

Certainly, it would be a mistake to equate the New Economic Policy and what we are doing now at a fundamentally new level of development. Today, there are none of those individual peasants in the country with whom to shape an alliance, which determined the most vital aims of the economic policy of the 20's.

But the New Economic Policy also had a more distant target. The task had been set of building the new society "not directly relying on enthusiasm," as Lenin wrote, "but aided by the enthusiasm engendered by the great revolution, and on the basis of personal interests, personal incentives and business principles. . . . That is what experience, the objective course of the development of the revolution, has taught us."

Speaking of the creative potential of the New Economic Policy, we should evidently refer once more to the political and methodological wealth of ideas underlying the food tax.

To be sure, we are interested not in its forms of those days that had been meant to secure a bond between workers and peasants, but the potentialities of the food tax idea in loosening the creative energy of the masses, enhancing the initiative of the individual, and removing the bureaucratic trammels that limited the operation of socialism's basic principle, "From each according to his abilities, to each according to his work."

In Lenin's last works, which were extraordinarily rich intellectually and emotionally, there emerged a system of views and the very concept of socialist construction in our country. This is an immense theoretical asset for the party.

Lenin's premature death was a terrible shock for the whole party and the Soviet people. The grief was immeasurable, the loss irreparable.

Struggles within the Party

The period after Lenin, that is, the 20's and the 30's, occupied a special place in the history of the Soviet state. Radical social changes were carried out in some 15 years. An incredible lot was squeezed into that period—both from the point of view of search for optimum variants of socialist construction, and from the point of view of what was really achieved in building the foundations of the new society.

Those were years of hard work to the limits of human endurance, of sharp and multifarious struggle. Industrialization, collectivization, the cultural revolution, strengthening of the multinational state, consolidation of the Soviet Union's international positions, new forms of managing the economy and all social affairs—all this occurred within that period. And all of it had far-reaching consequences.

For decades, we have been returning to that time again and again. This is natural. Because that was when the world's first socialist society had its beginnings, when it was being built. It was an exploit on a historical scale and of historic significance. Admiration for the exploits of our fathers and grandfathers, and the assessments of our real achievements will live forever, as will the exploits and achievements themselves.

And if, at times, we scrutinize our history with a critical eye, we do so only because we want to obtain a better and fuller idea of the ways that lead to the future.

It is essential to assess the past with a sense of historical responsibility and on the basis of the historical truth. This has got to be done, first, because of the tremendous importance of those years for the destiny of our country, the destiny of socialism.

Second, because those years are at the center of the everlasting discussions both in our country and abroad, where, along with a search for the truth, attempts are often made to discredit socialism as a new social system, as a realistic alternative to capitalism.

Lastly, we need truthful assessments of this and all the other periods of our history—especially now with perestroika in full gear. We need them not to settle political scores or, as they say, to let off steam, but to pay due credit to all the heroic [words missing] in the past, and to draw lessons from mistakes and miscalculations.

And so, about the 20's and 30's after Lenin. Although the party and society had Lenin's conception of building socialism and Lenin's works of the post-Revolution period to go by, the search of the way was not at all simple; it was marked by keen ideological struggle and political discussions.

At their center were the basic problems of society's development, and above all the questions of whether socialism could or could not be built in our country. Theoretical thought and practice cast about for the directions and forms in which to carry out socio-economic transformations, and how to accomplish them on socialist lines in the concrete historical situation of the Soviet Union.

Practical constructive work that called for a high sense of responsibility was the order of the day. Above all, the country squarely faced the question of industrialization and economic reconstruction without which building socialism and strengthening the defence capacity were unthinkable. This followed from Lenin's explicit directions, from his theoretical heritage. The question of socialist changes in the countryside, too, arose on the same plane and also according to Lenin's behests.

Thus, the question concerned large-scale and crucial matters, problems and objectives. And though, I repeat, the party had Lenin's guidelines on these issues, sharp debates erupted over them.

It is evidently worthwhile to say that even before and after the revolution, in the first few years of socialist construction, not all party leaders by far shared Lenin's views on some of the most important problems. Besides, Lenin's recommendations could not encompass all the concrete issues concerning the building of the new society.

Analyzing the ideological disputes of those times, we should bear in mind that carrying out gigantic revolutionary transformations in a country such as Russia was then, was in itself a most difficult undertaking. Historically, the country was on the march, its development was being sharply accelerated, all aspects of social life were changing rapidly and profoundly.

Reflecting the entire range of the interests of classes, social groups and strata, the needs and objectives of the times, the historical traditions and the pressure of urgent tasks, and also the conditions of the hostile capitalist encirclement, the ideological struggle was indissolubly intertwined with events and processes in the economy, on the political scene, in all spheres of people's lives.

In short, it was supremely difficult to get one's bearings and find the only correct course in that intricate and stormy situation. To a considerable extent, too, the character of the ideological struggle was complicated by personal rivalries in the party leadership.

The old differences that had existed back in Lenin's lifetime also made themselves felt in the new situation, and this in a very acute form. Lenin, as we know, had warned against this danger. In his "Letter to the Congress" he had stressed that "it is not a trifle, or it is a trifle which can assume decisive importance." And that was largely what had happened.

Their petit bourgeois nature took the upper hand in the case of some authoritative leaders. They took a factional stance. This agitated the party organizations, distracted them from vital affairs and interfered in their work.

The leaders in question continued to provoke a split even after the vast majority in the party saw that their views were contrary to Lenin's ideas and plans, and that their proposals were erroneous and could push the country off the correct course.

Trotsky and Bukharin

This applies first of all to Leon Trotsky, who had, after Lenin's death, displayed excessive pretensions to top leadership in the party, thus fully confirming Lenin's opinion of him as an excessively self-assured politician who always vacillated and cheated.

Trotsky and the Trotskyites negated the possibility of build-ing socialism in conditions of capitalist encirclement.

In foreign policy they gave priority to export of revolution, and in home policy to tightening the screws on the peasants, to the city exploiting the countryside, and to administrative and mil-itary fiat in running society.

Trotskyism was a political current whose ideologists took cov-er behind leftist pseudo-revolutionary rhetoric, and who in effect assumed a defeatist posture. This was essentially an attack on Le-ninism all down the line. The matter practically concerned the fu-ture of socialism in our country, the fate of the revolution.

In the circumstances, it was essential to disprove Trotskyism before the whole people, and denude its antisocialist essence. The situation was complicated by the fact that the Trotskyites were acting in common with the new opposition headed by Grigory Zi-noviev and Lev Kamenev. Being aware that they constituted a mi-nority, the opposition leaders had again and again saddled the party with discussions, counting on a split in its ranks.

But in the final analysis, the party spoke out for the line of the Central Committee and against the opposition, which was soon ideologically and organizationally crushed.

In short, the party's leading nucleus, headed by Josef Stalin, had safeguarded Leninism in an ideological struggle. It defined the strategy and tactics in the initial stage of socialist construc-tion, with its political course being approved by most members of the party and most working people. An important part in defeat-ing Trotskyism ideologically was played by Nikolai Bukharin, Feliks Dzerzhinsky, Sergei Kirov, Grigory Ordzhonokidze, Jan Rudzutak and others.

At the very end of the 20's a sharp struggle ensued also over the ways of putting the peasantry on the socialist road. In sub-stance, it revealed the different attitude of the majority in the Po-litical Bureau and of the Bukharin group on how to apply the principles of the new economic policy at the new stage in the de-velopment of Soviet society.

The concrete conditions of that time—both at home and in-ternationally—necessitated a considerable increase in the rate of socialist construction.

Bukharin and his followers had, in their calculations and the-oretical propositions, underrated the practical significance of the time factor in building socialism in the 30's. In many ways, their posture reposed on dogmatic thinking and a nondialectical assessment of the concrete situation. Bukharin himself, and his followers, soon admitted their mistakes.

In this connection, it is not amiss to recall Lenin's opinion of Bukharin. "Bukharin," he said, "is not only a most valuable and major theorist of the party; he is also rightly considered the favourite of the whole party, but his theoretical views can be classified as fully Marxist only with great reserve, for there is something scholastic about him (he has never made a study of dialectics, and, I think, never fully understood it)."

The facts again confirmed that Lenin had been right.

As we see, the political discussions of that time reflected a difficult process in the party's development, marked by acute struggle over crucial problems of socialist construction.

Collectivization and Centralization

In that struggle, which had to be endured, there took shape the concept of industrialization and collectivization.

Under the leadership of the party, of its Central Committee, a heavy industry, including engineering, a defense industry and a chemical industry abreast of the times, were built in short order practically from scratch, and the general electrification plan was completed.

The period under review also saw some losses. They were in a definite sense connected with the successes I have just referred to. People had begun to believe in the universal effectiveness of rigid centralization, in that methods of command were the shortest and best way of resolving any and all problems. This had an effect on the attitude towards people, towards their conditions of life.

A party and government leadership system of administrative command emerged in the country, and red tape gained strength, even though Lenin had warned about its danger in his day. And a corresponding structure of administration and planning began to take shape.

In industry—given its scale at the time, when literally all the main components of the industrial edifice were conspicuous—such methods, such a system of management, generally produced results. However, an equally rigid centralization-and-command system was impermissible in tackling the problems of refashioning rural life.

It must be said frankly: At the new stage there was a deficit of the Leninist considerate attitude to the interests of the working peasantry. Most important of all, there was an underestimation of the fact that the peasantry as a class had changed radically in the years since the revolution.

The principal figure now was the middle peasant. He had asserted himself as a farmer working the land he had received from the revolution and he had, over a whole decade, become convinced that Soviet government was his government too. He had become a staunch and dependable ally of the working class. An ally on a new basis, becoming convinced in practical terms that his life was increasingly taking a turn for the better.

And if there had been more consideration for objective economic laws and if more attention had been given to the social processes taking place in the village, if in general the attitude to this vast mass of the working peasantry—most of whom had taken part in the revolution and had defended it from the White Guards and the forces of intervention—had been politically more judicious, if there had been a consistent line to promote the alliance with the middle peasantry against the kulak, the village moneybag, then there would not have been all those excesses that occurred in carrying out collectivization.

Today it is clear: In a tremendous undertaking, which affected the fate of the majority of the country's population, there was a departure from Lenin's policy towards the peasantry.

This most important and very complex social process, in which a great deal depended on local conditions, was directed by predominantly administrative methods.

A conviction had arisen that all problems could be solved at a stroke, overnight. Whole regions and parts of the country began to compete: who would achieve complete collectivization more quickly. Arbitrary percentage targets were issued from above. Flagrant violations of the principles of collectivization occurred everywhere.

Nor were excesses avoided in the struggle against the kulaks. The basically correct policy of fighting the kulaks was often interpreted so broadly that it swept in a considerable part of the middle peasantry too. Such is the reality of history.

But, comrades, if we assess the significance of collectivization as a whole in consolidating socialism in the countryside, it was in the final analysis a transformation of fundamental importance.

Collectivization implied a radical change in the entire mode of life of the preponderant part of the country's population to a socialist footing. It created the social base for modernizing the agrarian sector and re-gearing it along the lines of advanced farming techniques; it made possible a considerable rise in the productivity of labor, and it released a substantial share of manpower needed for other spheres of socialist construction. All this had historical effects.

To understand the situation of those years it must be borne in mind that the administrative-command system, which had begun to take shape in the process of industrialization and which had received a fresh impetus during collectivization, had told on the whole socio-political life of the country.

Once established in the economy, it had spread to its superstructure, restricting the development of the democratic potential of socialism and holding back the progress of socialist democracy.

But the aforesaid does not give a full picture of how complex that period was.

What had happened? The time of ideological-political tests of the utmost gravity to the party was actually over. Millions of people had joined enthusiastically in the work of bringing about socialist transformations. The first successes were becoming apparent.

Yet at that time, methods dictated by the period of the struggle with the hostile resistance of the exploiter classes were being mechanically transferred to the period of peaceful socialist construction, when conditions had changed cardinally. An atmosphere of intolerance, hostility, and suspicion was created in the country.

As time went on, this political practice gained in scale and was backed up by the erroneous theory of an aggravation of the class struggle in the course of socialist construction. All this had a dire effect on the country's sociopolitical development and produced grim consequences.

Quite obviously, it was the absence of a proper level of democratization in the Soviet society that made possible the personality cult, the violations of legality, the wanton repressive measures of the 30's.

I am putting things bluntly. Those were real crimes stemming from an abuse of power. Many thousands of people inside and outside the party were subjected to wholesale repressive measures. Such, comrades, is the bitter truth. Serious damage was done to the cause of socialism and to the authority of the party. And we must say this bluntly. This is necessary to assert Lenin's ideal of socialism once and for all.

The Role of Stalin

There is now much discussion about the role of Stalin in our history. His was an extremely contradictory personality. To remain faithful to historical truth we have to see both Stalin's incontestable contribution to the struggle for socialism, to the defense of its gains; the gross political errors, and the abuses committed by him and by those around him, for which our people paid a heavy price and which had grave consequences for the life of our society.

It is sometimes said that Stalin did not know of many instances of lawlessness. Documents at our disposal show that this is not so. The guilt of Stalin and his immediate entourage before the party and the people for the wholesale repressive measures and acts of lawlessness is enormous and unforgivable. This is a lesson for all generations.

Contrary to the assertions of our ideological opponents, the Stalin personality cult was certainly not inevitable. It was alien to the nature of socialism, represented a departure from its fundamental principles and, therefore, has no justification.

At its 20th and 22d Congresses, the party severely condemned the cult itself and its consequences. We now know that the political accusations and repressive measures against a number of party leaders and statesmen, against Communists and nonparty people, against economic executives and military men, against scientists and cultural personalities, were a result of deliberate falsification.

Many accusations were later, especially after the 20th Party Congress, withdrawn. Thousands of innocent victims were completely exonerated. But the process of restoring justice was not seen through to the end and was actually suspended in the middle of the 60's. Now, in line with a decision taken by the October 1987 plenary meeting of the Central Committee, we are having to return to this.

The Political Bureau of the Central Committee has set up a commission for comprehensively examining new facts and documents pertaining to these matters and those known previously. Corresponding decisions will be taken on the basis of the commission's findings.

All this will also be reflected in a treatise on the history of the Communist Party of the Soviet Union, whose preparation is to be entrusted to a special commission of the Central Committee. This is something we have to do, the more so since even now there are still attempts to turn away from painful matters in our history, to hush them up, to make believe that nothing special happened.

We cannot agree to this. This would be disregard for the historical truth, disrespect for the memory of those who were innocent victims of lawless and arbitrary actions. Another reason why we cannot agree to this is that a truthful analysis must help us to solve today's problems of democratization, legality, openness, overcoming bureaucracy, in short, the vital problems of perestroika, or reorganization. That is why here too we have to be quite clear, concise and consistent.

An honest understanding of our enormous achievements as well as of past misfortunes, their full and true political evaluation, will provide real moral guidelines for the future.

The Great Patriotic War

In the West there is now much talk about the situation on the eve of the war. Truths are being laced with half-truths. This is being done especially zealously by those who are displeased with the results of World War II—political, territorial and social—by those who persist in scheming to amend those results. That is why they are interested in presenting the historical truth upside down, in garbling cause-and-effect relationships and falsifying the chronology of events.

In this context they are resorting to any lies to saddle the Soviet Union with the blame for World War II, the road to which was supposedly cleared by the Ribbentrop-Molotov Nonaggression Pact. This matter deserves being spoken about in somewhat greater detail.

Actually, it was by no means on Sept. 1, 1939, that World War II became a tragic reality. Japan's seizure of northeast China (the Manchurian Incident of 1931–1932), Italy's attack on Ethiopia (in 1935) and on Albania (in the spring of 1939), the German-Italian intervention against Republican Spain (1936–1939) and Japan's armed invasion of north and then central China (in the summer of 1937)—these were the initial conflagrations of World War II.

It is a different matter that in those days the West still pretended that this did not concern it or did not concern it enough to come to the defense of the victims of aggression. Hatred of socialism, long-term designs and class selfishness prevented a sober assessment of the real dangers.

Even more: Fascism was persistently being offered the mission of a strike force in an anti-Communist crusade. After Ethiopia and China, Austria and Czechoslovakia were flung into the furnace of appeasement, the sword hung over Poland, over all the Baltic and Danube states, and propaganda was being conducted openly in favor of turning the Ukraine into a wheat field and livestock farm of the Third Reich.

Ultimately, the main thrusts of aggression were being channeled against the Soviet Union, and since the scheming to divide up our country had begun long before the war, it is not hard to see how limited our options were.

It is said that the decision taken by the Soviet Union in concluding a nonaggression pact with Germany was not the best one. This may be so, if one is guided not by harsh reality, but by abstract conjectures torn out of their time frame.

In these circumstances, too, the issue was roughly the same as it had been at the time of the Brest peace: Was our country to be or not to be independent, was socialism on earth to be or not to be. . . .

The Great Patriotic War brought out to the full the talent of outstanding military leaders who had emerged from the midst of the people: Georgi Zhukov, Konstantin Rokossovsky, Aleksandr Vasilyevsky, Ivan Konev and other distinguished marshals, generals and officers, those who commanded fronts and armies, corps, divisions and regiments, companies and platoons.

A factor in the achievement of victory was the tremendous political will, purposefulness and persistence, ability to organize and discipline people displayed in the war years by Josef Stalin. But the brunt of the war was borne by the ordinary Soviet soldier—a great toiler of the people's own flesh and blood, valiant, and devoted to his country. Every honor and eternal glory to him!

Khrushchev and Brezhnev

It was the heroism of everyday work in those difficult postwar years that was the source of our achievements, of the economic, scientific and technical progress, of the harnessing of atomic energy, of the launching of the first spaceships, and of the growth of the people's economic and cultural standards.

But during this very same time—a time of new exploits by the people in the name of socialism—a contradiction between what our society had become and the old methods of leadership was making itself felt ever more appreciably.

Abuses of power and violations of socialist legality continued. The "Leningrad Case" and the "Doctors Case" were fabricated. In short, there was a deficit of genuine respect for the people.

People were devotedly working, studying, seeking new knowledge, accepting difficulties and shortages, but sensing that alarm and hope were building up in society. And all this gripped the public consciousness soon after Stalin's death.

In the middle of the 50's, especially after the 20th Congress of the Communist Party, a wind of change swept the country, the people's spirits rose, they took heart, became bolder and more confident. It required no small courage of the party and its leadership, headed by Nikita Khrushchev, to criticize the personality cult and its consequences, and to re-establish socialist legality.

The old stereotypes in domestic and foreign policy began to crumble. Attempts were made to break down the command-bureaucratic methods of administration established in the 30's and the 40's, to make socialism more dynamic, to emphasize humanitarian ideals and values, and to revive the creative spirit of Leninism in theory and practice.

The desire to change the priorities of economic development, to bring into play incentives related to a personal interest in work results, keynoted the decisions of the September 1953 and July 1955 plenary meetings of the party Central Committee. More attention began to be devoted to the development of agriculture, housing, the light industry, the sphere of consumption, and to everything related to satisfying human needs.

In short, there were changes for the better—in Soviet society and in international relations. However, no small number of subjectivist errors were committed, and they handicapped socialism's advance to a new stage, moreover doing much to discredit progressive initiatives.

The fact is that fundamentally new problems of domestic and foreign policies, and of party development, were often being solved by voluntaristic methods, with the aid of the old political and economic mechanism.

But the failures of the reforms undertaken in that period were mainly due to the fact that they were not backed up by a broad development of democratization processes. At the October 1964 plenary meeting of the party Central Committee there was a change of the leadership of the party and the country, and decisions were taken to overcome voluntaristic tendencies and distortions in domestic and foreign policies. The party sought to achieve a certain stabilization in the policy, and to give it realistic features and thoroughness.

The March and September 1965 plenary meetings of the party Central Committee formulated new approaches to economic management. An economic reform, and big programs for developing new areas and promoting the productive forces, were worked out and began to be put into effect.

In the first few years this changed the situation in the country for the better. The economic and scientific potential was increasing, the defense capacity was being strengthened, the standard of living was rising. Many foreign-policy moves enhanced the international prestige of our state. Strategic parity with the U.S.A. was achieved.

The country had at its disposal extensive resources for further accelerating its development. But to utilize these resources and put them to work, cardinal new changes were needed to society and, of course, the corresponding political will. There was a shortage of the one and the other. And even much of what had been decided remained on paper, was left suspended in mid-air. The pace of our development was substantially retarded.

At the April 1985 plenary meeting of its Central Committee and at its 27th Congress the party frankly identified the causes of the situation that had arisen, laid bare the mechanism retarding our development and gave it a fundamental assessment.

It was stated that in the latter years of the life and activities of Leonid Brezhnev the search for ways of further advancement had been largely hampered by an addiction to habitual formulas and schemes, which did not reflect the new realities. The gap between word and deed had widened.

Negative processes in the economy were gathering momentum and had, in effect, created a pre-crisis situation. Many aberrations had arisen in the social, spiritual and moral spheres, and they were distorting and deforming the principles of socialist justice, undermining the people's faith in it, and giving rise to social alienation and immorality in various forms. The growing discrepancy between the lofty principles of socialism and the everyday realities of life was becoming intolerable.

The healthy forces in the party and in society as a whole were becoming more and more acutely aware of the pressing need to overcome negative phenomena, to reverse the course of events, to secure an acceleration of the country's socio-economic development, and to bring about a moral purification and renewal of socialism.

It was in response to this extremely acute social need that the April 1985 plenary meeting of the Central Committee put forward the concept and strategy of accelerating the country's socio-economic development, and the course aimed at a renewal of socialism.

These were given more elaborate theoretical and political formulation in the decisions of the 27th Party Congress and subsequent plenary meetings of the Central Committee, and assumed final shape in the general policy of a revolutionary reorganization of all aspects of socialist society's life.

The perestroika idea rests upon our 70-year history, on the sound foundation of the basically new social edifice erected in the Soviet Union; it combines continuity and innovation, the historical experience of Bolshevism and the contemporaneity of socialism.

II

Perestroika

The changes taking place in the country today probably constitute the biggest step in developing socialist democracy since the October Revolution.

In reorganizing our economic and political system, it is our duty to create, first of all, a dependable and flexible mechanism for the genuine involvement of all the people in deciding state and social matters.

Secondly, people must be taught in practice to live in the conditions of deepening democracy, to extend and consolidate human rights, to nurture a contemporary political culture of the masses; in other words, to teach and to learn democracy.

The purpose of the radical economic reform begun in the country is to assure, during the next two or three years, a transition from an overly centralized command system of management to a democratic system based mainly on economic methods and on an optimal combination of centralism and self-management.

This presupposes a sharp expansion of the autonomy of enterprises and associations, their transition to the principle of profitability and self-financing, and the investment of work collectives with all the powers necessary for this.

The economic reform is no longer just plans and intentions, still less abstract theoretical discourses. It is becoming a part of life. Today a considerable number of enterprises and associations in industry, construction, transport and agriculture are working on the principles of self-maintenance and self-finance. From the beginning of next year, enterprises producing 60 percent of our industrial output will be operating on this basis. The law on the state enterprise (association) will have become effective.

In restoring material incentives to their rightful place and in paying more attention to their collective forms, we should not allow sociocultural, moral or psychological incentives to be underrated.

They are of exceptional importance for enabling relations of collectivism and comradeship and the socialist way of life to develop normally and our Soviet values to take firm root in the thoughts and actions of our people.

It would be a mistake to take no notice of a certain increase in the resistance of the conservative forces that see perestroika simply as a threat to their selfish interests and objectives. This resistance can be felt not only at management level but also in work collectives.

Nor can one really doubt that the conservative forces will seize upon any difficulty in a bid to discredit perestroika and provoke dissatisfaction among the people. Even now there are those who prefer to keep ticking off the slip-ups instead of getting down to combatting shortcomings and looking for new solutions.

Naturally, these people never say that they oppose perestroika. Rather, they would have us believe that they are fighting against its negative side effects.

But, comrades, isn't it time to stop trying to scare us with all sorts of slip-ups?

Of course negative side effects are inevitable in any undertaking, particularly if it is novel. But the consequences of marking time, of stagnation and indifference have a much greater impact and cost a lot more than the side effects that arise temporarily in the course of a creative effort to reshape the social fabric.

We should learn to spot, expose and neutralize the manoeuvers of the opponents of perestroika—those who act to impede our advance and trip us up, who gloat over our difficulties and setbacks, who try to drag us back into the past.

Nor should we succumb to the pressure of the overly zealous and impatient—those who refuse to accept the objective logic of perestroika, who voice their disappointment with what they regard as a slow rate of change, who claim that this change does not yield the necessary results fast enough. It should be clear that one cannot leap over essential stages and try to accomplish everything at one go.

III

Communism and the Future

The April 1985 plenary meeting of the C.P.S.U. Central Committee was a landmark in the development of Leninist thought along this line too. The new concept of foreign policy was presented in detail at the 27th Congress.

As you know, this concept proceeds from the idea that for all the profound contradictions of the contemporary world, for all the radical differences among the countries that comprise it, it is inter-related, interdependent and integral.

The reasons for this include the internationalization of world economic ties, the comprehensive scope of the scientific and technological revolution, the essentially novel role played by the mass media, the state of the earth's resources, the common environmental danger and the crying social problems of the developing world which affect us all.

The main reason, however, is the problem of human survival. This problem is now with us because the development of nuclear weapons and the threatening prospect of their use have called into question the very survival of the human race. . . .

The October 1986 meeting in Reykjavik ranks among the events which have occurred since the new stage in international affairs began, which deserve to be mentioned on this occasion and which will go down in history.

The Reykjavik meeting gave a practical boost to the new political thinking, enabled it to gain ground in diverse social and political quarters and made international political contacts more fruitful.

The new thinking, with its regard for universal human values and emphasis on common sense and openness, is forging ahead on the international scene, destroying the stereotypes of anti-Sovietism and dispelling distrust of our initiatives and actions.

It is true that, gauged against the scope of the tasks mankind will have to tackle to ensure its survival, very, very little has so far been accomplished. But a beginning has been made, and the first signs of change are in evidence.

This is borne out, among other things, by the understanding we have reached with the United States on concluding in the near future an agreement on medium- and shorter-range missiles. The conclusion of this agreement is very important in itself: It will, for the first time, eliminate a whole class of nuclear weapons, be the first tangible step along the path of scrapping nuclear arsenals, and will show that it is in fact possible to advance in this direction without prejudice to anyone's interests.

That is obviously a major success of the new way of thinking, a result of our readiness to search for mutually acceptable solutions while strictly safeguarding the principle of equal security.

However, the question concerning this agreement was largely settled back in Reykjavik, at my second meeting with the U.S. President.

In this critical period the world expects the third and fourth Soviet-U.S. summits to produce more than merely an official acknowledgement of the decisions agreed upon a year ago, and more than merely a continuation of the discussion. The growing danger that weapons may be perfected to a point where they will become uncontrollable is urging us to waste no time.

That is why we will work unremittingly at these meetings for a palpable breakthrough, for concrete results in reducing strategic offensive armaments and barring weapons from outer space—the key to removing the nuclear threat.

Toward a New World

What is the world going to be like when it reaches our revolution's centenary? What is socialism going to be like? What degree of maturity will have been attained by the world community of states and peoples? Let us not indulge in guessing. But let us remember that the foundations for the future are being laid today.

It is our duty to preserve our inimitable civilization and life on earth, to help reason win over nuclear insanity and to create all the necessary conditions for the free and all-round development of the individual and the whole of humanity.

We are aware that there is a possibility for continuous progress. We realize that it is not easy to insure it. But this does not frighten us. On the contrary, this inspires us, giving a lofty and humane purpose to our life and injecting it with a profound meaning.

In October 1917 we parted with the Old World, rejecting it once and for all. We are moving toward a new world, the world of Communism. We shall never turn off that road.

EDITOR'S INTRODUCTION

The reforms initiated by Gorbachev are viewed with suspicion by many Soviet workers who see in his demand for accountability a threat to their job security, and by party bureaucrats who see in his demand for more lower-level democracy a threat to their power. But there is one group that, on the whole, welcomed him: the intelligentsia, including the writers and artists who have struggled for years against the stifling effects of ideological purity campaigns. Yevgeny Yevtushenko, whose long poem "Babi Yar" made him famous in the West, has a fervently optimistic view of *perestroika*, which he explains in an interview conducted by Katrina vanden Heuvel which appeared in *The Progressive*, "Yevtushenko Feels a Fresh Wind Blowing," the first selection in this section. With a proper poet's egoism, he takes credit for the current ripple of liberalization: "We created a new generation with our poetry. We created the people who are now recreating our country."

Some artists are seizing the opportunity to examine past and current events with the kind of direct gaze that was never possible in a country where history is routinely fictionalized. A play about the nuclear disaster at Chernobyl in 1985, produced in four Soviet cities in 1987, was "the average Soviet citizen's best source of information about what really happened," according to the newsmagazine *Vienna*. The second selection, "Mad Russian," reprinted from *Film Comment*, is an interview conducted by Alexander Batchan with the Soviet critic Victor Dyomin and describes the recent progress made by Soviet filmmakers in lifting bans on controversial movies and taking more control over their industry.

Gorbachev's plans to reorganize Soviet society are complicated by a number of issues in addition to the intransigence of entrenched interests. One of these is the demoralization produced by the war in Afghanistan, a war that the Soviets have neither won nor lost but that has damaged party credibility and created a new class of disaffected veterans, as Bill Keller explains in the third selection, "Home from Afghanistan," taken from *New York*

Times Magazine. Keller mentions the close relations between the Afghans and the Tadzhiks, who live in a neighboring Soviet republic. The refusal of some of the country's many ethnic and religious minorities to assimilate into Soviet culture and to accept Russian control of their designated "republics" is the subject of Ronald Grigor Suny's "The Nationality Question," the fourth article, from *The Nation*.

Modernization of the economy is also hindered by the uneven pace of Soviet progress in technology. As Julian Cooper of the University of Birmingham notes: "There are peaks of Soviet achievement outdistancing anything in the West, but there are troughs of the most extraordinary depth: there are technologies in everyday use that advanced Western countries have relegated to industrial museums." The system, says Cooper, "inhibits the withdrawal of the obsolete." One of the Soviets' outstanding areas of achievement is space exploration, as is recounted in Michael D. Lemonick's article from *Time*, "Surging Ahead," the fifth selection. India and many Asian nations have long been customers of Soviet space services. In February 1988, for the first time, an American company bought satellite space on a Soviet rocket launch—an acknowledgment that the Soviet rocket program is now more reliable than any other.

YEVTUSHENKO FEELS A FRESH WIND BLOWING[1]

Yevgeny Yevtushenko is the Soviet Union's most famous and controversial poet. Born in Siberia in 1933, Zhenya, as he is more familiarly called, spent his childhood shuttling between Moscow and his Siberian birthplace of Zima Junction. At the age of fifteen, he joined his father, a geologist, in the southern republic of Kazakhstan, where he worked as a digger with a geological expedition. Yevtushenko returned to Moscow in the early 1950s and studied literature at the prestigious Gorky Institute. His poetry soon began to be published in the official journals and newspapers.

In the late 1950s and early 1960s, the years of Nikita Khrushchev's "thaw," Yevtushenko, along with such other young poets as Andrei Vos-

[1]Reprint of an interview conducted by Katrina vanden Heuvel, assistant editor of *The Nation*. *The Progressive*. 51:24–31. Ap '87. Reprinted by permission of The Progressive, 409 E. Main St., Madison, Wisconsin. Copyright © 1987 Katrina vanden Heuvel.

nesensky, articulated the discontents and aspirations of the first post-Stalin generation. In a country where popular poets sometimes achieve the celebrity of American rock stars and where culture is often an intense form of political expression, Yevtushenko's verse was read by millions of people, and his poetry readings electrified audiences across the broad expanse of the Soviet Union.

Yevtushenko developed an international reputation as a daring anti-establishment figure—a rebellious young man who assaulted Soviet dogma and conformity, who debated the merits of abstract art with Khrushchev, and who fervently protested, in poems such as "The Heirs of Stalin" and "Babi Yar," the legacy of Stalinism and official anti-Semitism. Even during the relatively liberal Khrushchev years, Yevtushenko was frequently and savagely criticized in the Soviet press for his outspoken views.

In 1964, Khrushchev was ousted and Leonid Brezhnev's conservative reign soon led to cultural stagnation and political repression. Yevtushenko adapted to the more conservative times, and his poems became more conformist in content and style. Yet he remained faithful in important ways to his own personal convictions. In 1968, for example, he sent a letter to the government protesting the Soviet invasion of Czechoslovakia, and in 1974 he sent a telegram to Brezhnev expressing concern for the safety of Alexander Solzhenitsyn, who had just been arrested.

Yevtushenko's position in Soviet culture and politics—that of rebel and envoy—has engaged and enraged readers and critics at home and abroad. He is defensive about suggestions that he has adapted to whatever political climate prevails in Moscow and that he has vacillated between defiance and conformity. Yevtushenko insists that he has never abandoned his unpublicized efforts in behalf of victimized Soviet writers and dissidents.

Whatever the full story, thirty years after he first burst onto the scene Yevtushenko is again a leading activist in the conflict-filled effort to reform and liberalize the Soviet system. Over the last two years, in speeches, articles, and poems, he has campaigned for *glasnost*, for openness in Soviet cultural and political life.

Americans will soon be able to sample Yevtushenko's most recent poems for themselves. In April, *Almost at the End*, a collection of his poems written during the Gorbachev period, including his controversial work "Fuku," will be published by Henry Holt and Company. Meanwhile, Yevtushenko has launched a new career as a filmmaker. His movie *Kindergarten* was shown in the United States last spring, and he is working on a new film about the Three Musketeers.

This interview took place in two parts and in two cities. Yevtushenko and I talked in March 1986 in New York City, and we continued the conversation at his home outside Moscow last December. He spoke in English during both interviews.

Yevtushenko is fifty-three. His blond, tousled hair is thinner, his face more lined, and his frame lankier. But his blue-gray eyes and unflagging enthusiasm still recall the brash young poet of the 1960s.

Q: How is Mikhail Gorbachev changing Soviet society?
Yevtushenko: He has changed the air over the soil. When I say

"air," I mean first of all a fresh wind which penetrates or tries to penetrate to all levels of our society. And by soil, I mean objective reality. I mean the economic situation. I mean the psychology of a people. The main change is a change of atmosphere.

It's been seventy years since the Soviet Revolution and seventy years from one point of view is a long time. But if you will remember how long the history of humanity is, it's a very short time. Our society is still very young, and I hope we are now entering the beginning of our maturity. One of the signs of the maturity of a person or the maturity of a society is being tolerant of difference. We were many times not tolerant, and I hope what's now happening, with the release of Sakharov and some other people, is a symbol of the maturity of a society that could permit human tolerance. And so we have big hopes now. We are living in a very promising time. I don't want to be a false prophet and idealize the future. But I have been working for this future, and I am working for this future, with my speeches, with my poetry.

Q: Could you give an example of how the society is becoming more tolerant?

Yevtushenko: For the first time in many years, we have incredible openness in our press—sometimes dealing with very painful questions, openly criticizing very high-ranking officials, including ministers, members of the government. For the first time, we are publishing in many of our newspapers editorials that are signed by people. This is wonderful, because it means people are taking on personal responsibility, showing personal points of view. There is a struggle against facelessness; that's what the main fight is now. It's very visible in the arts. There are more possibilities for talented, gifted people and happily fewer possibilities for mediocre ones, for one-sided minds, one-dimensional people, the knights of inertia.

Q: But won't these knights of inertia fight back?

Yevtushenko: There are always comrades—the "but-what-ifs"—who try to halt change. They do exist. And they always will. They barricade from their wooden minds any show of progress. I am absolutely sure they will not give up very quickly because they know what they will lose—their privileges. They will fight for them. But at the same time, they're a minority. A majority wants openness.

In many countries, many kinds of systems, you could find a mortal struggle between mediocre people and talented people.

Mediocre people have comfortable, soft armchairs under their asses. In my opinion, they have no ideologies. Their main ideology is their armchairology.

We have a Russian proverb that says, "Under the lying rock water can't flow." What we're trying to do is to move these rock-minded people, stone-minded people, and make our society more flexible, more vital and ready for innovations, for reforms. Times are changing. The old guard is getting very old. And they were educated in another time.

Q: What makes the new generation of leadership so different from the old?

Yevtushenko: Now in the Soviet Union, the people who are taking charge in all fields—including newspapers, factories, and regional party committees—are people who are not guilty of Stalin's crimes. They don't have spots of blood on their conscience. They don't feel guilty, and they are not guilty. That's why they don't have an inferiority complex. That's a very important nuance.

My hope is that they know what needs to be changed now. They are former engineers, they are former agriculturalists. They know industry and agriculture very well, and they know the daily needs of people much better. In Stalin's time, Party professionals were ordered to lead heavy industry, or to be responsible for vegetables, for agriculture, or roadways, or metro, or something. These people had no professional knowledge of such things. It was very destructive.

Q: To what extent is Gorbachev in the tradition of Nikita Khrushchev?

Yevtushenko: Khrushchev was a child of a certain epoch, of Stalin's era. He did wonderful things—he opened the borders of our country to foreigners, and he organized the first youth festival in 1956. He was a man who destroyed, as much as he could, the Iron Curtain, and he released so many people from our concentration camps. I think this man will go down in history in a positive way. But at the same time he belonged to Stalin's day. He was one of his Party leaders. Our new generation of leaders, they are not involved in such tragic mistakes, or even crimes.

About Khrushchev someone said many years ago, "He wanted to cross the abyss in two jumps." I think it's a very exact impression because he was a Stalinist, and at the same time an anti-Stalinist. He was a rebel against those epochs; he was slightly a rebel against himself.

So this was a man full of contradictions, but he made one heroic step which I think not only Russia but all humanity will never forget—when he made his speech at the Twentieth Party Congress, and he organized a commission which released so many innocent people.

Q: In how many jumps does Gorbachev want to cross the abyss?
Yevtushenko: First of all, I think he is not trying to jump; he is trying to make a bridge.

Q: Some commentators in America, including Alexander Haig, have said that Gorbachev is a neo-Stalinist.
Yevtushenko: That's absolutely. . . . Absolutely. . . . If he were neo-Stalinist, he could never support the sharpest anti-Stalinist creations, like some of the poems now being published.

Q: So you think he's part of the new anti-Stalinist movement?
Yevtushenko: I'm not telling you that he's specially anti-Stalinist.

Q: Wait a minute. You said you are an anti-Stalinist.
Yevtushenko: I am.

Q: Do you think Gorbachev is an anti-Stalinist?
Yevtushenko: It's difficult to give such a kind of definition for one politician.

Q: Is it too early to say?
Yevtushenko: No, no, no. I'm not saying that. I think this is a man of anti-bureaucratization.

Q: Why do you think people like Haig are misreading Gorbachev?
Yevtushenko: The so-called hard-liners are making their own business when they are trying not to notice these changes. Because otherwise their image of the Red Bear with long teeth wanting to cut the throat of innocent and peaceful Americans will collapse.

Your hard-liners explain their position by saying there are hard-liners in the Soviet Union. And our hard-liners are trying to close our openness, our democratization, because they are waving this image of American hard-liners. So they both need each other.

But even for them, for your hard-liners, because they are also human beings, it is a very dangerous game that they're playing; they are practically sawing off the branch on which they are sitting. Because of these hard-line games, even their lives are at stake, as well as the lives of the whole world.

Some of them, your right-wing people, by their characters, if they could live inside the Soviet Union, they would behave like the old guard of Stalin, like dogmatic Communists. And some American bureaucrats and right-wing journalists who take very anti-Soviet positions, I could imagine them living in the Soviet Union. They could make anti-American propaganda in the Soviet Union with no problem. They could say the same words. They're just the same people, but in reverse.

If you are a conformist in the United States, it means you are more or less a hawk. It's a very comfortable position, you know, but the hawk is everywhere a hawk. A hawk couldn't be a nightingale in another country. He will still be a hawk.

Unfortunately, there is an international nation of conformists. They just live in different countries. But happily, there is also an international nation of good people. They will always understand each other. But a third kind of people are in between them. There is a fence between them, a fence made of mugs. We're divided by this fence made of mugs, faces.

Q: Americans view the Soviet Union partially through Hollywood. During your tour of America last year, you did something most Americans haven't done: You saw *Rocky* and *Rambo* on the same day.

Yevtushenko: Yes, and the year before I saw *Red Dawn* and other great stuff. That was when I invented a word, "warnography." I don't think Mr. Sylvester Stallone himself is anti-Russian, or that he would like to eat live Russian children, or anything like that. For him, the Russians are like extraterrestrials, but frightening extraterrestrials. And probably when he made this film for commercial reasons, he forgot something very important: that the future of all humanity, including Mr. Sylvester Stallone's future, depends on Russian-American relations.

There isn't one movie in the United States where you can find even one good Russian who is *not* defecting from the Soviet Union. Unfortunately, these films remind me of how Japanese people were shown during the war. We Russians are not—happily not—at war with America, but it's a frightening sign when even before a potential war, the American cinema is already portraying all Russian people as if they were enemies. Such films create mistrust, mistrust creates missiles, and missiles create the danger of war, which will abolish everyone, including Mr. Stallone and all those teenagers who are applauding these films.

Q: How would you compare American cinema to Soviet cinema?
Yevtushenko: Our new films are more rebellious than yours.
They are sharper, not as conformist as American cinema. I'm not
speaking about independent American cinema; that's different.
But your mainstream commercial cinema is more conformist,
even more Stalinist, than in Russia at this moment. There is some
primitivization of Americans in Russian cinema, but in our films
about international problems, we never show Americans like wild
beasts, like animals. We never create, in our cinema, an image of
an enemy country or an enemy people like your *Rocky IV* or
Rambo.

The creation of the image of the enemy is self-destructive.
It's always connected with a kind of self-megalomania, self-
exaggeration, gigantomania. And the mother of gigantomania is
always an inferiority complex.

Q: Why has this image of the enemy been created?
Yevtushenko: Any kind of society, any state, needs an enemy. It's
terrible. It was George Orwell's point, if you remember. We
waste too much time in mutual accusations. I don't want to argue
with President Reagan, but he has argued many times with our
government. For instance, he once said Russia is a focus of world
evil. I don't blame him for saying this. I'm just trying to analyze
it. First of all, I think he wrote this expression in a rush, because
if he had thought more carefully about this phrase, he would have
realized that it is an anti-Christian definition. I'll explain why. All
Christianity is based on Dostoevsky's formula, "Everybody is
guilty in everything." You must first find the focus of evil inside
yourself. And afterwords, you can accuse others, but only by accusing yourself first.

And I don't like it when some dogmatic people in our country
try to show America as the whole center of world evil. I will never
say that America is the focus of evil. There are so many beautiful
people whom I know. When I wrote my famous poem "Between
the City of Yes and the City of No," I didn't mean that the City
of No was American society or Russian society. I think we have
some streets of No in America and some streets of No in the Soviet Union. The focus of world evil could never be concentrated
only in one country.

So the focus of world evil is inside all of us, that's human psychology. And we must be very careful in our expressions, because
we have now a war of words. But such wars, unfortunately, can

very easily be transformed into missiles and other terrible, terrible stuff.

Q: What role did you and your fellow artists play in bringing about the changes that are under way in the Soviet Union?

Yevtushenko: Who are these people who lead our country? They are people who were listeners of our poetry readings in the late 1950s and early 1960s. That's true. That's reality. Some people absorbed my message that bureaucracy is stifling them. We created a new generation with our poetry. We created people who now are recreating our country. For instance, there is a new openness in the Soviet Union. This is an echo of our poetry.

Q: Are you saying that writers and poets prepared the way for Gorbachev?

Yevtushenko: Of course. Absolutely. I'm sure. They absorbed our spirits. They were students—some of them were students squeezing without tickets on the balcony of our poetry readings.

I think my generation of poets did a lot of things to break the Iron Curtain. We wounded our hands breaking this Iron Curtain with our naked hands. We didn't work in gloves. Sometimes there were victories, sometimes there were defeats. Some retreats were preparatory, and sometimes we sat under the ground after a hail of insults. But our literature, our art, didn't come as a gift from the so-called upstairs.

We worked for it. We didn't get this as a gift. We forged this gift for ourselves and for future generations. Of course, we didn't think that we would produce new kinds of people. But it's happened. We've produced a new kind of person, a new-minded person. Poetry plays a great role in the Soviet Union, and so I am very happy that we worked for it not in vain.

Q: You mean you think that the poetry of your generation is the political soul of the new leadership?

Yevtushenko: I hope so. If I say this, it sounds immodest, but I hope so. I'm almost sure.

Q: What are some of the areas where you would like to see the policy of openness extended?

Yevtushenko: We now have what I think is an open discussion about our current problems. But in my opinion, we don't have enough openness when we speak about our past. Without having more open conversations about the problems of our past, we can't decide the problems of our present. There are some people who don't want to have open conversations about the tragedies of our past. So there are two points of view. There are people who don't want open speech, openness in our textbooks, or anything like that. Their point is, "Okay, that's our past. We don't want to repeat it. But why must they put salt on the open wounds? We just rehabilitated the wound so it could heal." That's their point of view. My personal point of view, which is shared by the majority of our writers, is that to put sugar on the open wounds is even more dangerous. Ever since ancient times, professional seamen have cured their wounds with salty water. It was the only way for them. Salt, honest salt, could be more helpful than dishonest sugar.

That's why I wrote a poem like "Fuku." In "Fuku" there are very important lines: "Someone who forgets yesterday's victims will be a victim tomorrow." That's probably my point of view on all of history, not only on Russian history. My hope is that now is a time for summing up in Russia. Summing up all of the positive and negative lessons of our experience in the first years of socialism. To be fearless builders of the future is only possible if we are fearless social archaeologists of our past. Yes, we must not only put salt on open wounds, we must dig into them as deep as possible, because there is still some infection which doesn't give us the possibility to be absolutely healthy.

Great literature is always a great warning. If we see some danger, we must prophylactically write about it. Even if it's very painful. This literature must be like acupuncture. We mustn't be afraid to put needles into the most painful points of the conscience. It's painful, it's unpleasant, but you might be saved. That's why I don't like so-called pleasant art.

Q: What about the artists who have left the Soviet Union? Are you angry at them for not staying and fighting to change your country?

Yevtushenko: I don't think I have any kind of moral right to be their judge. I understand only one thing: that it is a tragedy for a writer to be abroad, out of his own range. I couldn't imagine myself in exile. It would be the worst punishment to spend the rest of my life abroad.

Q: We get our image of the Soviet Union largely from people who have left. What about what those people say?

Yevtushenko: You can't generalize about all emigrés; they're all very different. For instance, Joseph Brodsky I think is a good poet, the best Russian poet who lives abroad. And I helped him, and he knows it, when he was in exile. I wrote a letter defending him. Then he came to the United States and began to say—not in the newspapers, but he began to say in so-called private circles—that I was one of the people who was guilty. He later asked for my forgiveness. You know, America, like Russia, is a big village. I asked him why he said such things. He told me, "I'm sorry, Yevgeny, when you are an emigré, sometimes you artificially force yourself to find someone to blame." That was a sincere answer.

Q: But don't you get angry?

Yevtushenko: I get angry because these people are full of ignorance and hatred. Such people are part of the focus of evil. They are morally not ready for mutual understanding. They don't want mutual understanding. But their ignorance is dangerous for themselves. Because if they don't want mutual understanding between such two great peoples, they are working for their own death, with all their screams, their cries, and always their declarations.

Q: What about Alexander Solzhenitsyn? You defended him in the Soviet Union.

Yevtushenko: Look, Solzhenitsyn, in my opinion, wrote some good books, some very good books: *One Day in the Life of Ivan Denisovich*, "An Incident at Krechetovka Station," his short stories, and there are some very beautiful pages in *Cancer Ward*. But in *Cancer Ward*, there are some very primitive pages, too. Because when a writer hates something too much, he ceases being a great writer, because hatred is a kind of blindness. A writer must have open eyes to see life.

I defended him many times, many times, until the last moment when he was arrested before he was sent abroad. He is a gifted writer, a very strong character as a man, and he wrote some books condemning the tragedy of the Stalin past, and I am very grateful to him. But in fighting against fanaticism, unfortunately, he became a fanatic. He put himself into a cage of his own design, a procrustean bed of his own schemes.

Q: You mentioned Brodsky's remark about you being one of the guilty. Your critics ask why the Soviet state, which will not tolerate others, tolerates you.

Yevtushenko: Some of the American press accuse some Russian writers of being conformist, not rebellious enough, et cetera, et cetera, et cetera. I am a victim of this accusation, because I am not in prison, I am not in a mental hospital, nothing like that. Such a writer's life is sometimes interpreted in your country as a kind of dishonesty.

But I am a poetician, not a politician. As a poet, I don't like any kind of borders, prisons, any kind of police, army, missiles, anything which is connected with repression. I don't like it. And I never glorified it. And I did everything that was possible. I am not God. Nobody is God—not even God himself.

I am doing everything to make life in my own country much better, freer in many ways. And I try, and I tried, and I will try, to help many people. I wrote a poem against anti-Semitism. I wrote a poem against Stalin and his era. I wrote many poems against bureaucracy.

You have a fighter, the *toreador*. You have the police and the public, those so-called observers. I've seen the public get unhappy when the *toreador* professionally and skillfully sneaks away from the *toro*'s horns. Unfortunately, inside many audiences is hidden the thirst to see real human blood. In the arena, I've seen some wonderful *toreadors* accused of being cowards. And they were not cowards. They didn't want to be killed by the bull. But there are some people who just observe your fight from a distance, and they are unhappy with it. They would like to idolize you. But if you fall down, with some horns on your head, it's only human nature. As Pushkin said once, "Only dead people can laugh."

Q: Why have you devoted so much of your writing to opposing the bureaucracy?

Yevtushenko: Because bureaucracy is based on indifference, and indifference is a kind of aggression. Indifference is a kind of war against your own people and against other people. One bureaucrat, for instance, who sits in his office and has the Picasso drawing with the dove of peace on the wall, he may be a pacifist, but at the same time he is in a permanent war with his people. He is an aggressor because he is indifferent.

But in my opinion, to accuse bureaucracy alone is too easy. To accuse governments is too easy a way out. I think all governments are far from perfection. But the rest of humanity is far from perfection, too. I disagree with the expression that every people has the government it deserves. No people deserve their government. In a way it's true. But when we accuse bureaucrats, sometimes we absolve ourselves. Sometimes we are responsible for the bureaucracy, the bureaucrats.

Q: You are called the rebel poet. Where did the first anger, the first urgency come from?

Yevtushenko: I am a child of the barracks. I am a child of the flea markets. I am a child of Siberian platforms. I am a child of the crowd. I am a child of lines, endless lines, for bread. And they helped me, these poor suffering people on lines, who can't write. They helped me. What I write is a way of paying them back. And I feel a responsibility to them.

Once I described myself in one of my poems as a writer for those who don't write. In my opinion, everyone can write a book. That's why I felt ashamed when I was at Babi Yar, standing and staring at mountains of rubbish over these nameless graves where many dead bodies were thrown like wood into this valley. Nobody had written about these graves. I'm not a mystical man, but I remember that moment. It seemed to me that I heard through the mountains of rubbish secret whispers of those who died, those murdered people who were asking me to write about what had happened. I felt them accusing me for having forgotten them. Do you understand? That made me ashamed. And my shame helped me to write "Babi Yar."

I am absolutely convinced that all poets, all real poets, are rebels. They could have been rebels in different ways. Let me make myself clear. You must not demand that all poets write political poetry, political declarations. You must not demand that. But it's my character.

A human being can be a rebel only if he is concerned about others more than about himself. When I use this word "rebel," I don't use it only in a political sense. Because as I said in one of my early poems, "Conversations with an American Writer," unfortunately in all centuries simple honesty looks like courage. Rebels are not only very famous people who make public statements. If someone doesn't give to others the possibility of engaging him in their hypocrisy, he is a rebel. Not famous, but a rebel. There are so many unknown rebels in the world, just simple, honest people. Any kind of honesty is rebellion.

Q: Do you sometimes feel you're not courageous enough?

Yevtushenko: Sometimes. I hope I am honest, but I don't think I am a courageous man. That is different. There is a special power when you can openly recognize your own weaknesses. That's why shame is the real and main engine of humanity. I feel shame for many things. First of all, I think shame must begin in yourself.

No one has the right to accuse an epoch, a century, a period in history, if he has no courage to accuse himself. I accuse myself of being criminally lazy. I haven't written many books, and they're probably dead in me now. Because I am too thirsty for life. I want to be everything, everybody, in every place, at the same time. I don't like people who are not thirsty for life. When they aren't curious, and lose their childish curiosity, and kill the child inside of them, they can't write poems.

So I accuse myself of not concentrating enough. Not being courageous enough. I can't accuse myself of betraying anyone— not in friendship, not in love, not in personal relationships.

Q: Do you fear, as you grow old, that you will lose the rebel inside of you?

Yevtushenko: There is a beautiful South American expression: "Where are the former incendiaries now? The incendiaries of all the revolutionary fires. Where are they? They are working as firemen. They are all of them in the firemen's service now." It's very easy to be progressive and rebellious when you're young, when you have no responsibility for others and you're responsible only for yourself. It's very easy. But if you are married, you have a first child, and then, as in so many former rebels' lives, the diapers of the child are like the white flag of capitulation.

I once wrote, when I was forty, a very sad poem about getting older. A friend of mine, a poet, reproached me. Don't take growing old too seriously, he said. There are just two dates in everyone's life: the date of birth and the date of death. And he said, you know, Don Quixote was old, but he wasn't old. And he said, don't lose the Don Quixote inside yourself, and you will always be young. It was good advice. Pasternak, when he was sixty-six years old, wrote beautiful, youthful poetry. And his writing was a great example for us. It's not really a matter of age.

Q: What is your impression of young people in the Soviet Union?

Yevtushenko: They're very different. When you ask me about them, I try to generalize. I see so many different faces, it's very difficult to generalize. But I think they are more informed about what is happening in the world. Most of them study foreign languages, unlike our generation. But now they get so specialized; they have the same danger in Russia that you have in America. To be a really great specialist, you must read so much technical literature. And we have one danger with this younger generation that they will be locked in the knowledge of their specialization.

Sometimes some of them don't know our own history, which is very dangerous. Dangerous.

Q: In one of your poems, you ask a sixteen-year-old, "How many people did Stalin kill?" And somebody says twenty or twenty-five, and then the highest estimate that you got was what?

Yevtushenko: Two thousand. They have a lack of knowledge about history. As I said in my Writers Congress speech of December 1985, we must rewrite our books about history, because if you don't know your own history, you can repeat mistakes. But generally I like our young people. They want what most Americans, all human beings, want. They would like to have a good job, a comfortable life, a good family, to have children, and not to be frightened by the threat of nuclear war.

Q: How hopeful are you that Soviet-American relations will improve?

Yevtushenko: Mr. Reagan has never been to Russia. I'm absolutely sure if, for instance, Mr. Reagan could sit down on the shores of Lake Baikal near a hunter's fire and drink vodka and speak with our fishermen, with workers, with others, he would be a different man, as would many other Americans. And many Russians would be different if they would come to America and sit near a hunter's fire in the Rocky Mountains and speak with Americans. I'm absolutely sure that would change their minds.

Both systems have some good features, some bad features. Probably if you find common mutual understanding, both societies, both structures could absorb the best features of each and we'll get an absolutely new structure in the future. But nobody knows. I don't know. I just want to be in my own place.

MAD RUSSIAN[2]

When news about a quiet revolt in the Soviet Filmmakers Union during its fifth congress in May 1986 had reached the West, it attracted the attention of many people but not necessarily Sovietologists or Russian émigrés. *Variety* headlined that Elem Klimov, hardly a household name

[2]Reprint of an interview conducted by Alexander Batchan, a New York–based film critic. This article first appeared in *Film Comment*, 23:48+, My./Je. '87. Copyright © 1987 by Alexander Batchan.

to the paper's readers, had been elected new president of the formerly docile group, although his name did not even appear on the officially approved list of nominees.

At the press conference in Moscow on June 20, Elem Klimov announced that a "conflict" commission was created to review all films held up by censors. On August 9, in an interview published in *Pravda,* Klimov also mentioned another newly formed commission, the "legal" one. "In the very near future," he promised, filmgoers will be introduced to several hitherto unknown pictures by Kira Muratova, Andrei Smirnov, Bulat Mansurov, Larisa Shepitko (his late wife). . . . The commission, he said, is dealing not only with specific films but also with the creative careers of certain directors, especially young ones, who for various reasons weren't allowed to make films. Now they have had an opportunity to resume their arbitrarily interrupted creative work."

Last fall, Klimov visited New York, Washington, and Los Angeles, promoting the largest showing to date of new and recent Soviet films in this country, which has been extended to 20 American cities. It includes formerly disgraced Sergei Paradjanov's new masterpiece, *The Legend of Suram Fortress,* and Alexei German's controversial picture about World War II, *Trial on the Road.* The latter was made in 1971 but released only last year and proclaimed by the Soviet film critics as the best film of 1986. "Our film industry has changed a lot," Klimov has been saying at numerous press conferences and public appearances in the West, "and will change still more."

Since he has been elected the first secretary of the Filmmakers Union, Klimov has spent much time abroad working to promote the new image of the Soviet cinema and Gorbachev's new policy of *glasnost,* which is largely responsible for the radical changes within the decaying Soviet film industry. During an interview with the *Los Angeles Times* last fall, Klimov said that he believes the political and artistic forces, working in opposite directions within the Moscow film community, have created a sense of daring that "we would be fools not to seize and use." In a second interview in the same paper, Klimov was asked whether he had opponents. He replied: "Many." Where are they? the reporter followed. "Everywhere," said Klimov.

One of the main opponents of the Young Turks headed by Klimov, the longtime chairman of the powerful State Film Committee (Goskino), Filipp Yermash, was removed from his position last December and replaced by another party functionary, Alexandr Kamshalov, who had been responsible for cinema at the culture department of the Central Committee of the CPSU. Yermash, one of the most conservative figures of Soviet cinema, was considered responsible for banning controversial films such as Klimov's *Agony,* recently released in this country as *Rasputin.* It was shelved for almost ten years, although it was awarded a prize in Venice in 1982. Gleb Panfilov's 1979 film, *The Theme,* was banned until recently, partly because it dared to raise the issue of recent Jewish emigration while not condemning the would-be émigré.

Tengiz Abuladze's *Repentance,* exposing the crimes of Stalin's henchman, the head of the secret police, Lavrenti Beria, had to wait for three years, as well as did Alexei German's second banned picture, *My Friend Ivan Lapshin,* which shows the misery of Soviet life in the mid-Thirties.

Now all those films are shown in Moscow to packed movie houses and openly discussed by the leading Soviet newspapers.

In another similar development, Klimov and his allies have been trying to lift ideological restrictions imposed on foreign films. Thus in early February, while visiting Paris, Klimov told reporters that soon Soviet movie fans will be able to see films by Federico Fellini. The Soviets have recently bought all of Fellini's pictures, including *8½*, which premiered at the Moscow International Film Festival 25 years ago and was given first prize. Yet it has never been shown to the Soviet public. The first Fellini picture Soviet audiences will see is *La Dolce Vita.*

Soviet audiences will also get to see Michelangelo Antonioni's *Red Desert* and two Milos Forman pictures, *One Flew Over the Cuckoo's Nest* and *Amadeus.* Not so long ago Forman and other Czech New Wave filmmakers were condemned for their participation in the Prague Spring of 1968.

The most dramatic releases will be the last two films of the émigré director Andrei Tarkovsky, who died in Paris last December. Tarkovsky's name was deleted from the film history textbooks and his films were banned after he decided to stay in the West in the early Eighties, when he was shooting *Nostalghia* in Italy. According to Klimov, authorities are negotiating for the rights to *Nostalghia* and to Tarkovsky's last Swedish-made picture, *The Sacrifice.* Meanwhile, the ban has been lifted from his Soviet films, and his name is mentioned in the Soviet press with great respect.

Yet another film made by émigré director Slava Tsukerman, *Liquid Sky,* which has become a cult classic in the West, has almost no chance of being shown in the Soviet Union in the near future. *Liquid Sky* might look too shocking for puritanical Soviet tastes. It will inevitably reach the Moscow and Leningrad underground videocassette markets, if it is not already there.

All those recent developments no doubt scare many a Soviet filmmaker or studio executive. As the director of *Ivan Lapshin,* Alexei German, said during his recent visit to the New Directors/New Films series in New York, for some of them it is difficult to get accustomed to the idea that so many things are allowed. This fact makes them quite perplexed. Their films will have to compete with the pictures of their more talented and controversial colleagues that previously had been banned, plus with the increased imported fare and the ever-growing video market.

At the news conference after the January plenum of the SFU, Elem Klimov said, "The situation will hardly change radically as long as we do not radically change the methods of making movies." One of the main changes confirmed at that plenary session was the shift of financial resources and control over creative aspects of filmmaking from Goskino to local studios. According to Klimov, that will lead to "greater democratization, greater freedom of action . . . and greater responsibility for the final result." Klimov also said that Goskino will not censor films any longer, and will instead coordinate joint projects and negotiate on behalf of the whole industry. Distribution will also be decentralized, and the emphasis will be placed on self-financing.

Rolan Bykov, one of the most popular Soviet actors and directors, whose *Scarecrow*—perhaps the first Russian film that insists that the individual could be morally superior to the Soviet collective—was seen by 55 million people, said: "He who calls the tune pays. This shift in responsibilities should provide real carte blanche for the artists." However, Bykov pointed out, "Now studios can also run the risk of going under, of getting ruined—a thing that had never before happened in a socialist society."

To avoid that risk Soviet filmmakers will have to be more attentive to public tastes. Klimov said that ticket prices will have to rise if we want films to bring profits. But that would not help so much as films playing to more people. Soviet filmmakers must learn the basics of a free enterprise system, with all its advantages and disadvantages, and at the same time figure out how to combine the new principles of *glasnost* with a centralized, ideological control that will not simply disappear.

Klimov has stated: "Studios will be led by exemplary citizens of our country, many of them Communists, who follow the current line of our party. The state leadership will remain." If this is so, what happens if the current party line changes, say, in a year or two, and the whole decentralization process collapses? It has happened in Soviet history before. And by loosening the control over the Filmmakers Union, Soviet authorities obviously want something in exchange: full movie houses at home and hard currency and prestigious awards abroad. Will they have enough patience to wait until Soviet filmmakers can repay their debt? The movies made under the new conditions won't be released until 1989.

These questions are among those I put to Victor Dyomin, renowned Soviet film critic and scholar, one of the secretaries of the board of the Soviet Filmmakers Union. Dyomin came to the United States at the end of March, together with Elem Klimov, Rolan Bykov, Eldar Shengelaya, Rustam Ibragimbekov, and other noted Soviet filmmakers to participate in an "Entertainment Summit" with their American colleagues. The Summit was organized by The Fund for Peace, and Mark Gerzon and Lindsay Smith of Mediators Productions.

—A.B.

Since you are the new president of the association of Soviet film critics, I suppose then you are the right person to ask what is going on in film criticism in the Soviet Union. There are two main film magazines: the monthly The Art of Film **and the bimonthly** The Soviet Screen. **Goskino, the state film committee, used to control both of them. Who is running those magazines now?**

Officially, Goskino should not have ruled them. The magazines should have been under the authority of both Goskino and the Soviet Filmmakers Union. In reality, though, the SFU indeed had no control over them, never. Hence any Goskino official, not just its chairman, but let us say a man responsible for distribution, had a right to delete the figures, thoughts, or conversational points that could have hurt his interests. All this caused a sharp criticism in the winter and spring of 1986, prior to our fifth congress.

At the congress, a sentiment was widely expressed that Goskino's activity was causing everybody anxiety and criticism.

Everybody else's but not our two film magazines which were under its control. Thus film magazines (in contrast to nonfilm publications) kept silent about Goskino's shortcomings and, as usual, praised the last awful pictures by Sergei Bondarchuk and Evgeni Matveev, without mentioning that those films turned out to be boxoffice flops. Goskino officials even wrote letters addressed to themselves which immensely praised the films in question, and then published these so-called readers' letters in their magazines. And so on.

Both the editors-in-chief of *The Art of Film* and *The Soviet Screen* have since had to resign. The new editor of *The Soviet Screen* is Yuri Rybakov, who is a very serious and responsible person. Hopefully, he will succeed in reorganizing its work. So far the situation with this magazine has been very difficult.

The Art of Film had started changing even before the new editor's arrival. Now he has assumed his responsibilities. His name is Konstantin Shcherbakov, also a very serious and knowledgeable man who supports our positions, the positions worked out at the fifth congress of the SFU. If you have seen the last issues of *The Art of Film*, in my opinion, those are the issues of a new magazine which reflects our reorientation ("*perestroika*"). There are very serious questions asked of the authorities and of the bureaucrats, and criticism of the past's poor attitude toward cinema. . . .

What happened at the State Film Institute (VGIK, The All-Union State Institute of the Cinema)? I have read that its students organized a conference where they demanded changes in the structure of film education.

The situation in the VGIK is very complicated: The first student revolt happened even before our congress. They gathered in April, and the SFU congress opened in May. VGIK students protested against the professors who cannot teach and offered a new mechanism of inviting new teachers approved by student votes. The students weren't taken seriously. But after the congress, when the SFU began to work in the right direction, and the VGIK and Goskino were subjected to strong criticism, it turned out that the VGIK students were right.

The truth of the matter is that the VGIK has an assembly line system of preparing new cadres. Under this system, creative talents are suppressed. The final product is a narrow-minded half-professional but surprisingly gifted person when it comes to vigilance, mistrustfulness, and an unwillingness to notice anything wrong with him- or herself. In this respect, the VGIK is quite successful: it manufactures like pancakes the so-called operated artists, which could be guided by remote control. This is the main danger of our times.

But what do you expect, if somebody like Bondarchuk admits into his class, say, 20 people, and is seen five or six times over a three year period? By the time his students are about to graduate, he cannot tell one from another.

Yet at the same time, in the capital of Soviet Georgia, Tbilisi, at the university, there is a department for theater directing but no film school, and without any permission from above, some very interesting film workshops are formed every year. There are no entrance exams. Talented young filmmakers are invited to participate in them. They are taught by the top professionals in the field.

For example, Eldar Shengelaya (the head of the Georgian filmmakers) arranged an internship for his four students on the shooting of his picture *The Blue Mountains*. That was a real on-the-job training for them without any dogmatic rules which would forbid them from working on a film.

I prefer such experiments, which take place in Tbilisi, to the solid, smothering approach at the VGIK, which boasts that some of their programs have not changed since 1962.

One suggestion to reform the VGIK is strongly supported by Elem Klimov: In September all students, old and new, should be sent out for internships. After that, all VGIK instructors should be thrown out, and the premises ought to be thoroughly disinfected. Then new teachers who can teach must be selected. Because today, the VGIK is a morass inhabited by untalented people who have entrenched themselves and, by pretending to be super-vigilant citizens, have managed not to convey to students any professional skills.

Let us assume that you will succeed in restructuring the system of education in filmmaking, cinema journalism, and theory. How many years before these changes will affect Soviet cinema?

This is a very serious question. We, the new people, with new ideas, upon becoming the leaders of the SFU, have shared the sweet dream that everything could be improved within one and a half to two years. Today we issue an appeal, and tomorrow ev-

erybody would respond to it by starting change from within. . . .
That was a period which Klimov calls an epoch of endless discussions (*"mitingovshchina"*). We agitated [amongst] each other for changes but thought that we were persuading everybody else. Now it turned out that there is another more important period, the period of [implementation], the epoch of work.

I will give you an example of how complicated our current situation is. First in September and then in November of the last year we discussed the films which all the Soviet studios were planning to produce—130 altogether. We looked at their plots, checked the directors' credentials, and concluded that 30 of the projects ought to be cancelled unconditionally. At that time we should have created an organizational mechanism to enforce such decisions. In fact, we had such an opportunity. The SFU members are also the members of cinematographers' bureaus at the studios, directors' bureaus, and screenwriters' bureaus, and we could have formed additional bureaus—such as a story editors' bureau. On the basis of these bureaus, we could have created an amalgamated bureau and appointed certain people from this bureau to be our representatives, the SFU commissars, so to speak, at the studios. Now those commissars could have had greater power than [simply] administration. And when the management of some studio wants to make a worthless film, commissars could say "no" and threaten to appeal to the power of the SFU.

We had serious arguments on that subject. I supported those who expressed moderate views, not the radicals. Today I think that maybe we made a mistake by not pursuing that idea. Because, despite our criticism, studio production plans have not changed. Only four or five mediocre projects have been cancelled. New production plans have been discussed, and we can see that neither Goskino nor the film studios want to make a single step toward reality. Our newspapers are now much more interesting than our movies.

Theaters raise serious problems in their productions more often than films. The same goes for our literature. But not for the film studios. This is our real situation today.

Under Klimov's direction, we have created a new model of film production where a bureaucrat has no power. This model is unique: artists will be giving orders to other artists. But so far nothing of the kind has happened—for the second year in a row.

The reconstruction in the film industry has more to do with releasing the old films which were banned than with making new, controversial pictures?

Yes, of course. This is what we can boast now. Films made two, four, six years ago are being shown now. They were made in a very strange time when our cinema was infected by the bureaucratic virus. Cinema only pretended that it was saying something. You know about this phenomenon in our society. Suddenly books come out that have no right to exist. They are the books for bureaucrats. There are also the whole symphonies written for the bureaucrats which can even be awarded prizes. They are performed only once because it's impossible to find a public to listen to them a second time.

There is a special term, "secretary literature." I am talking about novels written by the officials of the Soviet Writers Union. I mean the former secretaries that had held their positions before the recent writers' congress, although as you know the situation at that union has not changed much. They turned out to be less radical than the filmmakers union. As a result, half of the old leadership or even more were reelected.

But what do you do with all those worthless books? In this respect socialism has a great advantage over capitalism: By order from above, all city libraries will subscribe to a certain novel in six or eight parts. The novel will be published in 20 to 40 to 60 thousand copies and will reach library shelves, where it will stand quietly accumulating dust without being noticed by anyone. You can do this with books with the help of a socialist system. But it does not work when it comes to cinema.

You cannot bring people to the theaters by force. If he or she paid for the ticket and in 15 minutes left the screening room, we still count him as somebody who has seen the film. But more often than not he starts telling everybody not to go to this movie—very soon the public knows that this film is bad.

People are smart, and they know how to read our reviews. Here we come back to the problem of film criticism. When people read that a film is "a noble work of art calling for this or that, leading forward," they not only forget about the film but also stop reading the review. On the other hand, if they read, "Although this picture is talented, its creators have paid tribute to bourgeois taste with its cult of a fist and sex . . . ," they will also throw away the review. But because they will be rushing to see the movie.

There exists quite a magic situation—films made for the bureaucrats with reviews also written for the bureaucrats. We make movies the way we want, praise them the way we want—all in the family. But how about the audience? There is no audience for those films. Now the most important task is to win back the audience.

Pretty grim. How in such a Kafkaesque atmosphere did outstanding films like Rolan Bykov's *Scarecrow*, **Alexei German's** *My Friend Ivan Lapshin*, **or Tengiz Abuladze's** *Repentance* **get made?**
I would call it the law of polarization. Artists despised so much what was going on that they not only refused to speak the accepted language and maintain discourse at the accepted level but felt a contrary desire to do everything *their* way.

What happened, for example, with Tengiz Abuladze? Everybody knows now that he has made an interesting picture, *Repentance,* but not too many are aware of what happened prior to that. He went to Armenia with his preceding picture and was showing it in various clubs under very bad conditions—the projection and sound quality were terrible. Abuladze, as he recalled later, got very angry at the people who had organized the trip, and instead of going with them to the picnic he left Erevan earlier that day with his chauffeur. They were driving very fast to Tbilisi and were hit by a truck. Two other people in the car were killed but he survived, although he was badly wounded. He stayed in bed for four months and when he recovered he got this strange feeling that something extraordinary happened to him. As if somebody interfered on his behalf by saying, "Two people are enough: let this one stay alive."

Abuladze decided that if there is some purpose in his surviving the accident, he must make a masterpiece with no equals. Let them try to obstruct his work, but from now on he would not compromise.

From that accident springs this film about Stalinist terror, with a broader meaning. He even went to see Eduard Shevardnadze, then head of the Georgian Communist Party. Finally, he made this strange but great picture leading one to deep reflections. It is screened now in Moscow with tremendous success. *Repentance* is a very complex film. It represents a very sophisticated artistic play with facts, with reality. . . .

So having seen death, Abuladze felt like a free man. . . .
Yes [as if he thought]: "130 out of 145 directors make films for the authorities. You want to be praised by them. I am not going to think about it. I shall think about what is eternal, about my conscience, about my soul. It will be my repentance, the repentance of a generation. . . . "

Elem Klimov, when he was trying to make *Agony* (*Rasputin*), or Alexei German making his films, especially *Ivan Lapshin*, had similar feelings. They strived to counterbalance the situation which existed at the time: when hacks and vulgarians who could not do anything decent were in favor, they wanted to prove that it was still possible to make great films. This phenomenon of polarization in filmmaking then saves us now. But strictly speaking, we have not yet seen the new pictures created [that we hope will] result from our reconstruction, as a consequence of the ideas developed at our congresses.

HOME FROM AFGHANISTAN[3]

Aleksandr Simonov returned from the war in Afghanistan last summer, tanned and sinewy from carrying his weight in weaponry on mountain patrols.

In the tidy, three-room Moscow apartment he shares with his mother, grandmother and older brother, Simonov keeps two scrapbooks filled with snapshots from his army days. Showing them off to a visitor, he seems nostalgic for the camaraderie of war. Here he is, a boyish, bare-chested soldier striking a Rambo pose with a bazooka slung across his belly; here, lined up with his fellow paratroopers atop an armored personnel carrier; here, in his underwear clowning with comrades at a campsite in the Afghan desert.

"In Afghanistan," he declares, "I learned to love people."

A little probing, however, turns up less agreeable memories. Once Simonov was caught in a fusillade of rebel dum-dum bullets

[3]Reprint of a magazine article by Bill Keller, a correspondent in the Moscow bureau of the *New York Times*. *New York Times Magazine*. pp. 24+. F. 14, '88. Copyright © 1988 by The New York Times Company. Reprinted by permission.

that exploded against his flak jacket. At the base of his spine, the shrapnel has left a cluster of scars; they look like cigarette burns.

On another occasion, he and his buddies watched an errant rebel rocket hit a local bus, then rushed to pull survivors from the carnage. The 21-year-old soldier tells of trying to separate a baby from its dead mother, and having the tiny body come apart in his hands.

After all this, did Simonov, who is now a law student at Moscow State University, have any trouble readjusting to civilian life? "The first three months back home were pretty difficult," he admitted. "The air in Afghanistan is pretty rarified. Every night, I dream of war and of my fellow soldiers."

Then he suddenly turned away, covering his face with his hands and choking back tears.

During the past year, as *glasnost* has slightly lowered the wall of propaganda and secrecy surrounding the war, the hurt that Afghanistan has inflicted on Soviet society has become more evident. The aches of returning veterans like Simonov are the most visible, but not the only domestic pain caused by eight indecisive years of combat in a hostile country. The analogy often drawn between America in Vietnam and the Soviet Union in Afghanistan is glib in general and wrong in many particulars, but in critical respects, the similarity is keen. Wars, especially prolonged foreign wars of questionable purpose, do not confine their damage to the battlefield. They leave physical and emotional scars; they tear at the social fabric; they cast doubt on official policies.

For the Russians, the war in Afghanistan has contributed to drug abuse and draft evasion; it has encouraged a cynical malaise among the young, and among the intellectuals who make up one of Mikhail S. Gorbachev's core constituencies. The Soviet press recently published the complaints of mothers who wonder why the sons of top party officials escaped service in Afghanistan, and who suggest that the war would have been over long ago if the leaders' children were dying there, too.

The mounting domestic discontent—along with the damage Afghanistan has done to Gorbachev's peacemonger image and the sheer intractability of the war—appears to have convinced the Soviet leadership that some form of retreat is inevitable. Although the timetable of a withdrawal of the 120,000 Russian troops and of a cutoff of American arms to the Afghan rebels remains to be negotiated, Soviet Foreign Minister Eduard A. She-vardnadze, on a visit to Kabul last month, said he hoped to have the troops out by the end of 1988. Soviet officials now say that withdrawal no longer depends on reaching an agreement to leave behind a government in which Moscow's client, the governing People's Democratic Party of Afghanistan, plays a leading role. Indeed, talk of withdrawal is now so rampant at home that the Soviet leadership will have a good deal of explaining to do if it does not come off.

But wars, unlike sporting events, are not over when they're over. If the Soviet troops are brought home, there is a real danger that Afghanistan's civil war will continue, that the Afghan Government for which thousands of young Russians died will collapse, and that the Soviet Union will find itself with a self-destructing, chaotic Lebanon on its southern border. This prospect raises questions the Soviet authorities have not yet allowed to be asked in public—questions about the blame for the Afghanistan fiasco, and about the credibility of Soviet power.

Perhaps one million young men from the Soviet Union have served in Afghanistan since the invasion in December 1979. The Kremlin refuses to divulge the number of dead and wounded, but the State Department's most conservative estimate is 35,000 casualties, more than a third of them deaths. That does not include the many soldiers felled by malaria, jaundice, typhus, dysentary, hepatitis and heatstroke, or stung by scorpions in the eerie desert moonscape of Afghanistan.

The assimilation of Soviet veterans from Afghanistan seems, on the whole, less traumatic than the ordeal of many American veterans of the Vietnam War. But for many Russian youngsters, brought up to glorify the soldiers who fought in what their history calls "the great patriotic war" against German fascism, the Afghan adventure has been a disorienting experience.

"You go to war to fight one enemy, and when you get there, there's a real war there and it's difficult to understand who is fighting whom," said Aleksandr Simonov.

Because for years the Soviet press minimized the nation's involvement in Afghanistan, portraying the Soviet troops as non-combatant aides to the Afghan Army, veterans have found that their countrymen do not always understand what they went through.

"In 1984, we performed a combat operation in the Kandahar region," said Valery Burkov, a 30-year-old Air Force major. "But later I heard on Soviet radio that it was performed by Afghan troops. Of course, Afghans took part in it, but the ratio was their 10 to our 1,000. . . . There were lots of such cases. Our press distorts reality and weakens people's trust in anything that is said or written."

During the past year, a few Soviet writers have been able to report some of the tension and danger, even lunacy, of guerrilla war in a land of dubious loyalties. The accounts do not question the moral superiority of the Soviet troops, and the horror of war is toned down. But beneath the heroic paeans to Soviet soldiers, there is now an unmistakable subtext: It is a nasty business down there.

The most gripping accounts have been written by Artyom Borovik, a young journalist for Ogonyok, a popular weekly magazine. Borovik's stories of war-weary soldiers playing Rod Stewart tapes as they prepare for battle in a strange land, of bewildered troops confronting ambushes and mine fields, bear a striking resemblance to his favorite Vietnam book, Michael Herr's "Dispatches," and they have made him a celebrity among veterans.

At a crowded public meeting sponsored by his magazine in Leningrad not long ago, Borovik says, he recounted the torture of a Russian soldier by the rebels—they allegedly made an incision around the soldier's waist and pulled his skin up over his head like an undershirt. Afterward, one horrified woman whose nephew was fighting in Afghanistan came up to Borovik and implored him not to write about such things. "Before, it was easy waiting for our boys to return," she told him.

Borovik says he set out to portray the horrors of the war in order to combat public indifference toward the sacrifice of Soviet soldiers, and to embarrass officials into giving the veterans better treatment.

Valery Burkov, the airman, whose job was to travel with the infantry and call in air strikes, lost both legs at the knees when he stepped on a land mine in 1984. He now suffers with wretched wooden prostheses from a factory that has not been significantly modernized since it supplied World War II veterans. Wheelchairs and crutches are in short supply. Medical facilities are understaffed and often lack hot water and other basic amenities.

"I was wounded and needed serious medical care," recalled Sergei Sokolov, a pilot who was shot down by what he believes was an American-made Redeye missile. "In the hospitals and clinics, they were interested only in paperwork. I went around in an endless circle." While he waited, nursing his wounds, for housing authorities to give him an apartment, he lived with his pregnant wife and child in a house with no indoor toilet or running water.

Some of the veterans, humiliated by their disabilities in a society that tends to hide its invalids, seek refuge in special sanitariums rather than return to their families. Newspapers occasionally print letters from World War II veterans who question whether "the Afghantsi," as the veterans are commonly called, deserve the same advantages they receive, which include priority for scarce housing, a more desirable choice of vacation times, and the right to ride buses free and skip to the head of food and ticket lines.

Returning soldiers sometimes encounter citizens who ask about reports of Soviet attacks on innocent Afghan civilians or outright atrocities. These allegations, based on the stories of Soviet defectors, have not been discussed in the official press, but many Soviet citizens have heard them on Voice of America and other Western radio broadcasts.

"We are not sadists," Valery Burkov said, denying these allegations. "There were cases when we were provoked. Once the *dushmani* [the rebels] opened fire on us and we fired back, but it turned out there were only five *dushmani* and the rest were peaceful inhabitants. They suffered a lot, but it was not our fault."

Though no studies have been published to indicate the extent of the problem, it is believed that many Afghantsi turn to alcohol, and some to hashish, opium or even heroin to kill the nightmares that haunt them. "Poppy is everywhere in Afghanistan," said one recently returned Soviet officer interviewed in Dushanbe. "It's not forbidden there, and, well, some of our guys develop an easygoing attitude toward drugs."

Afghantsi have been blamed for beatings, rapes and drunken rampages in some cities, and for vigilante-style attacks on hippies and other youngsters who do not conform to their standards of patriotic behavior.

"They return from Afghanistan just like jets taking off," said Borovik, the journalist. "They want to remake society, to make it work maybe more like the army works. But many of them got accustomed to solving problems with Kalashnikov rifles or with fists.

"They have an allergy to bureaucracy. An invalid visits 10 places to get a card saying he is an invalid. Prosthetics are bad, terrible; they make the legs bleed. The doctor says, 'So what? I didn't tell you to go to Afghanistan.'

"We have to make our society understand that we *did* send these people to Afghanistan, and to think about how to re-integrate them into society. Otherwise, they may be a lost generation."

One of the few Soviet cities that has built a monument to honor a local hero of the Afghanistan war is Dushanbe, in the Soviet Republic of Tadzhikistan. Dushanbe is a city of squat, modern cement buildings ringed by the soaring Pamir mountains, and inhabited by a polyglot population of Tadzhiks, Uzbeks and Russians. From Dushanbe it is 75 heavily guarded miles to the Pyandzh River, across which rise the mountains of northern Afghanistan.

When I visited the city last month, officials took me to visit the former Grade School 37, which has been renamed for former student Aleksandr Mironenko. In 1980, Mironenko, so the story goes, was surrounded by an Afghan rebel band and rather than surrender pulled the pin on a hand grenade, killing himself and his captors. Each year, on the first day of school, Mironenko is eulogized, and last September, across the street from the school, the city installed a bust of the young soldier, inscribed with only his name.

In Dushanbe, there are few other outward signs of the war, but there is much evidence of Afghanistan. Because the Tadzhik language closely resembles the Farsi widely spoken in Afghanistan, many of the Afghan youngsters who have been brought to the Soviet Union for schooling and indoctrination came here—about 1,700 are studying in Dushanbe schools now, a local official said. There is an active border trade, which includes the legal exchange of Soviet consumer goods for Afghan oranges and olive oil, and a great deal of smuggling. Many Tadzhiks have relatives living in Afghanistan.

"Sometimes when we were in the *kishlaks,* the native villages, I forgot that I was in Afghanistan," said Mansour Sadykov, a Tadzhik from the town of Pyandzh who served as a commando in Afghanistan. "I felt that I was at home."

If the troops are pulled out, officials in Dushanbe say, Tadzhikistan will be an important way station for the increased trade and development projects Soviet authorities believe will be necessary to keep their hand in Afghan affairs. It will also be the first place to feel the spillover of whatever chaos is left behind.

Like Afghanistan, the Central Asian Republics of the Soviet Union are predominantly Islamic. Each night, Pakistan beams radio broadcasts to Soviet Central Asia that condemn Soviet aggression in Afghanistan and call for Islamic solidarity. Although the Communist Party has battled the influence of Islam at home with apparent success, local officials must look with discomfort on the prospect of Islamic fundamentalists—who are among the most zealous of Afghanistan's rebels—someday seizing control in Kabul.

In December, Dushanbe's Communist Party newspaper published a speech by the official who heads the Tadzhikistan K.G.B., which is responsible for maintaining security along the mountainous, 1,000-mile Afghan border. The K.G.B. chief charged that Moslem "prejudices," encouraged by neighboring Islamic countries, had led to an acute draft-evasion problem in the Soviet border provinces, sometimes with the acquiescence of local party officials. He warned that Afghan rebels "are stepping up their activity in provinces bordering on the U.S.S.R. The enemy is trying to transfer armed forms of struggle to Soviet territory."

Last March, the rebels fired a rocket into a matchstick factory in Pyandzh; in April, a rebel band crossed the border and killed two Soviet border guards. More recently, the Afghan rebels have been lobbing rockets into Soviet territory, which is common knowledge in Dushanbe, though unreported in the press.

Among soldiers who have served in Afghanistan, a common rationalization for the invasion is that if the Soviet Union had not stepped in, the United States would have—if not with military force, at least with eavesdropping installations. "The border is very long and it's difficult to close it because of the mountains," explained Aleksandr Simonov. "The C.I.A. would be a great threat. And if they deployed missiles there, I think that would be the end of everything."

One likely condition of a Soviet withdrawal would be a pledge by both superpowers to observe Afghanistan's neutrality, so Simonov's fears seem unlikely to be borne out. What is interesting, though, is that the kind of withdrawal Soviet officials now seem to be contemplating could undermine the carefully constructed rationalizations for which thousands of young men have died.

Simonov, like many veterans, has doubts about his Government's apparent determination to withdraw the troops. "I don't think they should be pulled out, because then the throat-cutting will really begin," he said. "There will be a sea of blood and fights all over the country between the different Afghan groups. At this stage, it's not the right time. When it's calm there, O.K. Each soldier will leave Afghanistan with pleasure."

For a large part of the population, the rationalizations for the occupation of Afghanistan have already unraveled. The depth of feeling against the war was evident one evening last November when hundreds of Muscovites packed the modern auditorium at the Moscow House of Film for a public meeting sponsored by Borovik's magazine.

Ogonyok regularly sponsors such "evenings" in theaters or small concert halls around the country, and they are a peculiar form of public therapy. The program usually begins with a lecture, a poetry reading, perhaps some songs. The audience passes forward slips of paper containing general questions or comments. The tamer questions are read aloud and discussed by the magazine's onstage panel, which usually includes journalists, cultural figures and other guests; the rest are filed away by the magazine as an informal measure of the public temper.

On this occasion, Borovik talked about his impressions from covering the war; Valery Burkov, the veteran, played the guitar and sang ballads about death in Afghanistan. In the blizzard of notes passed hand-to-hand to the stage, the angriest concerned the war. Here are a few that were not read aloud:

"Why don't you just come out and say that we don't need to fight in Afghanistan, that we don't need these heroes, these wounded, these homes for the crippled?"

"Don't you understand that until you call a dirty war a dirty war, any attempts to glorify this hopeless affair are in vain? You are only feeding the flame of tragedy."

"The main question about Afghanistan is not the truth about the horrors and the deaths, but why are we there?"

And this one, scribbled on a ticket stub, with the seat number judiciously blacked out: "Remember Vietnam!"

In a poll conducted by French and Soviet pollsters last October—the first published survey to touch on the question—more than half of the Soviet respondents said they favored a complete withdrawal of troops. The sentiment was much stronger among Russians aged 45 to 54, the generation of parents whose sons are eligible for conscription.

"In the first years of the war, our action seemed quite justified to the majority of people," said Gennadi S. Batygin, a sociologist and editor of the magazine *Sociological Research*. "It was common to hear such phrases as 'internationalist duty' and 'the interference of imperialism.' But in the past two years, the society has become a more open one, and that opened the eyes of a lot of people to the war. Not in the sense that we know more about it, but that we now face a diversification of opinion."

"Those who take the trouble of thinking about it consider the war to be our most important problem today," continued Batygin, stroking his goatee. "I agree with that view. All the rest—economic reform and so forth—is secondary to the war. I'm sure that if the war stops, we shall remove the largest obstacle standing in the way of *perestroika* [restructuring]. Our society cannot be open as long as the Afghan problem exists."

"I do not want to pass judgment on who is to be blamed," he added. "But I know it should be stopped. We must take all possible measures to stop it. Any compromises are permissible."

Batygin clearly speaks for a large portion of the educated Soviet public, and particularly for intellectuals. But the eagerness to be out of Afghanistan is tempered by a pessimism about what happens afterward, as a survey of young Russians, conducted for this article by the youth department of the official Novosti press agency, confirms.

Only a little more than half of those questioned said they considered the Soviet military involvement in Afghanistan to have been justified—a remarkable ambivalence about a war Soviet officials have been trying to justify for eight years. Yet almost half said the troops should not be withdrawn until a stable, neutral government can be left behind. More than a third of those queried—37 percent—agreed that "if the Soviet Union withdraws its troops, then a bloodbath may begin in Afghanistan," and less than a third (31 percent) disagreed. An overwhelming 65 percent agreed that "the Western powers want to establish control over Afghanistan in order to use it as a base against the Soviet Union."

Although the sample size (300 people) and the polling methods (a questionnaire distributed at Moscow schools and workplaces) leave a large margin for error, the results are consistent with those found in interviews for this article.

It seems that eight years of war and eight years of propaganda have succeeded in giving the Soviet public a sense that they have something important to lose in Afghanistan.

During the past few months, Soviet authorities have set out to contain the domestic impact of the war.

Last November, more than 2,000 military reservists, most of them Afghantsi dressed in their battle fatigues, converged on Ashkhabad, the capital of the Central Asian Republic of Turkmenia. Komsomol, the youth arm of the Communist Party, had organized the meeting in an attempt to assert control over independent Afghantsi organizations that had grown up spontaneously around the country, and to channel them in directions the party considers constructive.

Most of the veterans' groups had been innocent enough, meeting to swap war stories, provide moral and financial support for war widows, teach karate and boxing to students approaching draft age, and raise money to build monuments to fallen soldiers. But the groups were an embarrassment and a potential rival to Komsomol, which had virtually ignored the veterans.

Between sharpshooting matches and jeep-driving contests arranged for their entertainment, the former soldiers debated the merits of making their groups Komsomol adjuncts. Many soldiers felt it would mean endless bureaucracy and dilute their purpose. But in the end, Komsomol won over a majority of the veterans with offers of financial assistance and promises that the Afghantsi would have greater influence over policies governing veterans' benefits and training of future soldiers.

The council of military reservists created in Ashkhabad is governed by a 50-member steering committee consisting entirely of Komsomol and Communist Party members. By definition, veterans groups that choose to remain independent—and some have done so—are now outlaws. The documents published in the Komsomol press after the Ashkhabad conference downplayed the war, making no mention of the acute problems of disabled veterans or of the veterans' wish for a national memorial honoring their sacrifice, and focused instead on the need to cultivate patriotic thinking and physical fitness in Soviet youth.

In Moscow, Ashkhabad and Dushanbe, Komsomol organized meetings for me with veterans active in the new organization. Under the watchful eye of Komsomol choirmasters, Afghantsi in three-piece suits told me about the deep love of the Afghan people for the Soviet Union, the impressive fighting ability of the Afghan soldiers, the certainty that the rebels fight only because they are paid to do so, and the likelihood of peace after the troops withdraw. Their accounts of fraternal Soviet soldiers building public baths in the Afghan *kishlaks* and teaching Afghans to read reminded me of Borovik's description of the rosy press accounts in the early days of the war: "They gave the impression that Soviet soldiers were down there planting flowers."

The Komsomol-run group has opened a bank account that will be used to build two national memorials, one in Moscow and one in Tashkent. The memorials will not explicitly commemorate Afghanistan, however, but will honor all Soviet soldiers who "fulfilled their internationalist duty" in foreign campaigns, including those who fought in the Spanish Civil War, aided the Cuban Revolution, or helped quash the 1968 "Prague Spring" in Czechoslovakia. Moreover, the plan to build these memorials has not been widely publicized. There is still a powerful official hesitation about dealing directly with the consequences of the war.

The Soviet authorities, exercising their tremendous power to shape public opinion, have begun to lay the psychological groundwork for withdrawal. The reporting this winter on a major military offensive to reopen supply lines to the besieged city of Khost, in eastern Afghanistan, portrayed the Afghan Army as a fighting force that can stand on its own, a judgment that makes returning veterans laugh derisively. (In fact, as Western correspondents who visited Khost in January were told, Soviet firepower dominated the battle there, and even so the hold on the city was tenuous.)

The press has stopped referring to the Kabul Government as Socialist, subtly suggesting that withdrawal would not violate Moscow's obligation to defend fraternal Socialist states. The stature of Najibullah, the Soviet-backed Afghan leader, seems diminished, leading some Western analysts to believe he is being set up as the scapegoat if Afghanistan falls to pieces after Soviet troops depart.

Lately, Soviet officials have also come close to admitting that the decision to invade Afghanistan was a political mistake, the

product of "the old way of thinking" under former party leader
Leonid I. Brezhnev.

"If you take the, let's say, democratically thinking intellectuals, they believe the war was a mistake, and I think this opinion
will dominate when the war is over," Batygin, the sociologist, said.
"One can say that Brezhnev is to blame for it. That will comfort
many people, although of course the reality is more complicated."

But if the Soviet Union cannot even leave behind a stable
neighbor, let alone some assurance of a congenial one; if the retreat is even thought to leave the Soviet Union at some risk, then
the Afghanistan adventure cannot be so easily dismissed as the
foreign policy blunder of Leonid Brezhnev. Then it becomes
harder to escape certain questions: Who "lost" Afghanistan?
What will be the impact of such a defeat on a government whose
legitimacy rests so heavily on the invincibility of the Red Army?
What will be the reaction of client states like Nicaragua, Cuba and
Ethiopia? And how would the collapse of Afghanistan sit with the
Soviet military, which even now seems less enthusiastic about
withdrawal than the foreign ministry?

After his return from Kabul, Foreign Minister Shevardnadze
was asked whether Afghanistan had raised doubts among Russians about the uses of Soviet power abroad. "That's a very difficult question," he replied pensively. "We could discuss it until the
early morning hours."

"The invincibility of Soviet power is the last great myth of our
system," one young Moscow intellectual mused recently. "We can
accept sacrifice if we see a result, but we are psychologically unprepared to deal with the idea that we fought for nothing. That's
why the real problem of Afghanistan will emerge after it's over."

THE NATIONALITY QUESTION[4]

Mikhail Gorbachev recently suggested to visiting members of
Congress that the United States learn from Soviet experience and

[4]Reprint of a magazine article by Ronald Grigor Suny, professor of Armenian
and Russian history at the University of Michigan. *The Nation.* 244:808–10. Je. 13,
'87. Copyright © 1987 by The Nation Company, Inc.

set up separate states for blacks and other minority groups. His misunderstanding of America's racial conflicts was matched by his conviction that the problem of multinationality is best resolved by the Leninist program of territorial autonomy. Karl Marx had spoken on the czarist empire as the "prisonhouse of nations"; his ideological offspring in the Kremlin laud the *druzhba narodov* ("friendship of the peoples") in the Soviet Union, and predict that a unified Soviet people is being formed from the more than one hundred distinct ethnic groups in their vast country.

In stark contrast, Western analysts refer routinely to the Soviet "nationality problem" and foresee a "crisis." Whole careers have been based on expectations of a Moslem revolt. Last December's riots in Alma Ata, capital of Kazakhstan, confirmed in many minds that the Gorbachev government would find itself reaping the whirlwind of a seventy-year failure to solve this most threatening of Soviet dilemmas.

Although the goal of the *druzhba narodov* policy is to remove the continuing prejudices, inequalities and ethnic stereotyping that plague relations among Soviet nationalities, the typical Western view is that Soviet policy has consistently been directed toward "Russification." In that view, the histories of distinct peoples are merged into a single undifferentiated tale of oppression under an alien Marxist regime, the highlights of which are forced denationalization and the resultant explosion of nationalist resistance in the period after Josif Stalin's death. Only recently have a number of Western historians, sociologists, political scientists, and journalists begun to treat the non-Russian peoples not simply as a problem of regime manipulation but as part of a variegated process of nation-building under quite specific and extraordinary historical circumstances.

From their first days in power Soviet leaders were aware of the potential danger of anti-Russian nationalism. V. I. Lenin proposed a federal structure for the Soviet Union, the first state in the world to base territorial divisions on ethnicity. Although theoretically permitted to choose freely between joining the new Soviet federation or remaining independent, in practice most of the non-Russian republics lost their sovereignty and were integrated into the Soviet Union either through the activities of local Communist parties or forcibly by the Red Army. Lenin's policy of *korenizatsia* ("rooting," or nativization) in the 1920s promoted ethnic culture that was "socialist in content, national in form."

Several groups that had been on the verge of extinction—most dramatically the Armenians, who were the victims of Turkish genocide in the twilight years of the Ottoman Empire—were granted political, educational and cultural institutions.

In the 1930s, as Stalinism descended on the country, the process of ethnic nationalization was drastically curtailed. Despite his Georgian origins, Stalin began to reverse many of the gains of the non-Russians. At the end of World War II he went so far as to order the deportation of several small nationalities from their historic homelands to the deserts of Central Asia, ostensibly because they had collaborated with the Germans.

Only after Stalin's death, in 1953, did the contradictory effects of Stalinism fully reveal themselves. Ethnic consolidation had never stopped, and the national republics were more fully ethnic, both demographically and culturally, than they had ever been. By the late 1950s nativization had created an Armenia, for example, in which 89 percent of the population was Armenian; Tbilisi, the capital of Georgia, had a Georgian majority for the first time in centuries. As contact between peoples had increased, particularly in cities dominated by Russians, the potential for intermarriage, migration to distant cities and assimilation into Russian culture had also grown. The freer political atmosphere of the Khrushchev years permitted bolder expression of national feelings, and a dissident nationalism appeared in several republics— in Lithuania, where the Catholic Church served as a focal point; in the Ukraine; and even among Russians, who developed a radical nationalism with a neofascist flavor.

In dealing with the republics, both Nikita Khrushchev and Leonid Brezhnev applied a policy that might best be characterized as benign neglect. Local leaderships were given relatively free reign to run their republics as long as they managed to contain nationalist "deviations" within acceptable limits and to perform reasonably well economically. Those regional leaders had unusually long tenures, and the political machines they created were oiled by corruption, bribery, widespread black-marketeering and ethnic favoritism, particularly in personnel matters. The most flagrant abuses were in Transcaucasia and Central Asia.

Eventually, Brezhnev took action. In 1969, Geidar Aliev, a native of Azerbaijan who had made his career in the local K.G.B., was named first secretary of the Azerbaijan Communist Party and began a vigorous cleanup of the republic's political and economic apparatus. Dozens of officials were removed, and corruption was severely punished. Three years later, Eduard Shevardnadze, the Georgian Minister of Internal Affairs, took over in Georgia and for more than ten years tried to restore order. Although the results of those campaigns were mixed, the struggle against corruption was seen as the necessary first step toward reviving economic productivity. In November 1982, Brezhnev was succeeded by the former head of the K.G.B., Yuri Andropov, who launched a national campaign against corruption and for greater labor discipline.

In the past five years the policy of benign neglect has been replaced by a vigorous attempt to bring the benefits of economic modernization to non-Russian areas. Gorbachev and his associates argue for democratization in the party, more self-management in economic enterprises and renewed initiative by officials. Simultaneously, they are pushing for an integrated and more efficient Soviet economy. Such a program threatens the entrenched elites of the non-Russian republics. Democracy, claims Gorbachev, is not to be confused with local license to exploit the system, and he is determined to eliminate the abuse of power by ethnic political machines.

In late 1985, when Gorbachev replaced the party leaders of Tajikistan, Turkmenistan and Kirghizia with local nationals, there was little protest. But last December, when Politburo member Dinmukhamed Kunayev, who had headed the Communist Party in Kazakhstan since 1964, was replaced by a Russian, Gennady Kolbin, Kazakh students in the capital city surged into the streets, set cars on fire, smashed store windows and beat up passers-by. The Soviet press called them hooligans, but the anger of the students was genuine and clearly political.

Before Kunayev gained the party leadership, Kazakhstan had often had Russian bosses; Brezhnev had headed the party in the mid-1950s. But Kunayev's long reign had consolidated Kazakh influences in the party apparatus, the educational system and other institutions at a time when the Russian and European populations in the republic's cities and northeastern regions were growing rapidly. Slightly more than 40 percent of Kazakhstan's population is Russian; only a little more than one-third is Kazakh. The percentage of Kazakhs in the republic has been rising over the past thirty years, yet the only areas that Kazakhs dominate ethnically are the rural southern districts. Alma Ata, located in the south, is overwhelmingly Russian. It is not surprising that Kazakh students from the south, many of them not fluent in Russian, were among the instigators of the riots. As the Soviet Union lurches forward into economic modernization, the position of a people still living largely in rural areas and unable to speak Russian easily is particularly tenuous, unless special efforts are made by the state. Kunayev had tried to offset the demographic weakness of the Kazakhs in their own republic with a kind of affirmative action at both political and cultural levels, and perhaps anxiety about the loss of that privileged status added to the volatile mix that brought the students into the streets.

The events in Alma Ata starkly highlighted the difficulties faced by the Moscow-based reformers. Since the early 1960s the Soviet Union has been primarily an urban society, and it is precisely in the larger cities that the most serious confrontations between ethnic groups occur. Many Estonians in Tallinn, a city with an increasing Russian population, are so alienated from the Russians that they refuse to speak the official language. In Baku, relations between Azerbaijanis and Armenians remain tense. It is inaccurate to speak of the nationality question in the Soviet Union in terms of minority politics as it is understood in the West, for many ethnic groups form majorities in their home republics. In fact, the "minority problem" in the national republics revolves around how to deal with the Russian minority.

At this moment Gorbachev may be most politically vulnerable in the ethnic republics. The fear of Russian dominance is strong among non-Russians, even when the considerable benefits of Soviet development are acknowledged. For their own strategic and economic reasons the central authorities favor bilingualism, but ethnic intellectuals remain wary about any expansion of Russian instruction. When, in the spring of 1978, Moscow attempted to remove a clause from the Georgian constitution affirming Georgian as the sole official language of the republic, thousands of students demonstrated in central Tbilisi until Shevardnadze agreed to restore the disputed clause. That may be the most dramatic example of popular pressure forcing the state to abandon its plans for non-Russian peoples.

Gorbachev has yet to articulate any clear nationality policy, but he seems to have developed a greater realism about the power of separate ethnic cultures. An earlier official enthusiasm for the "fusion" of nationalities into a single Soviet people has quietly been tempered, and attention has been given to those social scientists, such as Iulian Bromlei, who have emphasized the development of ethnic culture as separate from the mode of production. Gorbachev's push for *glasnost* and democratization aims, potentially, toward greater cultural, even political, autonomy for nationalities.

Gorbachev's solution to the contradictions between his economic reconstruction and the Soviet Union's ethnic peculiarities has been to appoint reformist cadres in non-Russian areas. But the fiasco in Kazakhstan, as well as his failure to remove the leader of the Ukrainian party, Vladimir Shcherbitsky, early this year, demonstrated that ethnic political elites still retain considerable local support and power. Officials are aware that they must take national consciousness into account before it explodes into separatist nationalism, and Gorbachev's goal of a "single national economic complex" may have to adjust to the new public opinion of the national republics.

Recently, the government has begun to deal with the anomalous position of Soviet Jews, a "nationality" that since the 1930s has not had the same rights to its language and religious practices that ethnicities with their own national territory have enjoyed. The dilemma of Soviet Jews has been that they are in Soviet society but not of it; they are encouraged to assimilate but, at the same time, are regarded as outsiders. The solution for many has been to leave the country, yet the government has put innumerable obstacles in their way. (In practice, emigration is not a right for any citizen of the Soviet Union, but it has been given as a special privilege to those peoples—Jews, Armenians and Volga Germans—who have articulate supporters abroad.) Gorbachev appears to be trying to avoid the error of Brezhnev, who let Soviet Jews become pawns in the East-West struggle. As he extends his hand to the Soviet intelligentsia, a powerful ally in reform, he must resolve the dilemma of Jews, who have historically made up an important part of educated urban Russia.

Whether the consolidated and ethnically conscious nationalities that now make up half the Soviet population will be allies or opponents of Gorbachev's *perestroika*, or reorganization, is yet to be determined. The new generation of ethnic leaders, many of whom share his aspirations for economic and political reform, no longer have the option of satisfying their ethnic constituents by conspiring to rip off the system or pandering to nationalist sentiments. Yet they would ignore at their peril the voice of those whose aspirations have been too long denied. Whether the political and cultural demands of non-Russians can be met within the Soviet system or will require the empire's breakup, so desired by politicians and pundits in the West, depends on the depth and the extent of the current Soviet metamorphosis.

SURGING AHEAD[5]

Dominating one wall of the control room was an enormous display screen showing a map of the world. Superimposed on the map, a line traced the orbit of the Mir space station, with rings along it representing ground stations. Mir's position was marked by a blue-green light, which was moving slowly across the circle centered on Moscow. The flyby would take only eight minutes, after which the window of communication would close. The audio feed came through with startling clarity, as if Cosmonaut Yuri Romanenko were standing in the next room. "The work here is very interesting," he said in response to a question that had been posed in writing by Time *Correspondent Dick Thompson. "It brings us a lot of satisfaction."*

How does Mir compare with earlier Soviet space stations? "There is much more space," said Romanenko. "There is even room that can be used for living room. Atmospheric conditions are better, and all the instruments provide for good fresh air. It's much better than Salyut." Before another question could be asked, the light left the Moscow circle; the window had closed. Though all too brief, it was an extraordinary, exclusive exchange between an American journalist and an orbiting Soviet cosmonaut.

Just a few years ago that encounter in the Soviet Flight Control Center at Kaliningrad, a suburb 15 miles northeast of Moscow, would have been unthinkable. In the closed world of the Soviet space program, the most impressive launches were rarely announced in advance for fear of failure. Even then, the barest

[5]Reprint of a magazine article by staff writer Michael D. Lemonick. *Time.* 130:64+. O. 5, '87. Copyright © 1987 Time Inc. All rights reserved. Reprinted by permission from TIME.

details were released afterward—and only if the mission went just as planned. These days that characteristic secrecy seems to have evaporated, replaced with a confidence bolstered by the dawning international recognition that Soviet achievements in space are fast outstripping those of the U.S.

The new dynamism is drawn from a spirit of *glasnost*, or openness, that preceded the revolution Soviet Leader Mikhail Gorbachev is striving to bring to Soviet society. Moscow's venerable Institute of Space Research (known as IKI, its Russian acronym) now bustles with the comings and goings of an increasingly youthful, independent-minded cadre of Soviet space specialists. And along with them are growing numbers of foreign colleagues, many of whom have been invited to add their experiments to Soviet space missions. Visiting scientists need only a pass to wander the halls freely.

Such self-assurance on the part of the Soviet space establishment will be in ample evidence this week as IKI and its charismatic director, Roald Sagdeyev, sponsor a three-day extravaganza of seminars and speeches celebrating the 30th anniversary of the launch of Sputnik 1 in 1957. Called Space Future Forum, it will focus on the topic of international cooperation in space. Some 500 scientific luminaries from around the world plan to attend.

The Soviet conference is evidence that in their space program, openness is not just political fashion. Says Geneviève Debouzy, of the French space agency: "The seminars that ten years ago would have been given at the Goddard Space Flight Center are now given in Moscow." To the surprise of Americans, the Soviets' well-deserved reputation for a plodding, low-tech, assembly-line approach to space exploration has paid off. Says James Beggs, former NASA administrator: "There's been a habit in this country of thinking of the Soviets as stupid and that they steal all their technology. That's just not so."

Indeed, space experts in the U.S. and Europe are now conceding publicly what they would have found laughable a decade ago: although the Soviets lag far behind in electronic gadgetry, they have surged past the U.S. in almost all areas of space exploration. If unchallenged, Moscow is likely to become the world's dominant power in space by the 21st century. Says Heinz Hermann Koelle, a West German space-technology professor and former director of future projects at NASA's Marshall Space Flight Center: "American pre-eminence in space simply no longer exists."

Warns James Oberg, an expert on the Soviet space program: "If the Soviets can aggressively exploit this operational advantage, they can make us eat space dust for a long time to come."

In sheer numbers of launches per year, the Soviets inched past the U.S. in 1967, 66 to 58, and have stayed in front since. In 1983 they sent up 101 space shots, in contrast to 18 by the U.S. More impressive, Soviet cosmonauts have logged some 14 man-years in space, against less than five for U.S. astronauts. The knowledge of Soviet doctors and researchers about the medical and psychological consequences of long-term space habitation far outstrips that of their American counterparts. And with the twin Vega space probes, which photographed Halley's comet in 1986, Soviet scientists consolidated their reputation for gathering impressive scientific data from space.

The Soviets' launch capability took a quantum leap earlier this year when they successfully fired off Energia, a booster as powerful as the mighty Saturn 5, which the U.S. developed for the Apollo program and then scrapped in favor of the shuttle. With Energia, the Soviets can loft 100-ton payloads, vs. a maximum for the U.S. shuttle of 30 tons. That is enough to carry their shuttle, which is under development, or to orbit parts for a space station far larger than Mir, which could be a platform for a manned mission to Mars. Says Dale Myers, deputy administrator at NASA: "Energia is a pretty impressive machine. I would sure like to have it."

For all these accomplishments, Soviet microelectronics and computers are ten years behind those of the U.S. Military satellites sometimes break down in a matter of weeks. Photoreconnaissance satellites literally drop their film to earth for processing. The ultraconservative Soviet military is just now beginning to experiment with the techniques of electronic imaging developed by U.S. scientists years ago. Still, admits Geoffrey Briggs, NASA's director of solar-system exploration, "it's not clear that you need state of the art to be effective."

The Soviet drive into space is taking place while American space efforts are all but moribund. The U.S. space program has been virtually closed down since the space shuttle *Challenger* exploded in midair 73 seconds after lift-off in January 1986, killing all seven astronauts aboard, including Teacher Christa McAuliffe. The tragedy was more than a setback for NASA. It exposed the agency as an unwieldy, indecisive bureaucracy unsure of its direction and increasingly beset by the demands of the military and the Reagan White House.

NASA could handle awesomely complex missions like the Apollo landing on the moon in 1969 as long as it had plenty of money and control. But it has never established a long-range vision of the U.S. role in space. After its budget was cut in the early 1970s, the agency promised far more than it could finally deliver with the shuttle program. Even if launches resume on schedule, the orbiter *Discovery* will not fly until June 1988.

Meanwhile the Soviets are moving ahead. Next July the ambitious twin Phobos probes should be on their way to explore Mars and its moons. It is a mission worthy of Jules Verne. Harold Masursky, an astrogeologist who worked on the U.S. Viking missions to Mars, says the concept is "so damn complicated, it's just hair-raising." The Soviets plan to follow up on Phobos in 1992 by lofting another spacecraft, which will analyze Martian soil. Later in the decade, they want to use an unmanned probe to bring pieces of the planet back to earth, and have boldly suggested that the mission be jointly undertaken with the U.S.

But complex scientific missions are only part of the Soviets' push to dominate space. They are aggressively marketing their workhorse Proton boosters as a low-cost alternative to the European Space Agency's Ariane, China's Long March and, eventually, private U.S. rockets for launching commercial satellites. The Soviets are offering to sell high-resolution satellite photos of earth that could be used for mapping and assessment of agricultural and mineral resources. They plan to continue occupying Mir, which has been in orbit since February 1986. The space station has already been outfitted with an astronomical observatory module named Kvant. Additional modules are planned for materials processing, earth observation and biomedical research.

The Soviet space program had several notable early successes, including Sputnik 1, the first pictures from the dark side of the moon in 1959 and the first man in space, Yuri Gagarin in 1961. But its planetary-science program did not really take off until shortly after the appointment in 1973 of a 40-year-old scientist named Roald Z. Sagdeyev as head of IKI. From the outset, Sagdeyev started to shake things up. He took physicists out of their labs and put them on production lines to watch their experiments being built. Says Georgi Managadze, chief of IKI's active space experiments lab: "Sagdeyev follows every stage of manufacturing and testing."

The new director took some unprecedented and risky steps. He brought talented Jewish scientists into the institute. He began building a corps of young scientists and selecting projects based on their scientific value rather than the political standing of scientists. He fought for access to computers. Most important, and politically the riskiest, he introduced a potent measure of democracy into the Soviet program. "Before Sagdeyev," says Louis Friedman, executive director of the U.S. Planetary Society, "the Soviet space program was closed. Now they talk about their plans. They even argue in public. He has materially changed the way they do major projects." Declares Thomas Donahue, chairman of the National Academy of Sciences' space-science board: "He introduced *glasnost* into the space-science program years before Gorbachev."

Sagdeyev's era might have been short-lived except for one thing: it produced results. Among the first breakthroughs were Venera 9 and 10, projects started by Sagdeyev's predecessor, Georgi Petrov. In 1975 the two probes transmitted the first photographs of Venus' hellish surface. Imagers on the next two probes failed, but Nos. 13 and 14 sent back color photos plus a wealth of information on atmospheric, surface and subsurface chemistry. Then in 1983 came a pair of missions that stunned Western space scientists. Venera 15 and 16, in Venus' orbit, transmitted high-resolution radar maps of the planet's surface. The maps, says former NASA Administrator Beggs, "indicated a level of radar technology that we had not given the Soviets credit for." Says Masursky:

"They did first-class work."

Sagdeyev was already embarked on another project, one that could have ended his career. Called Vega, the mission was designed to approach and study Halley's comet. Sagdeyev chose to build Vega around the proven, off-the-shelf technology of the Venera probes. But he wanted the scientific instruments to be custom designed, even though the expertise was not available within the U.S.S.R. So he recruited scientists from nine countries, including the U.S., to join the project. That was unheard-of in security-conscious Soviet space circles. Recalls Sagdeyev: "Sometimes my opponents, in order to take over, were almost ready to say that I was too much for foreign cooperation. But if you have a belief that what you are doing is right, you can survive difficult times."

The gamble paid off spectacularly. On March 4, 1986, having swung by Venus to drop off scientific probes, Vega 1 trained its camera on the comet, then less than 9 million miles away, and relayed high-quality pictures to earth. Two days later, it came within 5,500 miles of the comet's heart. Although pelted by dust, Vega 1 revealed for the first time the dimensions and dynamics of the ten-mile-long nucleus.

The Vega mission put the world on notice that the Soviet Union would not take a backseat to anyone in space science. Admits NASA's Briggs: "They closed a big gap." But Sagdeyev has made it clear that catching up was only the beginning. He has now directed his considerable intellect, political capital and diplomatic charm to another high-risk international mission. If all goes according to plan, the Phobos probes will take off next summer for Mars. When they reach the Red Planet some 200 days and 118 million miles later, they will orbit for a time, taking data on solar physics. The first Phobos will match orbits with the moon for which it is named, a chunk of rock about 14 miles across believed by many astronomers to be an asteroid captured by Mars' gravity. The other will be a backup.

Phobos will glide between 98 and 260 ft. above the moon's surface—"something similar to a cruise missile," quips Sagdeyev—and drop an instrument-bearing minilander to record data on the moon's soil. One experiment involves a laser that will emit short bursts of energy, each vaporizing a square millimeter of surface into a cloud that can be analyzed by the probe's spectrometer. "You can pick up such exploded material from many different places," says Sagdeyev. "In the end you have a chemical map of the surface of Phobos—if you are lucky."

But there is more than luck involved, as Western experts make clear. "The Phobos mission," says Cornell Planetary Scientist Carl Sagan, "is not just world class. It is novel, diverse and appropriate. The whole idea is very clever." Notes Gerhard Neukum, of the German Aerospace Research Establishment: "The Mars mission is fantastic. It carries a huge set of instruments. They did it with Venus. Now they have focused on Mars, and it is to be expected that they will be equally successful." In fact, each of the probes will carry 25 instruments—an enormous number, considering that the U.S.'s complex, much delayed Galileo probe to Jupiter has only 16.

Sagdeyev has even higher expectations for the Mars Sample Return mission, now being planned for the late 1990s. The idea is for the spacecraft to make a soft landing on the planet and send a rover to gather soil samples on a yearlong trek over the surface. Then about 2 lbs. of material would be returned to earth for detailed analysis. In Sagdeyev's plan, the U.S. would supply the rover, plus advanced electronics to guide it from an orbiting mother ship.

Sagdeyev's enthusiasm for robot probes, however, brings with it an inevitable tension: in the U.S.S.R., just as in the U.S., the unmanned and manned programs compete for budget dollars, and so far the manned missions have been the big winners. But, says Sagdeyev, "99% of what man can do in space can be done by robots." The statement irritates his comrades at Soviet mission control. "This crew has done 100 repair jobs," scoffs Victor Blagov, the deputy flight director, arguing that humans are needed to deal with unanticipated situations. Snaps Stepan Bogodyazh of Glavkosmos, the Soviet equivalent of NASA: "You need people there to test the instruments. The cosmonaut is a researcher, and this is a laboratory."

As with their unmanned missions, the Soviets have made a virtue of slow, steady progress in the manned program. While the U.S. jumped quickly from orbital flights to moon missions to the now defunct Skylab to the shuttle, cosmonauts have steadily plied earth orbits for nearly three decades. The Soviets perfected their launch techniques by using substantially the same rocket that sent Gagarin into orbit in 1961. While they lost the race to the moon for want of a large booster, they remedied the situation last May, when the 170 million–hp Energia rocket blasted off its pad at the Baikonur Cosmodrome, near Tyuratam in Soviet Central Asia.

The new rocket will make possible the deployment of larger, more sophisticated Soviet space stations. Says Bogodyazh: "There will be a Mir 2." Explains Alexander Dunayev, head of Glavkosmos: "Space stations weigh up to several dozen tons. What's needed are stations that weigh several hundred tons. We should soon learn to build big structures out there, not tens of meters but kilometers across, multifunctional platforms. Cosmonauts may well live there permanently. And from these structures, there may be flights to other planets." If so, then first on the agenda, undoubtedly, would be Mars.

The lure is strong. Mars is the only other known planet that may be habitable—and thus the only realistic location for a space colony. That makes it a logical target for the Soviets, who are committed to establishing a permanent presence in space for both scientific and military reasons. Besides, the national prestige resulting from a visit to Mars would be immense.

The greatest problem: the physiological stress of a mission that could take up to three years. The Soviets learned early that humans are not built for a low-gravity environment. On a long-duration flight in 1970, which lasted 18 days, the cosmonauts did no physical conditioning. After they landed, it was almost three weeks before they could walk. Now it is well established that space travelers begin to lose muscle tone almost immediately and that calcium starts leaching from bones in low-gravity environments. Today, thanks to intensive research, Soviet space explorers returning to earth from 200-day-plus missions can walk unaided in three days and recover completely within three weeks.

The prescription: constant physical therapy. Each day, Mir cosmonauts put in an hour on an exercise bicycle and another on a treadmill. For 16 hours a day, they are required to wear a suit crisscrossed with a web of elastic cords so that any movement in any direction forces the cosmonauts to strain against the counterpressure. It is no pleasure. "They do it because their health depends on it," says Deputy Flight Director Blagov. "They cannot miss a single day. Without the work load, there may be calcium loss and decrease in leg muscles. The body takes away what it doesn't use." Sagdeyev is convinced that the health dangers of a Mars mission would be manageable. "The first year is O.K.," he says, "so two or three years are probably also O.K."

Psychological problems too are likely on a long flight. To keep motivation sharp and productivity high, the Soviets pay plenty of attention to the space station's livability. The interior of Mir, for example, has been painted in two colors to provide the crew with a sense of floor and ceiling. On Mir, cosmonauts get two days off each week and have special radio hookups so they can talk with their families and with virtually any sports figure, scientist or celebrity they choose.

The Soviets have shared their knowledge about long-term spaceflight, mostly through informal contacts rather than formal publication. Says one NASA specialist: "We have a book summarizing these lessons. We've got their diets. We try to make our people very aware of what the Soviets have done, because our own experience is all short duration and our data base is very old."

Nonetheless, says Nicholas Johnson, author of the book *Soviet Year in Space*, "the Soviets still have much to learn before they can reasonably responsibly put together a Mars mission." They need, for example, a reliable propulsion system for their interplanetary space capsule; at least two of the later Salyut systems had propulsion failures. The Soviets are weak, Johnson says, in communications technology. "They know they do not have the best technology," he observes. But they are working on it.

Similar shortcomings plague the *glasnost*-proof, supersecret Soviet military space program. At any one time, say U.S. intelligence analysts, the U.S.S.R. is operating some 150 satellites, and perhaps as many as 120 are believed to be performing military missions. For hours each day, say intelligence analysts, Soviet Cosmos military satellites drift over the U.S., photographing missile silos and naval deployments. Other Soviet spacecraft lurk with sensitive electronic ears that can pick up telephone conversations in Washington, while Meteor weather satellites monitor conditions over key U.S. targets. Soviet infrared satellites watch for the telltale heat signaling a launch of U.S. ICBMs. At the military launch site in Plesetsk, 500 miles northeast of Moscow, crews stand ready to launch additional intelligence satellites at a moment's notice.

"They have a very active military space program in numerical terms," says the Brookings Institution's Paul Stares, author of the recently published book *Space and National Security*. "But simple numerical comparisons of space activity can be misleading. In every possible way, our satellites are superior to theirs." Since 1972, for example, the Soviets have been struggling to establish a continuous early-warning launch-detection satellite system. Since these satellites generally have short life-spans, says a Washington analyst, "the Soviets are forever launching those early-warning systems." As a result, the Soviet brass are less prone than their American counterparts to depend heavily on them. Says Johnson: "The military environment will not collapse without those satellites. They are there simply to enhance and increase the efficiency of Soviet ground-based systems."

Some Western experts, notably U.S. Defense Secretary Caspar Weinberger, charge that the Soviets have a working satellite-killer system in place. Administration officials suspect that military research is under way aboard Mir. Indeed, a classified intelligence report this summer described a Star Wars–like test in which a laser on Mir located and tracked a Soviet dummy ICBM. U.S. observers like Soviet Space Expert Oberg find such assertions "highly implausible." Still, he does not believe for a moment "that Mir is a completely nonmilitary station." Says Oberg: "The microchips they make in space don't go into video arcades in Moscow. They go into missile guidance." He points out that the Soviets "have been pursuing a space-weapons program for 20 years and lying about it. We have to adjust to the fact that they do pretty nasty things in space weapons."

Despite mutual and growing distrust between Washington and Moscow on the military uses of space—a contrast to increasing cooperation in limiting nuclear weapons—Sagdeyev's plea for U.S. cooperation on the Mars Sample Return mission seems to be serious and genuine. Argues Sagdeyev: "If we start progress in this area, it could create a much better political climate."

Should the U.S. consider cooperative missions like the Mars project a legitimate pathway back into space? Or should it view Sagdeyev's emphasis on international cooperation as an attempt by the Soviets to gain access to Western technology? Sagdeyev has repeatedly assured U.S. scientists that his only interest is in building the most advanced space probes. The experience of U.S. and European scientists with Soviet space programs has been mixed. Says University of Chicago Physicist John Simpson, who had a comet-dust analyzer on Vega: "I was allowed into their inner labs to supervise the installation of the experiment directly on board their spacecraft. That had never been done before." Simpson says the Pentagon was not pleased, but notes, "There was nothing in those instruments that can benefit the Soviets militarily." To allay the fears of Western governments, the Soviets have promised that foreign satellites will be left sealed until launch, thus ensuring that no secrets of advanced technology will be stolen.

Others express frustration with Soviet managerial clumsiness. Wolfgang Pietsch of West Germany's Max Planck Institute for Extraterrestrial Physics, whose team has an X-ray detector in the Kvant module, first learned that the experiment had finally been launched when it was announced on East German radio. Says Andrea Caruso, head of Europe's Eutelsat satellite cartel: "From a business point of view, they still have a lot to learn. I keep corresponding with them, and they keep sending me back telexes in Russian. It's a disaster."

For the U.S. to embrace fully Sagdeyev's concept of wide-ranging cooperation with the Soviets would mean a radical rethinking of the U.S. space program. Indeed, the very concept of a space race between the superpowers—at least in the nonmilitary sectors—would become outmoded. Does it really matter who is ahead in space? "Yes," answers NASA's Myers unequivocally. "It has always been the goal of the United States to be the leader in space."

That, and the fact that sending sophisticated technology into the U.S.S.R. would be risky, suggests that the U.S. is unlikely to take up Sagdeyev's offer. U.S.-Soviet cooperation and the rising fortunes of the Soviet space program have posed troubling questions for Washington that cannot be ignored. Can the U.S. forge a consistent, long-range policy for space? What kind of resources will it take for America to recapture its position as the leading space power? Considering the Soviet lead, is it possible to catch up? It is up to the Reagan Administration, which is currently reevaluating the future of the crippled U.S. space program, to supply the answers.

III. HOW WE SEE THEM

EDITOR'S INTRODUCTION

The relationship between the Soviet Union and the United States at times resembles a hall of mirrors: each defines its own foreign policy in terms of what is perceived to be the foreign policy of its adversary. Given the lack of trust between the two, it is not surprising that throughout the postwar period both nations have tended to frame their rivalry in the language of a Manichean struggle between light and darkness. The Soviets have always considered regular denunciations of American "capitalist imperialism" to be a necessary feature of their political discourse, even during periods of detente. The demonism of the "Commies" has likewise been an eternal theme of the American right wing, but rarely has a U.S. president so baldly identified communism with the devil as did Ronald Reagan in his 1983 speech "The Evil Empire," reprinted from *Speeches of the American Presidents* as the first selection. (President Reagan has since been at pains to moderate his verbal attacks as his administration seeks to negotiate a variety of arms treaties with the Russians.) In an article reprinted from the *Bulletin of the Atomic Scientists*, Marshall D. Shulman puts this "good vs. evil" rhetoric into historical perspective; he documents the political misperceptions on both sides that have brought the superpowers to an impasse, and calls for a dose of rationality in future relations.

The third selection, by Richard Schifter, assistant secretary for human rights and humanitarian affairs, and taken from the *Department of State Bulletin,* points out a distinction between the American and Soviet political systems that makes mutual understanding difficult, if not impossible. The U.S. constitution, notes Schifter, guarantees the rights and freedoms of the individual and explicitly limits the power of the national government, while the Soviet constitution, although ostensibly modeled after the American, guarantees the unlimited and permanent authority of the ruling elite—the Soviet Communist Party—at the expense of individual rights. Both systems fear the fundamental premises of the other. W. W. Rostow, one of the original architects of postwar

American Soviet policy, maintains in the fourth selection, from *Foreign Affairs,* that, despite these deep differences, the superpowers now have it within their grasp to end the cold war. Rostow believes, however, that the goal requires the kind of steady American foreign policy that has not been in evidence for many years.

What kind of opportunity does the rise of Mikhail Gorbachev present to the West? Will he create a more open Soviet Union, one that will eventually evolve toward some form of democracy? Or is he the most formidable adversary since Stalin, charming the West while forging a more efficient and dangerous empire? There is as yet no certain answer to these questions, argues Charles William Maynes in the final article, taken from *Foreign Policy,* but the U.S. must take the risk of fresh, creative diplomacy before the opportunity passes.

THE EVIL EMPIRE[1]

There is sin and evil in the world, and we are enjoined by Scripture and the Lord Jesus to oppose it with all our might. Our nation, too, has a legacy of evil with which it must deal. The glory of this land has been its capacity for transcending the moral evils of our past.

For example, the long struggle of minority citizens for equal rights, once a source of disunity and civil war, is now a point of pride for all Americans. We must never go back.

There is no room for racism, anti-Semitism or other forms of ethnic and racial hatred in this country. I know you have been horrified, as have I, by the resurgence of some hate groups preaching bigotry and prejudice. Use the mighty voice of your pulpits and the powerful standing of your churches to denounce and isolate these hate groups in our midst. The commandment given us is clear and simple: "Thou shalt love thy neighbor as thyself."

[1]Excerpted from an address by President Ronald Reagan, delivered on March 8, 1983, in Orlando, Florida, before the National Association of Evangelists.

But whatever sad episodes exist in our past, any objective observer must hold a positive view of American history, a history that has been the story of hopes fulfilled and dreams made into reality. Especially in this century, America has kept alight the torch of freedom—not just for ourselves but for millions of others around the world. And this brings me to my final point today.

During my first press conference as president, in answer to a direct question, I pointed out that as good Marxist-Leninists, the Soviet leaders have openly and publicly declared that the only morality they recognize is that which will further their cause, which is world revolution.

I think I should point out I was only quoting Lenin, their guiding spirit, who said in 1920 that they repudiate all morality that proceeds from supernatural ideas or ideas that are outside class conceptions; morality is entirely subordinate to the interests of class war; and everything is moral that is necessary for the annihilation of the old exploiting social order and for uniting the proletariat.

I think the refusal of many influential people to accept this elementary fact of Soviet doctrine illustrates an historical reluctance to see totalitarian powers for what they are. We saw this phenomenon in the 1930's; we see it too often today. This does not mean we should isolate ourselves and refuse to seek an understanding with them.

I intend to do everything I can to persuade them of our peaceful intent; to remind them that it was the West that refused to use its nuclear monopoly in the 40's and 50's for territorial gain and which now proposes 50 percent cuts in strategic ballistic missiles and the elimination of an entire class of land-based, intermediate range nuclear missiles.

At the same time, however, they must be made to understand we will never compromise our principles and standards. We will never give way our freedom. We will never abandon our belief in God.

And we will never stop searching for a genuine peace. But we can assure none of these things America stands for through the so-called nuclear freeze solutions proposed by some. The truth is that a freeze now would be a very dangerous fraud, for that is merely the illusion of peace. The reality is that we must find peace through strength.

I would agree to a freeze if only we could freeze the Soviets' global desires. A freeze at current levels of weapons would remove any incentive for the Soviets to negotiate seriously in Geneva, and virtually end our chances to achieve the major arms reductions which we have proposed. Instead, they would achieve their objectives through the freeze.

A freeze would reward the Soviet Union for its enormous and unparalleled military buildup. It would prevent the essential and long overdue modernization of United States and allied defenses and would leave our aging forces increasingly vulnerable. And an honest freeze would require extensive prior negotiations on the systems and numbers to be limited and on the measures to insure effective verification and compliance.

And the kind of freeze that has been suggested would be virtually impossible to verify. Such a major effort would divert us completely from our current negotiations on achieving substantial reductions.

Let us pray for the salvation of all those who live in totalitarian darkness, pray they will discover the joy of knowing God.

But until they do, let us be aware that while they preach the supremacy of the state, declare its omnipotence over individual man, and predict its eventual domination of all peoples of the earth—they are the focus of evil in the modern world.

It was C. S. Lewis who, in his unforgettable "Screwtape Letters," wrote:

"The greatest evil is not now done in those sordid 'dens of crime' that Dickens loved to paint. It is not done even in concentration camps and labor camps. In those we see its final result. But it is conceived and ordered (moved, seconded, carried, and minuted) in clear, carpeted, warmed, and well-lighted offices, by quiet men with white collars and cut fingernails and smooth shaven cheeks who do not need to raise their voice."

Because these "quiet men" do not "raise their voices," because they sometimes speak in soothing tones of brotherhood and peace, because, like other dictators before them, they are always making "their final territorial demand," some would have us accept them at their word and accommodate ourselves to their aggressive impulses.

But, if history teaches anything, it teaches: Simple-minded appeasement or wishful thinking about our adversaries is folly—it means the betrayal of our past, the squandering of our freedom.

So I urge you to speak out against those who would place the United States in a position of military and moral inferiority. You know, I have always believed that old Screwtape reserves his best efforts for those of you in the church.

So in your discussions of the nuclear freeze proposals, I urge you to beware the temptation of pride—the temptation blithely to declare yourselves above it all and label both sides equally at fault, to ignore the facts of history and the aggressive impulses of an evil empire, to simply call the arms race a giant misunderstanding and thereby remove yourself from the struggle between right and wrong, good and evil.

I ask you to resist the attempts of those who would have you withhold your support for this administration's efforts to keep America strong and free, while we negotiate real and verifiable reductions in the world's nuclear arsenals and one day, with God's help, their total elimination.

While America's military strength is important, let me add here that I have always maintained that the struggle now going on for the world will never be decided by bombs or rockets, by armies or military might.

The real crisis we face today is a spiritual one; at root, it is a test of moral will and faith.

Whittaker Chambers, the man whose own religious conversion made him a "witness" to one of the terrible traumas of our age, the Hiss-Chambers case, wrote that the crisis of the Western world exists to the degree in which the West is indifferent to God, the degree to which it collaborates in Communism's attempt to make man stand alone without God.

For Marxism-Leninism is actually the second oldest faith, he said, first proclaimed in the Garden of Eden with the words of temptation: "Ye shall be as gods." The Western world can answer this challenge, he wrote, "but only provided that its faith in God and the freedom He enjoins is as great as Communism's faith in man."

I believe we shall rise to this challenge; I believe that Communism is another sad, bizarre chapter in human history whose last pages even now are being written. I believe this because the source of our strength in the quest for human freedom is not material but spiritual, and, because it knows no limitation, it must terrify and ultimately triumph over those who would enslave their fellow man.

For, in the words of Isaiah:

"He giveth power to the faint; and to them that have no might
He increased strength. But they that wait upon the Lord shall re-
new their strength; they shall mount up with wings as eagles; they
shall run, and not be weary."

FOUR DECADES OF IRRATIONALITY:
U.S.-SOVIET RELATIONS[2]

In his recent book, *The Cycles of American History*, Arthur
Schlesinger recalls a lecture by the British historian Sir Herbert
Butterfield at Notre Dame University during the early Cold War
years. Entitled "The Tragic Element in Modern International
Conflict," Butterfield's talk suggested that the historiography of
international conflict has characteristically gone through two
phases.

In the first or "heroic" phase, historians portray a struggle of
right against wrong, of good people resisting bad. Then, as time
passes and emotions subside, historians enter the second,
"academic" phase, when they seek to understand the motives of
the other side, and to define the structural dilemmas that so often
underlie great conflicts between masses of human beings. Thus
he notes, the "higher historiography" moves on from melodrama
to tragedy. Butterfield's two phases, prescient at the time he
wrote, are useful for a retrospective examination of the course of
Soviet-American relations over the past four decades.

Hostile Camps and Containment Doctrine

Recall that it was 40 years ago that the United States went
through one of the most remarkable transformations in American politics. It was a period when the matrix of the Cold War was
established—a period of heroic accomplishments and of serious
mistakes.

[2]Reprint of an article by Marshall D. Shulman, senior lecturer and former director of the W. Averell Harriman Institute for the Advanced Study of the Soviet
Union, Columbia University. *Bulletin of the Atomic Scientists.* 43:15–25. N. '87. Reprinted by permission of the *Bulletin of the Atomic Scientists,* a magazine of science and
world affairs. Copyright © 1987 by the Educational Foundation for Nuclear Science, 6042 S. Kimbark Ave., Chicago, Illinois 60637.

Within the space of a few months there was a massive turn-around in U.S. policy, from a period of collaboration with the Soviet Union as the "gallant ally" that had contributed heroically and with great loss of life to the defeat of the Nazi armies, to an alarmed and belated response to the problems of the postwar world—particularly the emerging Soviet dominance in Eastern Europe and a perceived Soviet threat to the Balkans and to Western Europe.

In March 1947 the Truman Doctrine not only provided $400 million in aid to Greece and Turkey, which Britain, impoverished by war, was no longer able to supply, but also announced the commitment to resist Soviet expansionism anywhere. "It must be the policy of the United States," President Truman declared, "to support free peoples who are resisting attempted subjugation by armed minorities or by outside pressures." In June the Marshall Plan was launched, an effort of unprecedented scale to restore the economic vitality and political confidence of Western Europe. In July George Kennan published an article in *Foreign Affairs* under the pseudonym "X," since he was a State Department employee at the time. In the article he articulated the premises of the containment policy: "The main element of any U.S. policy toward the Soviet Union must be that of a long-term, patient but firm and vigilant containment of Russian expansive tendencies."

On the Soviet side, 1947 was the year of the establishment of the Cominform, the Communist Information Bureau, the successor to the Comintern. Perceiving the Marshall Plan as part of a U.S. and British effort to undermine Soviet efforts to establish a cordon in Eastern Europe against a revival of a German threat, Stalin developed the Cominform as an instrument of tightening his control over that area and over the communist parties of France and Italy. And, as we now know, plans were made at that founding meeting for the coup in Czechoslovakia the following February.

We can only conjecture about what degree of control Stalin originally intended to establish in Eastern Europe, based upon the ambiguous wartime discussion of a sphere of "friendly states" in Eastern Europe, but a convulsive tightening of control to totalitarian levels followed, accompanied by a heightened militancy in communist parties the world over. The signal for this militancy was given by Andrei Zhdanov, one of two leading Politburo members under Stalin, in a speech at the founding meeting in which he posited that the world was now divided into two hostile camps.

For the Soviet Union, however, the crucial question was how to forestall the rearmament of Germany and its inclusion in the Western camp. But in the 1948 Berlin blockade the Soviet Union failed to prevent the unification of the Western zones of Germany. One paradoxical effect of the North Korean attack on South Korea two years later was that it stimulated the formation of the Federal Republic of Germany, along with the beginnings of its rearmament and its inclusion in NATO, whose organization had been catalyzed by the heightened Soviet militancy.

In the swift interactions of that period, during which conflicts of interest were raised to a level of total hostility, we can see in retrospect elements of what Butterfield described as the movement from melodrama to tragedy.

There were, to be sure, some positive achievements in the extraordinary measures taken by the U.S. leadership to mobilize support from a volatile and reluctant public for the defense of the West. Among these, three were of particular importance:

• In the face of its long tradition of isolation from "foreign entanglements," the United States became firmly committed, with bipartisan support, to accepting its global responsibilities.

• The restoration of the West European economies and political confidence laid the basis for the Atlantic Alliance, which gave organizational expression to the defense of shared democratic values, and provided stimulus and encouragement to the formation of supranational institutions for the management of economic, political, and military collaboration.

• The containment policy worked. Its success rested not only, and perhaps not primarily, upon the reversal of postwar demobilization and the creation of a military balance, but also on its demonstration that where the United States effectively addressed local sources of political weakness and upheaval, as in Western Europe, it was able to foreclose opportunities for the expansion of Soviet influence and control.

However, there were also some negative consequences of the way in which support was mobilized for these accomplishments:

• The notion of containment became increasingly military and global. By overemphasizing the military aspect of containment, the United States contributed to the militarization of its own economy and also forced the pace of military competition. In extending containment to the Third World, the United States became preoccupied with the military and East-West aspects of local conflicts, obscuring its understanding of the local causes of conflict situations. This attitude led to misguided efforts in Vietnam and Central America.

• In the effort to loosen congressional purse strings to fund military programs, the Greek-Turkish aid programs, and the Marshall Plan, U.S. officials exaggerated and oversimplified the Soviet challenge as an ideologically driven effort to conquer the world. Anticommunism became the American ideology, the central principle of U.S. foreign policy. Thus the primitive stereotypes of the Soviet Union which took form at that time have continued to dominate U.S. thinking and discussion of the complex reality of the Soviet Union.

Perhaps it is inherently difficult for democratic societies to respond in a measured way to their problems, and perhaps it is inevitable that democratic leaderships should be impelled to resort to hyperbole in alerting their publics to the dangers they face; but the consequences of such hyperbole also inevitably become counterproductive and difficult to control.

George Kennan has written recently that when he published the X article he did not see the Soviet Union as a military threat, and thought the fears that the Soviet Union might overrun Western Europe were exaggerated:

What I was trying to say in the *Foreign Affairs* article was simply this: "Don't make any more unnecessary concessions to these people. Make it clear to them that they are not going to be allowed to establish any dominant influence in Western Europe and in Japan if there is anything we can do to prevent it. When we have stabilized the situation in this way, then perhaps we will be able to talk with them about some sort of a general political and military disengagement in Europe and the Far East—not before." This, to my mind, was what was meant by the thought of "containing communism" in 1946. (George F. Kennan, "Containment Then and Now," *Foreign Affairs,* Spring 1987, pp. 885–90)

In clarifying the ambiguities of his X article, Kennan was responding to criticism by Walter Lippmann at the time the article came out—that military containment was not feasible, and that the purpose of U.S. policy should be to seek a settlement that would lead to the withdrawal of all foreign forces from the continent of Europe. (Walter Lippmann, *The Cold War: A Study in U.S. Foreign Policy*, New York: Harper & Brothers, 1947) How this was to be done Lippmann did not say, but Kennan returned to the disengagement theme in his later Rieth lectures (see George F. Kennan, *Russia, the Atom and the West,* New York: Harper & Brothers, 1957), and to the theme he had earlier advanced—which Averell Harriman had rejected as unacceptable to the American people—of some kind of spheres settlement. Presumably, the settlement reached would give the Kremlin sufficient reassurance against the establishment of regimes in Eastern Europe hostile to the Soviet Union, tempering the degree of control over the area that the Soviet leaders felt it necessary to exercise.

Whatever Kennan's intentions may have been, then or later, the American people interpreted the X article as demonstrating the necessity for the military containment of a Soviet Union ideologically driven to seek unlimited expansion. This was what Butterfield called the first or "heroic" phase of the conflict. Americans were seeing the world in terms of good versus evil; and although some—including Kennan—have since made the transition to a more analytical and differentiated understanding of the conflict, the Manichean dichotomy has had a persistent life, reemerging in our own day with considerable political force as the "evil empire" theme, making for primitive analysis and irrational responses.

In fact, over the four decades since the end of World War II, the Manichean view has dominated U.S. policy toward the Soviet Union, with the exception of brief periods under President Eisenhower, in the last year of the Kennedy administration, and in the so-called détente period under President Nixon—all of which not only proved short-lived and abortive, but were followed by backlash reactions that intensified the conflicted relations.

The Roots of Anti-Soviet Fundamentalism

The central theme of this dominant view is that Soviet expansionist behavior is so inherent to the nature of the Soviet system that it can be modified only by bringing about fundamental changes in the Soviet system. This view rests upon the belief that the revolutionary ideology remains in full force as a driving determinant of Moscow's foreign policy; that the Soviet system needs to expand in order to hold its leadership in power, to claim legitimacy, or to validate its view of history in ideological terms; and that the messianic tradition in prerevolutionary Russia and its continental expansion reinforce the ultimate aspirations of Marxism-Leninism. The further belief is that the problems of the Soviet regime are of such magnitude that external pressure could precipitate a collapse or compel the leadership to accept fundamental changes that would weaken it.

In its formative period 40 years ago, this view was shaped by arguments drawn from the X article, that "Soviet power . . . bears within itself the seeds of its own decay," and that "the United States has it in its power to increase enormously the strains under which Soviet power must operate, to force upon the Kremlin a far greater degree of moderation and circumspection than it has had to observe in recent years, and in this way to promote tendencies which must eventually find their outlet in either the breakup or the gradual mellowing of Soviet power." Throughout subsequent years, the dominant view retained its fixation upon Stalinism as the unchanging and unchangeable model of Soviet behavior, intractably hostile, unlimited in its aspirations for world dominance.

Logically, the policy that derived from this view has been directed toward forcing the Soviet system to change its fundamental character. Since the belief was that the Soviet Union understands only the language of force, it was argued that pressure and overstrain would compel the Soviet leadership to capitulate, to make concessions, to contract from its extended positions, or, ultimately, to collapse.

It followed also from this view that U.S. security could be assured only by military superiority; that productive arms control agreements were not possible with a nation of such a character; and that arms control negotiations could only be disadvantageous to the United States, leading to unilateral disarmament. Although military programs have sometimes been justified as necessary "bargaining chips," in practice, given this disbelief in seeking security through arms control, the result has been the continued intensification of the military competition, in pursuit of superiority.

Given these policies, there has not been—nor could there be expected—any other outcome than a continuation of the conflict relationship and of the intensification in military competition. Although the underlying assumptions have not generally been clearly and openly articulated, these themes have continued ascendant in American political life, and still constitute the hidden agenda that has dominated policy during most of the past decade, despite rhetoric that is sporadically used to obscure its fundamental purpose.

This confrontational view has persisted because relations between the United States and the Soviet Union are powerfully influenced by the interaction of complex political forces within each of these countries. On the U.S. side, three factors need particular emphasis in explaining why American policy toward the Soviet Union has tended to be less than rational:

• *Familiar psychology mechanisms, most often operating below the conscious level, tend to make very real conflicts of interest between the United States and the Soviet Union appear absolute and therefore intractable.* The subject is shot through with emotions, areas of dark uncertainty, fear, prejudices, and primitive stereotypes. Much of what Americans would wish to know about the Soviet Union is not known and may be unknowable, and therefore preconceptions are projected into these dark areas—partly from hopes and partly from fears.

Some of the psychological concepts developed to deal with interpersonal relations suggest applications to the way Americans tend to perceive the Soviet Union. Anxiety originating in many sources, including the hazard of nuclear destruction; displacement; denial; and projection are obviously relevant factors. The familiar "we-they" phenomenon—the tendency to apply separate standards to the good "in group" and the bad "out group"—leads Americans to look with indulgence on their own actions and with harsh severity on the Soviets': Soviet military programs reflect hostile intentions; American military programs are defensive. The expansion of Tsarist Russia and the Soviet Union to the Pacific proves Russian and Soviet intentions to conquer the world; the continental expansion of the United States was a matter of right. Soviet activities in the Third World are manifestations of aggression; U.S. interventions are altruistic. Soviet espionage is traitorous; American espionage is patriotic. (This double standard, of course, applies with equal force to Soviet perceptions.) An obvious consequence of this "we-they" mechanism is that public discussion on this subject in the United States is dominated by simplified and polarized stereotypes.

It may be inevitable that people and leaderships should regard other nations in this way, but a greater awareness of the operation of psychological mechanisms can free us to distinguish what is real from what is fancied in our perception of each other, and to move in some small measure toward greater objectivity. It is a fundamental condition for the transition from Butterfield's first phase to the second, more analytical phase.

• *U.S. policy toward the Soviet Union has been greatly influenced by the vicissitudes of American politics.* Sine the mid-1970s the United States has experienced a conservative political tide in domestic politics and a resurgence of nationalism in foreign policy. The external ideological focus of this mood has been expressed in anticommunism as the main organizing principle for foreign policy; it has created a reaction against what is viewed as the weakness of the "liberal illusions" of the previous period by bringing about support for policies of greater activism and military strength against a perceived heightened threat from the Soviet Union. A hardening of popular attitudes toward the Soviet Union resulted from that nation's moves in Angola, Ethiopia, and Afghanistan, as well as from Moscow's actions against human rights and from continuing military buildup. These feelings were intensified by a backlash from the unrealistic expectations aroused by the détente period, as well as by a widespread sense of impotence stemming from the United States' experience in Vietnam and with the hostages in Iran, and by the passing of the period of American military superiority.

The intellectual foundation of these sentiments derived from the neoconservative movement, which returned to the ideological fundamentalism of the postwar period in its approach to the Soviet Union, but is generally nationalist rather than internationalist in its foreign policy. In the prevailing climate, these views created powerful political support for a strong anti-Soviet posture, and they discredited policies directed toward arms control, reduced tension, and measures of cooperation with the Soviet Union. The most serious liability a politician could incur was to be labelled soft on communism and weak on defense.

• *The third factor to determine U.S. policy toward the Soviet Union has been the absence of rationality in decision making on military policy, the autonomy of the military establishment, and its increasing influence on U.S. foreign policy and domestic society.* Decisions on defense policy, from research and development to the acquisition of weapons systems and deployment decisions, result from the interplay of parochial pressures and interests, rather than from an overarching determination of the national interest. Even if a president were to seek disinterested but competent counsel on defense policy concerns, there has been no mechanism to provide for such counsel since the abolition of the President's Science Advisory Committee. Today, such policy decisions depend on the outcome of bargaining between the military services, on the influence of the defense contractors, and on the economic and political interests of congressional districts.

Defense expenditures, which have approached $2 trillion in the past six years and now constitute approximately one-third of the U.S. federal budget, have come to dominate the economy. These funds have become a primary source of support for scientific research, and have deflected scientists and facilities from civilian to military purposes—a factor in the U.S. decline in advanced industrial technological innovation.

Even more relevant to the immediate subject, however, is the progressive weakening of civil control over the autonomy of the military establishment in driving the competition with the Soviet Union. George Kistiakowsky testified eloquently about how Eisenhower came to feel increasing despair at his inability to control the Pentagon. Eisenhower observed the Pentagon driving up estimates of presumed Soviet capabilities in order to get larger appropriations, on which military careers and profits for military contractors depended. He enlisted Kistiakowsky's help in an unsuccessful effort to exercise control over the Strategic Air Command, whose inflation of targeting requirements led to overkill beyond reason.

The most crucial aspect of U.S.–Soviet relations is the military competition between the two countries. It is evident that the mindless increase in weapons programs, driven by parochial interests on both sides, has locked the two countries into a rising spiral, with its consequent tensions, apprehensions, and costs serving the interests of neither. This process has created an arms race that is the prime source of the world's insecurity. It is sometimes said that arms control has been tried and has failed to reduce weapons, or to prevent new weapons from taking the place of those that are limited. One major reason why this has appeared to be the case is that political leaders have felt it necessary to protect existing or planned weapons systems in which the military establishment had an interest, in order to forestall military opposition to the proposed agreements.

The Soviet Evolution

The Soviets obviously have also been far from rational in managing relations with the United States, and some of the same factors that affect U.S. policy have operated in the Soviet Union with equal or greater force. Soviet domestic politics, including in some periods factional conflicts, have been an important determinant of policy. Although Soviet military institutions are structurally different from their U.S. counterparts, rivalries among the military services, competition among the design bureaus, a persistent pattern of overinsurance in military affairs, the extensive military influence over civilian society, and, during certain periods, the relatively greater autonomy of the military establishment have resulted in short-sighted military decisions that did not serve Soviet interests. Misperceptions of the United States and the outside world generally stemmed from the same psychological mechanisms operating in the United States, magnified by ideological rigidities that have shaped the perceptions and expectations of the leadership, and compounded in the past by a parochial unfamiliarity with the outside world.

The Marquis de Cuistine and other travellers to Russia in earlier centuries described the country in terms that in many respects bear a striking resemblance to the Soviet Union today— just as Alexis de Tocqueville's descriptions of the United States and the American character 150 years ago still have some contemporary application. In prerevolutionary Russia, travellers noted autocratic and repressive institutions, xenophobic suspicions, extreme secrecy, ambivalent feelings toward the West, and a messianic impulse—all of which still sound familiar. And travellers to the Soviet Union today are often struck by the sense of history that overhangs the present.

It is, however, misleading to assign such weight to historical continuity that it obscures significant elements of change in the Soviet experience. The Soviet Union is not a static society. In its own way, it has followed the normative life cycle of all revolutionary movements, and the Soviet political culture is significantly different from what it was during earlier periods.

Alexander George, in his commentary on Nathan Leites's *A Study of Bolshevism,* observed that Lenin, by conscious effort, sought to create a "Bolshevik character" by reversing certain traditional aspects of the Russian character, in particular "those qualities of the reform-minded Russian intelligentsia of the nineteenth century that had, in Lenin's judgment, proven to be quite unsuitable for the task of making a successful revolution." Repressing strands of thought extolling freedom, which had been an element in the Russian intellectual tradition, the Bolshevik political culture created by Lenin laid the basis for the Soviet totalitarianism that was to come to fuller development under Stalin. It is not to this aspect of Lenin's legacy that Gorbachev refers when he claims Leninist sanction for his reforms, but to Lenin's later "new economic policy" and his writings on the use of cooperatives as a legitimate form of socialism.

The system on which Stalin put his stamp accelerated the primary transformation of the country from an agricultural to an industrial society—a process that had in fact begun in the middle of the nineteenth century. His coercive methods—the logical application of the "Bolshevik character" created by Lenin, but with less tactical flexibility than Lenin might have shown—forced the pace of industrialization and created a powerful military machine which enabled the country to survive the war with Nazi Germany. It did so at terrible human cost, however, and Stalin's rigid and ruthless totalitarianism and police-state methods became increasingly counterproductive, stifling initiative and innovation.

Even during Stalin's lifetime, a few bold voices, to their cost, called for changes required by the country's passage into a more advanced stage of industrialization, but it was not until 30 years ago, under Khrushchev's leadership, that a major effort was made to break the Stalinist mold. Although his impetuous ways and his frontal challenges to powerful interest groups frustrated his efforts and brought him down, Khrushchev must be credited with a bold effort to smash the Stalinist godhead, and to begin a process of reform that would be carried forward unevenly by others. Kosygin and Andropov both sought to implement domestic modernization, and Brezhnev attempted to continue the rationalization of foreign policy begun by Khrushchev; but Kosygin lacked political support, Andropov's term in office was too brief, and Brezhnev in his later years was to find a consensual style of leadership unsuited to the enforcement of a consistent policy.

This background is necessary to make the point that Gorbachev's reforms did not spring into existence suddenly, by some form of immaculate conception. They represent the continuation and maturation of a process that has extended over three decades, and reflect a growing awareness on the part of many—although still a minority—that the system developed by Stalin had become increasingly dysfunctional. And while one man and his personal qualities may now largely determine how much of the transformation is ultimately achieved, it should be understood that his efforts are part of a process that reflects a logic of necessity for moving the system to a new historical stage of development.

The details of Gorbachev's reform program are by now familiar. His political slogans are the equivalent of John Kennedy's "Let's get the country moving again!" One word he uses is *perestroika*, which can be translated as "restructuring" or better, "reformation"; and another, *glasnost*, meaning "openness" or "candor," has now entered the American lexicon. We shall concern ourselves here with the aspects of his reform program that most directly affect Soviet-American relations, and with the much debated questions about how Gorbachev's efforts should affect U.S. policy toward the Soviet Union.

The heart of Gorbachev's program is to modernize the Soviet economy. The economy he inherited was marked by declining growth rates approaching stagnation, low productivity, widespread corruption, and a massive and lethargic bureaucracy. Most important of all were the lag in the advanced technological sector of the economy behind that of all other industrial states, and a system that tended to discourage innovation and initiative. The starting point for Gorbachev was a recognition of the worldwide revolution in science and technology—an idea that has been discussed fitfully at lower levels in the Soviet Union for more than a decade. The new phase of the industrial revolution, he has said, centers on advanced technology, computers, electronics, robotics, genetic engineering, information processing, and automated production. In these areas the Soviet Union was falling farther and farther behind, and if this were not corrected, the country would find itself not even a second-class power in international competition.

There have been debates in the United States about whether the economic reforms so far proposed by Gorbachev are as "radical" or "revolutionary" as he has proclaimed. Some say he has moved too slowly, and that his program is mostly talk and little action. But those who hold this view seriously underestimate his political problems, the immensity of his task in turning around a vast economy, against the resistance of an entrenched bureaucracy, a lethargic and conservative population, and a party organization that fears for its own power in the wake of drastic change.

It is an endeavor that will take many years, and he has proceeded slowly, cautiously, and with consummate political skill. Step by step he is making personnel changes that will in time give him the political base he needs for structural changes, as well as administrators and managers who will be competent to exercise the initiative he has called for. At this point we can only take an agnostic position on his chances for complete or even partial success. A number of years may pass before it will become clear how much he has been able to do. Some observers from abroad have said that he faces organized opposition within the Communist party and in other powerful bureaucratic interest groups—the military, the KGB, the economic ministries—and that these groups may eventually bring him down. But there is no clear evidence on this matter.

What is clear is that in Gorbachev's efforts to deal with what he calls "the human factor," to inculcate more initiative and participation at the grass-roots level—a transformation no less profound than was Lenin's creation of a "Bolshevik character" out of old Russian traditions—he faces a monumental task. Those who have watched television reports of his speeches around the country may have grasped a sense of this. On one side of the split screen is Gorbachev in his populist style trying to explain and persuade the crowds around him that *perestroika* has to begin within themselves, while on the other side is a sea of bewildered and passive faces of people trying to understand a concept that is far beyond their experience. Some express fear that outspokenness might expose them to reprisals if the line should change, as the Cultural Revolution followed the "let one hundred flowers bloom" campaign in China. Some feel comfortable with their present arrangements; they fear the chaos and anarchy that might result from upsetting changes, and from new and unfamiliar ways of doing things.

The Gorbachev Opportunity

What is more directly relevant to our concerns is the political side of Gorbachev's program. For essentially economic reasons—to raise productivity, participation, and initiative—he has sought the support of the creative intelligentsia with campaigns of democratization and *glasnost*. As a check on the bureaucracy, he has sought to widen the limits of permissible criticism. And he has encouraged an easing of censorship, the release of some dissidents, a reform of legal institutions, and an open discussion of some hitherto forbidden subjects in Soviet history, including the crimes of the Stalin era.

Here the results of Gorbachev's efforts are dramatically evident. The Soviet press has been transformed in ways that most of us would not have thought possible. There is a more open news policy toward disasters and shortcomings—particularly since Chernobyl. Investigative reporters and letters to the editors have raised questions not only about venalities and abuses on the part of local officials and even the KGB officials, but also about the special stores available to privileged officials, and the special schools for their children. Plays, movies, books, and literary and historical journals have begun to deal with subjects long prohibited. Multiple-candidate elections with secret ballots have been talked of for the workplace and for local party organizations, although so far only the most gingerly experimentation has occurred.

A number of ideological inhibitions have been breached in the political and economic discussions. Greater wage differentials, unemployment, bankruptcy, and the encouragement of entrepreneurial activities on the farms and in the service sector through cooperatives have had Gorbachev's endorsement. Although, as we have seen, Gorbachev has been selective in claiming ideological sanction from Lenin, his claim has some support from young party idealists who had continued to regard Lenin as representing the true line of the Revolution, from which Stalin was seen as an aberration.

These political changes entail obvious risks, for it is always a time of danger when rigid political systems open the door to some reduction of central control, and expectations may outrun the system's tolerance. The Soviet leadership occasionally cautions against excesses of criticism, and Gorbachev himself has made it clear that control will continue to be exercised from the center, and that the new openness will not be allowed to degenerate into anarchy. He has insisted that the one-party system will be preserved, although he has sought to achieve the functional equivalent of a multiparty system by encouraging debate within the party.

In an article in the Spring 1987 *World Policy Review,* Robert C. Tucker noted "something of historic import" in these changes: "Today, a society has again begun to emerge from under the shroud of what has been an all-encompassing state." Circumscribed as these changes may be, they undoubtedly have the possibility of leading to a system transformation—perhaps the "mellowing" to which Kennan referred. Gorbachev is pragmatic rather than ideological in his approach; he advances no blueprint or final characterization of the mix of the new and the old. But historically it has sometimes been the case that changes made in response to immediate felt needs have had effects that go beyond anything that was intended or foreseen. If these changes should continue and not be reversed by some upheaval in Soviet politics, they will have a bearing on one of the central elements in the American debates on the fundamental nature of the Soviet system.

Gorbachev's foreign policy, and policies on defense and arms control, are subordinate to his concerns with the domestic economy. This is a period of turning inward for the Soviet Union. Gorbachev has insisted that his domestic priorities require tranquility abroad, and not adventurism. There is a general recognition in the Soviet Union that the activism of the 1970s under Brezhnev proved costly, first because it incurred economic liabilities the country cannot afford, and second because it damaged relations with the United States.

In what he has called the "new thinking" required in the world, Gorbachev has put primary emphasis on the need to avoid a nuclear catastrophe, and to establish a dialogue and mutual understanding with the United States. His secondary emphasis has been on global problems: the interdependence of the world economy, in which he sees the Soviet Union inextricably involved; the plight of the developing countries and their massive debt burden; and environmental concerns.

The time has come, he has said, for a turning point in U.S.–Soviet relations; for a sober, pragmatic reassessment of the relationship on both sides. Despite the military influences he sees as dominating American policy, he believes the national interests of both countries can and should lead to an easing of the military competition, as is required by the economies of both countries. As he put it in a colorful image, we should not be like "two dinosaurs circling each other in the sands of nuclear confrontation."

Remarkably enough, the Soviet Union has sought doggedly to engage the United States in productive dialogue and negotiations, as unpromising as this prospect has appeared to them on repeated occasions. Although not wanting to take the role of supplicants, the Soviet leadership has persisted in seeking even modest agreements with the Reagan administration, if more comprehensive agreements prove unattainable. Their hardheaded calculation is that the situation cannot be allowed to drift while new weapons systems are developed on both sides, and the Soviet Union would be obliged to continue to divert into the military sector resources sorely needed for the modernization of Soviet industrial technology.

The depth and seriousness of Gorbachev's concern over the dangers of nuclear war and the costs of the military competition cannot be doubted. The Soviet Union is more serious about its interest in engaging the United States in productive negotiations on arms control than ever before in history. But it is also clear that Gorbachev is walking a tightrope. He cannot afford to have the Soviet Union appear weak or intimidated by pressure; but he also feels the need to avoid taking actions that would fuel the notion abroad of a renewed "Soviet threat." This calls for a carefully calibrated policy, which has so far been evident. One can only speculate about the domestic pressure he must take into account. While some among the Soviet military leaders appear to support his policies, on the ground that a strong industrial base is necessary for the future of Soviet power, there are hints that others are concerned about the effect of cuts in their services, stemming from arms control agreements or budgetary reductions.

Several elements in Gorbachev's "new thinking" bear watching. One is his emphasis upon the "mutuality of security." As he said at the 1986 party congress: "We can never be secure while the United States feels itself insecure." If this view were to become dominant in the Soviet Union, it would show more insight than either superpower has shown before and could improve the prospect for negotiations. He has also observed that the Soviet Union has no need of an external enemy, breaking with Stalin's reliance upon a "capitalist encirclement" to justify military programs. His questions about Soviet military requirements suggest he is beginning to follow logic to the concept of sufficiency, as the United States did during a brief, earlier period. In the broader aspects of foreign policy, he has recognized the interdependence of states in the world economy, and has accepted the implication that autarchy is impossible at a time when economic problems are international.

These are "tender shoots" that might wither or flower, depending upon internal and external circumstances. But what they suggest is the possibility that the Soviet Union may have moved a long way from the "two camp" doctrine of hostility toward a period when, if encouraged, it would recognize its own interest in playing a more constructive role in the international system and in international economic institutions. This too could have an important effect on the debate within the United States on the prospects for a more constructive relationship with the Soviet Union.

What follows if we look at the course of American–Soviet relations in this way?

First, it seems clear that the confrontationist view that has dominated U.S. policy toward the Soviet Union is based upon assumptions that were questionable to start with, and are increasingly inapplicable to the Soviet Union as it has been changing over the years. It is a view that can have no outcome other than the continuation of an unregulated nuclear military competition which will be an increasing danger to U.S. security and a continuing distraction from other important foreign policy problems, whose resolution becomes more difficult as long as the two great powers are locked into a confrontational relationship.

Second, while it is too soon for summary judgments about prospects for the success of Mikhail Gorbachev's efforts to reform the Soviet economy and modernize the Soviet system, the steps he has taken over the past two years present an opportunity to put the U.S.–Soviet relationship on a more sensible footing. In the first instance, the United States should, in its own interest, explore the possibilities now available to stabilize and moderate the deterrent balance between the two countries, in nuclear weapons and in conventional weapons and forces, and to open dialogues at many levels on bilateral and multilateral economic, regional, and political problems, holding open the possibility of cooperative action.

But U.S. policy should also be formulated from the outset on the basis of a long-term evolutionary purpose. If the initial negotiations are successful, they should be seen as opening the way to a long-term shift—perhaps over decades—in the balance between competition and cooperation, with the purpose of drawing the Soviet Union into a constructive involvement in both the international system and the international economy.

Third, Americans should recognize that if they cannot respond productively to the opportunities presented by the Soviet Union, because of the persistence of the fundamentalist ideological views that have dominated U.S. policy in the past, the consequences will be disadvantageous to U.S. interests:

• Strains in the Atlantic Alliance will become increasingly serious.

• Other foreign policy problems—regional, political, and economic—will become increasingly difficult.

• To the extent that U.S. actions have an effect upon Soviet developments—perhaps marginal, but nevertheless significant— Gorbachev, if he survives politically, is likely to be driven to carry forward his reform efforts in a climate of hostility. The mobilization this would entail would diminish the chances for easing the repressive aspects of the Soviet system and the likelihood of changes in the Soviet system and foreign policy that the United States would wish to see.

Fourth, many of the most urgent U.S. foreign policy problems—the arms race, the budget deficit, the trade imbalance, the large Third World indebtedness, the sources of conflict among the developing countries—can only be solved within an international framework, which is out of reach so long as the nation continues to be preoccupied and obsessed by the political and military competition with the Soviet Union, and gripped by a nationalist fervor that undermines international institutions.

Finally, the key to U.S. movement in these directions is in its domestic political life. What is needed is a strong, politically effective constituency that supports an enlightened view of U.S. security interest in moderating the military competition and relations with the Soviet Union, along with a return to the bipartisan spirit of internationalism that characterized the immediate postwar years.

Is it reasonable to expect politics to be rational? Not wholly, for it is a human enterprise and shares the fallibilities of human nature. But it is not unreasonable to expect the American people to have a clearer and more enlightened understanding of their own self-interest, and some concept at least of how they would like to use their country's great, if now declining, influence in the world.

If this is not possible, we shall arrive at Butterfield's last and tragic phase in international conflicts, when, as he said, "in historical perspective we learn to be a little more sorry for both parties than they knew how to be for one another."

THE SOVIET CONSTITUTION: MYTH AND REALITY[3]

If we were asked to identify the passage or passages in the Constitution of the United States that best characterize the nature of our government, I would assume that a good many of us would point to the Bill of Rights, particularly the First and Fifth Amendments. If the same question were asked with regard to the Soviet Constitution, I, for one, would select four key provisions.

First and foremost, I would direct attention to Article 6, which states:

The leading and guiding force of Soviet society and the nucleus of its political system, of all state organizations and public organizations, is the Communist Party of the Soviet Union. . . . The Communist Party . . . determines . . . the course of the domestic and foreign policy of the U.S.S.R., directs the great constructive work of the Soviet people, and imparts a planned, systematic and theoretically substantiated character to their struggle for the victory of communism.

I would then move back to Article 3 and note the following words:

[3]Reprint of an address delivered by Richard Schifter, assistant secretary for human rights and humanitarian affairs, on August 10, 1987, before the American Bar Association. *Department of State Bulletin.* 87:34–7. O. '87.

The Soviet state is organized and functions on the principle of democratic centralism. . . . Democratic centralism combines central leadership with local initiative and creative activity. . . .

Next, I would drop down to Article 39, which states:

Enjoyment by citizens of their rights and freedoms must not be to the detriment of the interest of society or the state. . . .

I would round out these quotations from the Soviet Constitution with Article 59, which reads as follows:

Citizens' exercise of their rights and freedoms is inseparable from the performance of their duties and obligations.
Citizens of the U.S.S.R. are obliged to observe the Constitution of the U.S.S.R. and Soviet laws, comply with the standards of socialist conduct, and uphold the honor and dignity of Soviet citizenship.

The Role of Lenin

The Soviet Constitution is a lengthy document, containing altogether 174 articles. A number of them would, at first blush, remind us of guarantees of individual freedom which are the hallmark of basic charters in true democracies. To understand their meaning and significance in the Soviet setting, we need to comprehend fully just what the role of a constitution is in the U.S.S.R. and how constitutional provisions must be read in the context of the Soviet Union's basic notions of the relationship between the governing and the governed.

In seeking to construe our own Constitution, we often refer to the *Federalist Papers* and other writings of the Founding Fathers. Similarly, the Soviet Constitution should be interpreted in light of the writings of the Soviet Union's Founding Father. That person is, of course, Vladimir Ilyich Ulyanov, whom the world has come to know as Lenin.

In using the term Marxism-Leninism, we often lose sight of the individuals to whose teachings we thus refer. They were, in fact, persons who differed markedly from each other. Karl Marx was a theoretician, who proclaimed to the world his purportedly scientific analyses of economics and history and who predicted future historic trends on the basis of his analyses.

Lenin, by contrast, was an activist. His writings are free of abstruse theory. They are how-to-do-it kits on seizing and holding power. To be sure, these writings were not entirely original. Their basic theses can be found in Machiavelli's *The Prince*, written close to 400 years before Lenin put pen to paper.

After having become familiar with Marx's writings, Lenin committed himself to helping history along by seeking to establish first in Russia and then throughout the world his own notion of Marx's vision of an ideal society. With single-minded devotion to his cause, he applied himself to the goal of taking power in Russia, a goal which he reached in the fall of 1917.

Lenin, we must note, had competition among the revolutionaries who, like he, tried to depose the czar and Russia's ruling aristocracy. His competitors included advocates of capitalist democracy as well as leftwing revolutionaries, some of them fellow Marxists. What distinguished most of them from Lenin was that, in one way or the other, they subscribed to the ideas of the role of government and of the dignity of the individual which were the essence of the teachings of the Enlightenment. These teachings, let us recall, are, indeed, the teachings to which our Founding Fathers subscribed and which provided the ideological base on which our system of government is built.

Lenin rejected these teachings, derisively referring to them as "bourgeois liberalism." His basic precepts were that the power of the state must be seized and held by an elite group, which he viewed as "the vanguard of the revolution." That vanguard was the Bolshevik faction of the Russian Social Democratic Party, which later renamed itself the Communist Party. Not long after the Bolsheviks had taken power, one of Lenin's disciples and a principal leader of the new Soviet state, Grigory Zinoviev, had this to say in his report to the 11th Congress of the Soviet Communist Party:

[W]e constitute the single legal party in Russia; . . . we maintain a so-called monopoly on legality. We have taken away political freedom from our opponents; we do not permit the legal existence of those who strive to compete with us. We have clamped a lock on the lips of the Mensheviks and the Socialist Revolutionaries. We could not have acted otherwise, I think. The dictatorship of the proletariat, Comrade Lenin says, is a very terrible undertaking. It is not possible to insure the victory of the dictatorship of the proletariat without breaking the backbone of all opponents of the dictatorship. No one can appoint the time when we shall be able to revise our attitude on this question.

Within the party, decisionmaking, according to Lenin, was to be concentrated at the very top. As semantic games are often played by the Soviets and as the term "democracy" is assigned an important role in that context, let me share with you the following quotation from Lenin:

Soviet socialist democracy is not in the least incompatible with individual rule and dictatorship. . . . What is necessary is individual rule, the recognition of the dictatorial powers of one man. . . . All phrases about equal rights are nonsense.

It is against this background that we must read the term "democratic centralism," as it appears in Article 3 of the Soviet Constitution. It means that the people in the central position call the shots. Lenin made no bones about his intention to establish a dictatorship.

The Soviet Constitution as an Educational and Propaganda Instrument

We must understand, therefore, that the Constitution of the U.S.S.R. is not, like our Constitution, a document that spells out the powers and form of government as well as its limits and the inalienable rights of the individual. In a Leninist state there are, by definition, no limits to the power of government. There are no inalienable rights of the individual. Law is made and altered at will by the leadership. The powers of the leadership cannot be limited by an overarching document that would deprive a leadership group of its freedom to act as it sees fit. Nor can the assertion of the right of an individual stand in the way of the leadership's determination of what is good for society.

The Constitution of the U.S.S.R. is, therefore, an educational and propaganda instrument. Any provisions contained in the Constitution which might facially suggest that freedom of the kind that we know exists are effectively modified by the key phrases in Articles 3, 6, 39, and 59 to which I referred earlier.

Let me offer an illustration of what I mean. The equivalent of our First Amendment is contained in Article 50 of the Soviet Constitution, which reads as follows:

In accordance with the interests of the people and in order to strengthen and develop the socialist system, citizens of the U.S.S.R. are guaranteed freedom of speech, of the press, and of assembly, meetings, street processions and of demonstration.

Starting from our notions of civil liberties, we might read this article to mean that citizens of the U.S.S.R. are guaranteed freedom of expression and that that grant of freedom accords with the interest of the people and strengthens the Soviet Union's system of government. But that is not the way Article 50 is understood in the Soviet Union. The way Article 50 is applied, freedom of speech, of the press, of assembly is granted *only if it accords with the interest of the people and if it strengthens and develops the socialist system*. And who is to decide what is in the interest of the people and what strengthens and develops the socialist system? The answer is, of course, found in Articles 3 and 6 of the Constitution. What is in the interest of the people is decided by the Communist Party and ultimately by the central leadership, the Politburo. That is why a law that makes defamation of the socialist system a crime is constitutional. Defamation, which in Soviet practice means speaking unpleasant truths, is presumed not to strengthen the socialist system.

Let us take a look at another constitutional provision dealing with civil liberties. Article 52 reads as follows:

Citizens of the U.S.S.R. are guaranteed freedom of conscience, that is, the right to profess or not to profess any religion, and to conduct religious worship or atheistic propaganda.

Indeed, in the Soviet Union today, anyone may profess a religion. But nothing in the Constitution prohibits the Communist Party of the Soviet Union from banning anyone who professes religion from its membership and, therefore, from advancement to any position of leadership and responsibility in Soviet society. Furthermore, while the right to conduct religious worship is guaranteed, this phrase has not been construed to mean that any group of citizens may conduct religious worship at any time in any place of their choosing. Laws have been promulgated which allow religious associations to form and register with the authorities of the state. If they are registered and if they do receive permission to use a house of worship, worship in that place at times authorized therefore is permitted. Any group which worships without appropriate authority can be and often is punished severely.

How does all of that comport with the constitutionally guaranteed right "to conduct religious worship"? The Soviet answer would be that the right to conduct religious worship exists. The Constitution, they will say, does not guarantee a right to *unregulated* religious worship.

To understand how religion may be practiced in the Soviet Union, we, as American lawyers, should think of the way the securities industry functions in the United States. Just as you may practice religion in the Soviet Union, you may engage in the securities business in the United States. But to engage in the securities business in our country, you must operate within the regulations issued by the Securities and Exchange Commission. If you act outside the regulations, you may, indeed, be punished. That is the way it is with the practice of religion in the Soviet Union. If you act within the regulations laid down by the Religious Affairs Commission, you will not run into any problems. If you act outside these regulations, you violate Article 227 of the criminal code of the Russian Soviet Federated Socialist Republic or the corresponding code sections in the criminal codes of the other republics. Article 227 makes it a crime to participate in a group which "under the guise of preaching religious doctrines and performing religious rituals is connected with . . . inciting citizens to refuse to do social activity or to fulfill obligations. . . ."

The penalty imposed upon violators is customarily 3 years of deprivation of freedom. For leaders of such a group, it is 5 years.

Gorbachev and Glasnost

In light of the news that has come out of the Soviet Union within the last 8 months or so, you might ask whether we cannot expect some fundamental changes in the roles of the party and the state under Mikhail Gorbachev and *glasnost*. My answer to this question would be "no." Gorbachev is deeply committed to carry on in the spirit of Lenin and, as I noted at the outset, dominance of the state by a single party, control of the party by a self-perpetuating leadership group, and subordination of the individual to the interests of the state, as defined by the leadership, are the essential elements of the teachings of Lenin. In fact, Gorbachev made precisely that point in his statement to the Communist Party's Central Committee Plenum in January of this year when he emphasized that "the principle of the Party rules under which the decisions of higher bodies are binding on all lower Party committees . . . remains unshakeable."

What Gorbachev and his friends are attempting to strip from the operations of the Soviet system, in the name of *glasnost*, are the features of oriental despotism initially imbedded in the Leninist construct by Joseph Stalin. These include severe punishment for the mere expression of dissenting opinions, rigid limitations upon allowed literary expression, state control over all other forms of artistic endeavor, punishment for criticism of any state official or any official action, etc. Under *glasnost* all of these Stalinist controls are to be relaxed. The petty tyrannies of local officials are to be ended, as efforts are made to have the lower levels of the bureaucracy operate under the rule of law. But, and this is a point that must be kept in mind, there are to be limits to the relaxation. Nothing is or will be allowed that might threaten the control of the state by the party, as guaranteed by Article 6 of the Constitution. Gorbachev and his colleagues reject, as did Lenin before them, "bourgeois democracy." Their goal is to return to the practices of the Soviet system in the early 1920s, in the time of Lenin and the years immediately after his death. Their notion is to live by Lenin's precepts, not to abandon them.

It is important to note in this context that Stalinism is now being stripped from the Soviet system for the second time. It was initially exorcised by Nikita Khrushchev, back in the 1950s. It evidently sprouted again after Khrushchev's removal, even though not driven by paranoia of the same intensity as under Stalin. What the Soviets really should ask themselves is whether a Leninist system, without any checks and balances, will inevitably, over time, develop Stalinist features and whether, therefore, in the absence of fundamental change, Gorbachev's *glasnost* is not likely to go the way of Khrushchev's thaw, with the country returning to another form of despotic rule.

As I have noted, the Soviet governmental system is characterized by an absence of checks and balances, by an absence of a constitutional framework which guarantees individual rights against the highest state authority. It is for that reason that the operation of the entire system is so critically dependent on the outlook and attitude of the person or persons who at any one time control the principal levers of power in the Soviet Union. As Dr. Koryagin—the Soviet psychiatrist who has recently been released from prison—has had occasion to observe, the somewhat greater freedom of expression now allowed in the Soviet Union is not *guaranteed*, it is *permitted*, and permission can at any time be withdrawn.

Though the Soviet leadership does not appear to have any present intention of abandoning the basic precepts on which its system of government rests, that does not mean that no change will ever occur. Having gotten in recent months at least a whiff of greater freedom, some Soviet citizens might be willing to learn how other societies go about the task of assuring respect for individual rights. And who would be better equipped to talk to them about this subject than those whose professional responsibility it is in a democratic country to see that the rights of the individual are protected?

It is for that reason that I want to end my remarks with an appeal to you. If the ABA/Association of Soviet Lawyers agreement is renewed, I sincerely hope that American participants will try to learn how the Soviet system works, will learn to understand the facade which the Soviet Constitution presents, a facade behind which any Politburo directive can supersede any alleged constitutional guarantee. I hope that American participants will not be shy about explaining to the Soviet lawyers they meet the difference between a constitution which a country's political leadership can manipulate at will and one which with the help of an independent judiciary can, indeed, shield the individual citizen against oppressive government. In responding to you, a good many of your interlocutors will parrot the party line, but deep down they will understand what you are talking about.

ON ENDING THE COLD WAR[4]

The Truman Doctrine and the Marshall Plan were the decisive initial moves in an effort to stem a postwar Soviet thrust for hegemony in western Eurasia that had been gathering momentum in the bleak winter and early spring of 1946–47. The historical circumstances pose two related questions: Why did the enterprise seem in Moscow a possible dream? Why did the U.S. reaction to the Soviet pursuit of its objective come late? The American delay imparted, as lagged responses and feedback generally do, a cyclical character to the U.S.-Soviet relationship which was to persist and yield three distinct cycles over the next four decades.

A full answer to the first question surely involves mixed impulses of fear and ambition deeply rooted in Russia's history and collective memory, elements of ideological commitment and

[4]Reprint of an article by W. W. Rostow, Rex G. Baker Jr. Professor of Political Economy, University of Texas at Austin. Reprinted by permission of FOREIGN AFFAIRS, No. 4, 1987. Copyright © 1987 by the Council on Foreign Relations, Inc.

evangelism, and more mundane variables of geography, resources and technological capacity. But the cold war can be viewed more simply. It has arisen from the fourth major effort in the twentieth century by a latecomer on the world scene to enlarge its power at the expense of earlier front-runners already at or beyond the inherent limits of their international stature. Stripped of details, the past century has witnessed two attempts by Germany, one by Japan and, since 1945, one by the Soviet Union to achieve strategic hegemony in their respective regions, although Soviet ambitions in the cold war evidently came to reach much farther—as did Germany's at the peak of its ambitions.

II

Think for a moment of how things stood in 1870 when Bismarck rounded out the German Empire with his three small wars. Britain accounted for 32 percent of the world's industrial production; Germany, 13 percent; France, 10 percent; Russia, 4 percent; and across the Atlantic, the United States, 23 percent. The Japanese, only two years beyond the Meiji Restoration, were not in this company.

The German takeoff began in the 1840s; the Japanese, in the 1880s; the Russian, in the 1890s. By 1914 Germany had acquired all the then existing major technologies, as had Japan and the Soviet Union by 1941. These three challengers had come, in my vocabulary, to technological maturity which, in the era, required some 60 years beyond the takeoff. By 1936–38 the shares of world industrial production reflected the relative decline of Britain and France, the rise of Russia and the appearance of Japan in the arena of power: Britain had 9 percent; Germany, 11 percent; France, 5 percent; Russia, 19 percent; the United States, 32 percent; Japan, 4 percent. World War II canceled out for a time two of these players, gravely weakened two others, and left a proud, ambitious but war-torn Soviet Union and an undamaged United States economically rehabilitated from the Great Depression.

My first proposition is, then, that it was not unreasonable for Soviet planners, as Allied victory because increasingly certain after the great turnaround in the autumn of 1942—at Stalingrad and at both ends of North Africa—to set their sights high for the postwar extension of Soviet power. There is ample evidence that they did.

But what about the United States? After all, as the war ended it was the greatest industrial power in the world, producing almost half the world's output and enjoying a monopoly on nuclear weapons. But the United States was also unilaterally disarming. It was behaving as if it were about to repeat its convulsive withdrawal from responsibility of 1919–20. American behavior appeared every day to be confirming President Roosevelt's opening statement at Yalta, in which he made what Churchill described as the "momentous" prediction that the United States would not keep a large army in Europe and that its occupation of Germany could be envisaged for only two years. Anyone who wishes to understand why the Soviet Union cautiously concluded that it might dominate Europe should examine the course of American politics and policy in 1945–46. Robert J. Donovan, in his biography of Truman, correctly designated 1946 a "disastrous" year.

This poses the second question: Why was the American reaction to the Soviet movement toward European hegemony so late?

The full answer lies in the same variables that explain Russian behavior: history, ideology, geography and economic capacity. But we should begin with a narrower question: Did some special dispensation of grace exempt the United States from the latecomer's impulse to seek regional hegemony?

By no means. The American takeoff came about the same time as Germany's, in the 1840s and 1850s. The American instinct to deploy its new power was expressed, in the first instance, in consolidating its authority across the American continent, and then in asserting itself in the Pacific, the Caribbean, Central America and Mexico. But however strong the imperialist impulse may have been among some Americans of the pre-1914 generation, it was reined in by three forces: an ideological sense among a good many other Americans that imperialism was incompatible with the values and institutions on which American society was built; disconcerting confrontations with nationalism in areas that resisted American intrusion (for example, in the Philippines and Mexico); and, starting in 1917, the recurrent problem of dealing defensively with the efforts of latecomers to achieve hegemony at a time when Britain, which had managed the balance for almost a century after 1815, could no longer cope without our active engagement.

When American energy was focused on the rounding out and consolidation of the North American continent, we had a positive sequence of objectives and were capable of taking the initiative or acting swiftly—and sometimes brutally—to exploit unexpected opportunities. But when we inherited part of the task of fending off thrusts for hegemony in Europe or Asia our central mission in protecting the national interest became negative and defensive. We acted reluctantly, late, and usually in a context of crisis. To this day our traditional political rhetoric makes it difficult—almost embarrassing—to articulate the quite sensible balance-of-power strand in the national interest.

Nevertheless, if one were to play over the last seven decades without a soundtrack—putting aside the rhetoric, debates and oscillations of American foreign policy—the United States has behaved in times of crisis in a consistent way. We have consistently acted as if we were mortally endangered should a single power or coalition achieve hegemony in Western Europe, in Asia, or in both. We have also, of course, reacted systematically since the 1920s whenever a major extracontinental power threatened to install substantial military force in this hemisphere. In the nuclear age we have reacted consistently whenever we have judged ourselves potentially threatened by a first strike that might radically reduce our second-strike capability, or whenever our allies have been placed under heavy diplomatic pressure backed by an explicit nuclear threat.

But the acceptance by an effective majority of American citizens that the nation had abiding interests in the balance of power in Europe (and Asia) came hard. Even in World War II it required the attack on Pearl Harbor and Hitler's declaration of war on the United States to resolve the deeply rooted national schism concerning the nature of our interests in Eurasia. As many have noted, this is a problem reaching back to John Winthrop's time and our self-image as a "city upon a hill"; to Washington's Farewell Address almost 170 years later; and to the many other occasions when Americans felt impelled to distinguish their society, values and posture on the world scene from those of the wicked Old World. We tended to await times of acute crisis, when U.S. interests—strategic, ideological and economic—palpably converged, before acting forcefully to restore the balance of power in Eurasia. That is what happened in 1917 and 1941. The spring of 1947 was also such a time, and the Truman Doctrine and Marshall Plan resulted, providing between them a posture comfortable for a substantial majority of Americans. Thus ended the first cold-war downswing of 1945–47, giving way to the contentious upswing of the first cycle.

III

There have been three distinct cold-war cycles, measured peak-to-peak from an American perspective: 1945–55, 1955–73 and 1973–87. The first cycle might be called the Truman-Stalin duel. It began, as I have suggested, with a descent from a wartime peak in the relative power of the United States. This retrogression was marked by U.S. weakness and confusion in 1945–46, including rapid unilateral reductions in effective military strength. This interval was also marked by progressive movement toward the division of Germany and Europe. Then in 1947 came the first two of three belated American cold-war reactions—the Truman Doctrine and the Marshall Plan—followed two years later, in the wake of the blockade of Berlin, by the creation of NATO.

As Europe quieted down into a stalemate along the Elbe in 1948–49, the scene of intense action shifted to Asia. There, Mao Zedong moved toward victory in China while the French continued to fight the Viet Minh to maintain their hold in Indochina. Guerrilla warfare erupted in Burma, Malaya, Indonesia and the Philippines; and the Korean War was planned (according to Khrushchev) in Moscow early in 1950 by Stalin and Mao at Kim Il Sung's instigation. Following the death of Stalin in 1953, a truce was quickly negotiated in Korea, and Mao, in his somewhat idiosyncratic style, turned to domestic development. Asia, like Europe, seemed to have settled into a postwar stability. The exception was the struggle in Indochina; and the conflict, after eight years, appeared to be sealed off by the Geneva Accords of 1954. The Austrian State Treaty and the Geneva summit of 1955 seemed to signal a possible subsidence of the cold war after a decade of thrust and counterthrust amid the dishevelment of post–World War II Eurasia.

But in 1955 the second cycle was, in fact, already under way, its contours foreshadowed by Khrushchev's nuclear threat, made in Birmingham during his visit to Great Britain, and by the Soviet-Egyptian arms deal. The Soviet thrust consisted of thermonuclear-tipped missiles—used to apply political pressure on Western Europe—and the extension of the cold war into the Middle East, Africa, South Asia and, before long, Latin America.

Soviet momentum accelerated after Sputnik I was launched in October 1957 and after an optimistic communist summit meeting was held in Moscow in November of that year. The tone of that meeting was well captured in Mao's keynote address at the University of Moscow, in which he argued that "the East Wind is prevailing over the West Wind. That is to say, the forces of socialism have become overwhelmingly superior to the forces of imperialism."

Soviet initiatives followed in the Congo, in Indochina, where war was revived in 1958 by Hanoi, and in the Caribbean, where Castro rose to power in 1959. Nuclear blackmail assumed a quite lucid, operational form with Khrushchev's on-again, off-again ultimatum on Berlin, with its explicit threat to Western transport routes.

This was what confronted John Kennedy when the second turnaround began. The American response to nuclear blackmail built up to related climactic crises in Berlin in 1961 and early 1962 and the Cuban missile crisis of October 1962. The Congo gradually settled down under U.N. auspices; and the 1962 Geneva Accords on Laos appeared to have again yielded calm in Indochina. But, as in the first cold-war cycle, there was a second round of conflict, including the movement to substantial conventional war in Indochina in 1964–65, the Malaysian-Indonesian *konfrontasi* and an attempted communist coup in Indonesia, and an exacerbation of the multiple conflicts of the Middle East. The latter conflict reached a temporary climax in the 1967 Arab-Israeli war; the Indochina conflict in the peace agreement of January 1973.

It was in this second round that the protracted test between communist and non-communist methods of modernization in the developing regions, launched with President Truman's 1949 Point Four, was fully joined.

With the beginning of the normalization of U.S.-China relations, the Nixon-Brezhnev summit meetings and the first Strategic Arms Limitation Talks treaty, there was an interval in the early 1970s during which it appeared the cold war might be subsiding.

Then came the third cycle. It was triggered by the convergence of the self-destruction of an American president via Watergate, throwing the whole political system out of balance for the better part of the 1970s, and the underlying schisms, traumas and uncertainties generated by the protracted U.S. military engagement in Southeast Asia. The result was not only a remarkable period of unilateral reduction in U.S. military expenditures relative to GNP, but an across-the-board weakening of American will to deal with strategic reality. Perhaps a bit to their own surprise, Soviet planners, conducting their correlation-of-forces analyses in 1973–75, perceived the most attractive array of opportunities since Sputnik I—or perhaps even since Roosevelt's opening statement at Yalta. As in the 1955–73 cycle, there was an exercise in nuclear blackmail against Europe—this time with the SS-20 missile buildup. There were new thrusts, exploiting Cuban and Vietnamese forces, into the Caribbean and Central America, Angola, Ethiopia, Yemen and Indochina, permitting the acquisition or strengthening of important Soviet naval and air bases. Finally, there was the Soviet invasion of Afghanistan in 1979. This triggered the third belated, reactive turnaround in U.S. policy, echoing those of 1947 and 1961.

Eight years after the turnaround of 1979, the United States and the Soviet Union are in a phase of relative political equilibrium (like 1953–55 and 1969–73) that might be translated into either a movement toward ending the cold war or yet another phase of befuddled American weakness, ambitious Soviet activism, a belated U.S. response and a fourth cycle.

On the hopeful side, the votes of the European parliaments on the cruise and Pershing missiles in the early 1980s put an end to the second Soviet attempt at nuclear blackmail. The expansion of U.S. military budgets since 1979 has improved the overall military balance. Nationalist resistance to communist intrusions in Central America, Africa, South Asia and Southeast Asia, supported by the United States and others, has thus far prevented Soviet consolidation of the apparent gains of the 1970s. On the other hand, recent domestic economic policy has put U.S. social and defense outlays into conflict. The connection between U.S. strength and the pursuit of a more stable peace, confused by the Reykjavik summit, has not been made clear to the American people or their major allies. And the Iran/contra imbroglio threatens to weaken U.S. military and foreign policy on a broad front, as did Watergate from 1973 to 1979.

IV

I have, with purpose, evoked this dreary 40-year saga as if the sole powerful force at work in the world arena were the U.S.-Soviet cold-war duel and as if each of the three cyclical rounds of the duel were of equal significance to the relative power of the two major contestants. Neither proposition is true.

It was historically understandable, if not quite inevitable, that the Soviet Union would make a bid for hegemony in Eurasia after 1945 and that the United States would react, even if belatedly. In fact, power in the post-1945 world arena was never wholly duopolistic and became progressively less so. Consequently, the geopolitical stake for each side in each of the three cycles of the cold war progressively diminished, while the stake for each side in avoiding a nuclear exchange increased with the buildup in the stockpiles of nuclear weapons and the improvement of technologies for their accurate delivery.

After all, the first round (1945–55) directly concerned regions and nations that still determine the strategic balance in Eurasia. It settled the initial postwar political and strategic orientation of Western Europe, Germany, Eastern Europe, Japan, China and India. The second round (1955–73) related to the Eurasian balance in a somewhat more oblique way: the Berlin crisis and the diplomatic and psychological threat to Western Europe via nuclear missiles; the acceptance or rejection of Soviet missiles in the western hemisphere; and the future balance of forces in Southeast Asia and the Middle East.

The intensity of the Soviet nuclear blackmail threat via the SS-20 in the third round, with its denouement in the votes of West European parliaments, did not match the intensity and raw drama of the Berlin and Cuban missile crises 20 years earlier. Similarly, the ample supply of trouble generated in recent years in Southeast Asia, South Asia, the Middle East, Africa and the Caribbean does not appear to have had quite the immediate strategic importance of the earlier crises in the Third World.

The implications of this point should not be misconstrued. The shift of the East-West struggle to what might be regarded as more peripheral areas, where Soviet support was thrown behind local communists when opportunity for incursions was created or otherwise occurred, does not mean that these initially limited efforts to enlarge communist power could not have affected the central power balance if ignored by the United States and others who opposed Soviet hegemony. The incursions in each of these regions, if unchecked, could have yielded major shifts in the Eurasian or western hemispheric power balance. Nevertheless, the crises of the third round (1973–87) have had distinctly less initial specific gravity than their predecessors.

Why should this be so? One reason is that the orientation of the major strategic regions was settled in the first cold-war cycle and has not been subsequently upset. There have been, of course, some substantial shifts: the defection of Yugoslavia from the Soviet orbit, the Sino-Soviet schism and the communist successes in Cuba, Nicaragua and Indochina. But it is also the case that quietly, erratically, the capacity of the developing regions to resist intrusion and to shape their own destiny has been increasing. In part, nationalism, always fundamental, has gathered strength. In part, economic, social and technical progress under noncommunist auspices has reduced the possibility of external manipulation. The members of the Association of Southeast Asian Nations, for example, used to good effect the time painfully bought in Vietnam between 1965 and 1975 and rallied together rather than collapsed when Saigon fell. At the moment, the major threats to these countries stem from domestic instability rather than overt external aggression of the kind that engulfed Indochina. In the Middle East the Iranian revolution, the Iran-Iraq war and the tragic internecine struggle in Lebanon show that the countries of the region are not wholly the playthings of cold-war manipulation or ideology and will increasingly go their own, not always attractive, ways. Indeed, historians may well assess the rising power of nationalism and the demonstration of the superiority of non-communist over communist methods of modernization as more significant over the past two generations than most of the cold-war clashes, serious though they were.

Still another somewhat related trend has been quietly at work reshaping the world arena of power over the past two generations: the relative decline in the economic power of the Soviet Union and the United States as Western and Southern Europe, Japan, the developing countries of the Pacific Basin, and some of the more advanced developing countries in other regions have moved forward more rapidly. The combined gross national product of the United States and the U.S.S.R. may have declined from about 44 percent to 33 percent of the global product between 1950 and 1980.

To sum up thus far: the three rounds of the cold war have conformed to a pattern of Soviet initiative and belated U.S. response, reflecting the historical roots and asymmetrical character of the struggle. There was nothing self-limiting about this long succession of thrusts, and their containment required considerable efforts by the United States and others. Nevertheless, the issues at stake in each round have been increasingly less fundamental to the strategic position of the two central players. This is partly because the capacity of the Soviet Union and the United States to influence the behavior of the developing nations has progressively declined with the rise in power and assertiveness of nationalism and the overall strengthening of their economic foundations. The Soviet Union and the United States have maintained over these 40 years the two greatest concentrations of nuclear power. These have proved to be useful almost exclusively to assure mutual nuclear deterrence, although the U.S.S.R. unsuccessfully mounted two major exercises in nuclear blackmail. But usable military power, as well as economic capacity, has tended to diffuse away from both superpowers; and the costs of all-out war have steadily increased for both parties.

In short, barring an irrational stumbling into nuclear war, the underlying historical forces at work would appear to decree that the Russian latecomer's drive for hegemony—like the earlier efforts of Germany and Japan—will fail. If the United States were to engage in such a hegemonic effort, it also would fail.* The second half of the twentieth century has proved a bad time for empires. The 21st century promises to be worse. The question is: Can we bring the cold war to an end without the kind of major conflict that ended the German and Japanese efforts, which, in a nuclear age, would constitute a disaster for all humanity?

V

The possibility of a soft landing for the cold war is strengthened by two related revolutions that have been proceeding concurrently over the past decade. One is a major technological

*There are, of course, those who believe the United States has been engaged in a hegemonic effort. I would underline that my argument is based, in part, on the distinction between hegemony and maintaining a balance of power. The former requires much more direct control of other states than the latter, where the objective is essentially negative, that is, to deny hegemony to any other power.

revolution generated in the advanced industrial countries, the other an educational revolution mounted in the more advanced developing countries, which is putting them in a position to absorb and apply the new technologies. What can be observed, for example, in South Korea's remarkable race to high-tech status is what we can expect increasingly over the next several generations in the developing regions.

Taken together, these revolutions are accelerating the diffusion of power away from both Washington and Moscow and posing domestic challenges that render the ideological aspects of the cold war increasingly anachronistic. The logic of these revolutionary forces calls for a quite different, still difficult, but potentially more benign U.S.-Soviet relationship.

To validate these bald assertions requires that we examine a bit more closely the dual revolutions and the challenges they pose for both the older and newer industrial societies.

The technologies that moved from invention to innovation in the mid-1970s include microelectronics, genetic engineering, a batch of new industrial materials, lasers, robots and various new means of communication. They have four distinctive characteristics: a close linkage to areas of basic science also undergoing revolutionary change; a capacity to galvanize the old basic industries as well as agriculture, forestry, animal husbandry and the whole range of services; an immediate relevance to developing countries to a degree depending on their stage of growth; and a degree of diversification such that no single country is likely to dominate them as, for example, Britain dominated the early stage of cotton textiles and the United States the early stage of the mass-produced automobile.

While the old industrial countries of the North have been spawning this glamorous, much discussed revolution in technology, the developing regions of the South have been mounting a little-noted human revolution of their own.

Overall, the proportion of the population aged 20–24 enrolled in higher education in what the World Bank calls "lower middle income" countries rose from 3 percent to 10 percent between 1960 and 1982; for "upper middle income" countries the figure increased from 4 percent to 14 percent. For Brazil, fated to be a major actor in this drama, the proportion rose from one percent in 1965 to 12 percent in 1982. In India, with low per capita income but a vital educational system, the figure rose from 3 percent to 9 percent. To understand the meaning of these figures, it should be recalled that in 1960 the proportion for the United Kingdom was 9 percent, for Japan 10 percent.

There has been, moreover, a radical shift toward science and engineering. In India, for example, the pool of scientists and engineers has increased from about 190,000 in 1960 to 2.4 million in 1984—a critical mass exceeded only in the United States and the Soviet Union. In Mexico the annual average increase of graduates in natural science was about 3 percent, and in engineering 5 percent, in the period 1957 to 1973. From 1973 to 1981 the comparable figures were an astonishing 14 percent and 24 percent, respectively—an almost fivefold acceleration.

Even discounting for problems of educational quality, the potential absorptive capacity for the new technologies in the more advanced developing countries is high. Their central problem—like that of most advanced industrial countries—is how to make effective use of the increasingly abundant scientific and engineering skills they already command. This requires, in turn, an ability to generate and maintain flexible, interactive partnerships among scientists, engineers, entrepreneurs and the working force.

These figures, signaling a surge in technological absorptive capacity, mark the arrival of a stage when national growth rates are, under normal circumstances, at a maximum. Despite current vicissitudes, India, the developing countries of the Pacific Basin (including China) and those containing most of the population of Latin America are likely to absorb the new technologies and move rapidly forward over the next several generations. Much the same would happen, I believe, if the Middle East could find its way from its chronic bloodletting to a twentieth-century version of the Treaty of Westphalia, which ended the Thirty Years' War in 1648.

Thus, if my view of what lies ahead is broadly correct, the world economy and polity face a familiar adjustment in which latecomers narrow and finally close the gap with front-runners. But this time it is likely to occur on an unprecedented scale. The advanced industrial countries (including the U.S.S.R. and the East European nations) now constitute about 1.1 billion people, or approximately one quarter of the world's population. At least 2.6 billion people, about 56 percent, live in countries that will, I estimate, acquire technological virtuosity within the next half century. Moreover, population growth rates in the decades ahead will be higher in the latter group than in the former. We are talking about a great historical transformation.

This transformation poses major challenges to the United States, Western Europe, Japan and the Soviet Union—as well as to the newcomers.

VI

The United States, Western Europe and Japan need to explore the possibilities opened up by the new technologies and to apply them across the board to basic industries, agriculture and the newer service industries. Only by so doing will they be able to maintain economies of sufficient productivity and flexibility to support and enlarge their affluence in the face of the sustained competitive test ahead. I believe this requires a historic shift in the pattern of domestic politics in the Western world.* The shift is away from a more or less decorous struggle over how real national income, assumed to be automatically expanding, should be distributed. It can be argued that this has been the dominant pattern of politics since Bismarck initiated his welfare legislation in the 1870s. The required shift is toward a cooperative effort that embraces business, labor and government as well as the scientific, engineering and entrepreneurial sectors and the working force to ensure that real national income in the advanced industrial countries will continue to expand in the face of increasingly severe international competition.

For historical reasons, Japanese politics is, for the moment, well oriented for the tasks ahead. Since Commodore Perry turned up in Tokyo Bay some 130 years ago with his squadron of black ships, the interaction of the external world with Japanese pride and ambition has yielded a succession of crises that have strengthened the nation's sense of unity and common purpose. Since the mid-1950s Japan's economic position in the world has been the focus of that sentiment. Japan's challenge will be to maintain a sense of clear, common purpose when it shifts, as it inevitably must, from an obsessive focus on maximizing its export surplus to a wider spectrum of domestic and external objectives.

*See for example my elaboration of this point in *The Washington Post*, Dec. 28, 1986.

In the West the transition is necessary to maintain not only politically and strategically secure societies but also societies sufficiently well poised to manage peacefully the adjustment that must take place as the newcomers approach technological maturity.

Clearly, the world that emerges as the developing regions absorb the new technologies is not going to be dominated by any one power. But the lesson of the past four centuries is that the diffusion of technological competence can generate dangerous neomercantilist conflicts. Mutual survival in a nuclear age requires that we now do a better job with this kind of structural transition than has been done by our predecessors since the British challenged Dutch primacy in the seventeenth century.

What does a better job require? The general formula for a peaceful adjustment of front-runners and latecomers was set out first by David Hume in 1758 in explicit opposition to mercantilist doctrine. He noted two facts, confirmed by later experience: the older front-runner can gain from the enlarged two-way trade induced by the rapid rise of a latecomer; but to enjoy that advantage and hold his place in the queue, the front-runner must vigorously exploit his technological and other relative advantages and adjust flexibly to the inevitably intensified competition. Hume concluded that the original front-runner could do well and benefit, on balance, from the rise of the latecomer if he remained "industrious and civilized."

In our time, that evocative phrase implies a response at three levels. First, the individual nations of the West and Japan must react at the national level with vigor and resilience to the new technologies and the intensified competition within the world economy. A successful adjustment is unlikely if the major countries of the Organization for Economic Cooperation and Development are defensive, bedeviled with unsolved problems and grasping for evasive short-term economic solutions.

Second, if a mercantilist fragmentation, likely to intensify rather than end the cold war, is to be avoided, something new and difficult, but not impossible, will be required. Western Europe, Japan and the United States will have to generate collectively the leadership none can now provide alone. This means designing and abiding by new rules of the game for trade, capital movements and domestic policy in the extraordinarily internationalized economy that has emerged. On the basis of such rules, they will have to work with each other and with the developing regions to exploit the new possibilities and make the peaceful adjustments cooperation could render realistic and mutually profitable. And, I would add, as the latecomers move forward, they must gradually assume an increasing degree of responsibility for the viability of the international system as a whole. The United States grossly failed this test between the two world wars—with tragic results. Japan now confronts this test, and before long so will South Korea, Taiwan, Brazil and the other aspiring, fast-moving latecomers, especially India and China.*

Third, to manage this dynamic process of mutual support and adjustment in a civilized way to the common advantage, global rules of the game in trade and finance will require an underpinning of regional organization. That should be the central mission for an intergovernmental Pacific Basin organization, the subject of endless symposiums but virtually total governmental inaction. This is also the next task for the Organization of American States and the Inter-American Development Bank—not to try out of nostalgia to recreate the old Alliance for Progress but to assure that Latin and North America move forward with steady, mutual support as the former makes the transition to full technological maturity, coming to grips along the way with debt and other acute problems.

But what about the Soviet Union? As Mikhail Gorbachev is quite aware, the Soviet Union also confronts related domestic and foreign policy challenges in the face of the dual revolutions now under way. The challenges are captured in his oft-stated assertion that, if the Soviet Union does not restructure its institutions to permit an acceleration of scientific and technical progress, its global stature will be reduced and its hopes for a higher standard of living will be endangered. Put in such general terms, the problems on the Soviet agenda are similar to those confronting the United States; in both cases they require important institutional and political changes for their solution.

Take, for example, an issue posed by the new technologies. By accident of history, the United States and Russia emerged with quite different methods for organizing science and technology.

---

*The decisive role for Asian and global stability of relations between India and China is the closing theme of my book, *The United States and the Regional Organization of Asia and the Pacific, 1965–1985*, Austin: University of Texas Press, 1986, pp. 158–161. That study also suggests an operating agenda for an intergovernmental organization for the Pacific Basin.

The Russian government, modeling its arrangements on those of early eighteenth-century Western Europe, built up over the subsequent two centuries a distinguished Academy of Sciences, which was carried forward and greatly expanded in the Soviet Union. Its many institutes contain a high proportion of the U.S.S.R.'s best scientists and engineers, but their ties to those beyond their bureaucracies are often limited. This did not matter so much in the era of steel, electric power plants, cement and other technologies rooted in the pre-1914 world, although Soviet productivity in these classic older sectors remains lower than it might have been, in part because the capacities of Soviet scientists and engineers have not been effectively brought to bear in the Soviet civilian economy. As Soviet leaders are aware, the problem is now much more serious with respect to the new round of technologies. The flexible, interacting, day-to-day linkage of the institutes to the production process required for the generation (as well as the diffusion) of the new technologies is proving difficult to bring about without radical institutional change.

These linkages are somewhat easier for the United States. Two useful and gracious institutions in Philadelphia (the American Philosophical Society) and Boston (the American Academy of Arts and Sciences) attest that we, too, found inspiration in the British Royal Society and the French Academy, respectively, during the eighteenth century. But our tradition is better symbolized by the land-grant colleges. We are fortunate that our academic institutions generally accept the proposition that basic university research may be legitimately addressed to the problems of the active world, and that two-way contacts across academic boundaries can be mutually beneficial, albeit sometimes complex. I suspect that, for some time, the United States will do quite well in generating new technologies.

A second and quite distinct problem is to assure that the new technologies are promptly introduced into the sectors where they are likely to prove cost-effective. Here the United States (as well as the U.S.S.R.) had difficulties, as the condition of the American automobile, steel, machine tool, textile and other basic industries attests. In some sectors we have spawned entrepreneurs who, whatever their virtues, find it difficult to deal creatively with their research and development departments. Their considerable expertise never prepared them for a world where a 30-percent per annum obsolescence rate is common. The application of short-run profit maximization in a sector where the linkage of management to R&D is weak can yield a result not unlike that induced by the setting of quantitative production goals by a central planning organization. The common result is sluggishness in exploiting new technologies or, in the American case, the pursuit of cheap labor by relocating overseas. Yet in other U.S. sectors, such as electronics, chemicals and aerospace, the management-R&D linkage works quite well. These are industries that, in effect, arose out of laboratories—an origin that has left its mark.

Overall, the problem appears more acute in the Soviet Union than in the United States. In fact, all socialist countries, including those most willing to reform, have found it difficult to provide incentives for technological innovation in industry.

Well over a century ago, contemplating the contest he saw ahead between democracy and socialism, John Stuart Mill, who viewed socialism seriously and with considerable sympathy, concluded that the choice would probably hinge on "which of the two systems is consistent with the greatest amount of human liberty and spontaneity." The challenge is particularly profound in the U.S.S.R., as Gorbachev appears to perceive, although there is no basis for American complacency. The paradoxical fact is that both superpowers are now in the grip of major productivity crises.

The Soviet domestic changes required to meet the challenge must take place at a time when the relative rise in economic and technological stature of the developing regions is palpably moving the more advanced countries among them beyond the reach of superpower hegemony. Meanwhile, the thrust for national independence and increased human freedom is certain to rise with the passage of time and the succession of generations in Stalin's East European empire. Even now, Soviet control is diluted in quite different ways in Romania, Hungary, Poland and East Germany as Moscow makes concessions to gathering historic forces in order to hold on to what it now regards as necessary to the security of the U.S.S.R. The pressure to find some alternative way to satisfy legitimate Soviet security interests in Europe is bound to increase.

Under appropriate circumstances, all this could lead Soviet policy to reflect what Soviet leaders and analysts almost certainly suspect: that the emerging world arena is not one capable of sustained domination by Moscow or any other single power, and that the appropriate historical role of the U.S.S.R. will be to join the older and newer industrial powers in managing as peacefully as possible the somewhat precarious transition already under way.

VII

I believe a peaceful transition of this kind is possible but not certain. It is possible because forces are at work that in time may make an end to—or a gradual withering away of—the cold war logical and safe for leaders of both the Soviet Union and the United States. But ending the cold war will not be simple. Diplomatic and military history will not end. The Soviet Union and the United States both have abiding interests to protect as nation states; they will have to look after those interests. And a new flow of difficult, but hopefully more benign, problems will arise. In fact, exit from the cold war should be viewed as a process—probably protracted—of getting from here to there. It should be carried forward by steps that permit each side to feel confident as it supplants one set of relations with another. With its unsettling mixture of grandiose objectives, chicanery and transparent propaganda, and with its minimal attention to the process of getting from here to there, Reykjavik will remain a model of how not to proceed.

What, then, in rough outline, would a working agenda for ending the cold war look like? Initial understandings would have to be reached in three critical areas.

The first would, of course, be the nuclear arms race. Here three conditions would have to be satisfied: a thoroughly inspected U.S.-U.S.S.R. nuclear balance sufficient to guarantee, at lower overall force levels, secure second-strike capabilities but no capacity for nuclear blackmail; agreements on nuclear force ceilings with other nuclear weapons powers; and, against this background, a drive to implement more firmly the Nonproliferation Treaty. The path of wisdom may alter as we learn more; but I would be skeptical of solutions that eliminated nuclear weapons, wholly relied on the Strategic Defense Initiative or totally eliminated elements of SDI as part of stable deterrent systems. Evidently, problems of immense complexity are embedded in these conditions, even under circumstances of maximum goodwill among the parties.

The second area would be a reorganization of NATO and the Warsaw Pact in ways that allowed an increased scope for national political freedom in Eastern Europe and guaranteed agreed force levels, securely inspected, for residual NATO and Warsaw Pact forces. The most complex issue certain to arise is the degree and character of German unity. But the objective can be simply stated: the U.S.S.R. would have to decide to accept a balance of power rather than a hegemonic solution to its legitimate security interest in Eastern Europe; that is, a solution guaranteeing that no other major power dominates Eastern Europe, rather than Soviet domination of the region. On this proposition basic U.S. and Soviet interests firmly overlap.

Finally, the third condition: the settlement of regional conflicts with a cold-war dimension and the development of new longer-run rules of the game. In the short run, intimate Soviet ties to Hanoi, Havana and Kabul might provide the basis for settlements in which the existing government would remain but would be effectively confined within its own borders without the presence of external military forces. But, clearly, no guarantees can be given to Moscow or Washington regarding the long-term political orientation of the countries concerned. (As this is written, the Soviet Union appears to be experimenting with a resolution of this type in Afghanistan; its terms do not appear consistent with prompt success.) This would work only if the United States and the U.S.S.R. agreed that henceforth they would live with outcomes determined by strictly local historical forces—an evidently difficult condition to live with given habits built up over the past 40 years. The Middle East would, of course, be extremely difficult to sort out in these terms, given the limited powers of the United States and the U.S.S.R. in the region. But, as elsewhere, those powers would be formidable if rooted in a joint conviction that the cold war was no longer a sensible framework for the conduct of U.S.-U.S.S.R. relations or the superpowers' respective relations with others.

In all cases, U.S.-U.S.S.R. understandings would be basic to a successful outcome, but the interests of many other states would be involved. Negotiations would therefore be complex. Moreover, the outcome would be stable only if new common rules were established and validated by successful experience. But once the expectation was established that all were engaged in transforming the cold war into something more desirable, the process might move forward quite briskly.

VIII

I am reasonably confident that this kind of scenario of how the cold war might end is realistic in that it conforms to historical forces likely to persist and gather strength. My uncertainty, however, is serious and comes to rest on two critical questions: one concerns the U.S.S.R., the other the United States.

The set of changes in Soviet relations with the United States, Western and Eastern Europe, and the developing regions implied by this scenario is quite significant. So are the changes required in Soviet society and its institutions to render the economy efficient and capable of absorbing in all sectors the remarkable flow of new technologies. As Marxists should be the first to acknowledge, technological changes of this magnitude require changes in politics, the language of politics, and the texture and institutions of social life. To use Khrushchev's good phrase, the age of "steel-eaters" is over.

It is easy to take the view that the Soviet political leadership, by some combination of Russian history, communist doctrine and institutional vested interest, is and will remain so deeply committed to indefinite expansion that only defeat in bloody war could bring about a resolution of the cold war—that is, the emergence of a Soviet Union which, like other latecomers, would come to accept fully that hegemony was beyond its grasp and that its primary task was to look after more conventional national interests in an increasingly complex, multipolar world by encouraging balance. Soviet leaders may even fear that such a change in perspective would undermine fatally the legitimacy of Communist Party rule over Russia. I am inclined to believe that, with the passage of time, the problem of legitimacy, however real it may have been earlier, has diminished. Perhaps the turning point was the Soviet role in the defeat of Germany in World War II. At the moment, one cannot help feeling that the viability of Soviet domestic rule hinges rather more on the progress of the economy than on the continued expansion of Soviet power. But Russia is unlikely to be exempted by history from the slow-working but stubborn and rising insistence of human beings on political systems that provide dignity and increasing degrees of human freedom. What matters, however, are not the views of external observers but the views of those who operate and live within the Soviet system.

In any case, I would judge that it is on the willingness of the Soviet leadership to make the requisite domestic changes that a soft landing depends; but the posture of the United States might affect that willingness to the extent that it generates in Moscow a sense of insecurity, security or revived hopes for hegemony.

This brings me to the second uncertainty: Is the United States, as a society, capable of a reasonably steady military and foreign policy? We have oscillated since 1945 between evasive illusions and feverish, belated efforts to halt or roll back Soviet expansionist initiatives launched to exploit those intervals of American myopia. We have survived on the basis of Dr. Samuel Johnson's dictum: "Depend upon it, Sir, when a man knows he is to be hanged in a fortnight, it concentrates his mind wonderfully." But our survival by periodic, belated, convulsive exertion has exacted great costs and imposed great risks on humanity in a nuclear age. After 40 years of cyclical behavior the leaders of both political parties ought to be able to unite on the need for a steady, long-term military and foreign policy.

Moreover, despite certain natural advantages, it is still to be demonstrated that American society and its political process will, in fact, make the necessary outlays for education and research, find a new generation of entrepreneurs and otherwise accept the discipline and flexibility that the age of the new technologies demands. Our performance thus far—especially at the level of national politics—suggests a society that prefers to go down in the style to which it has become accustomed rather than to grapple with reality.

Thus a soft landing from the cold war is an American as well as a Soviet responsibility; for a steady America, strong but not aggressive, paying its way in the world, conscious of the reality of its own interests as well as the legitimate interests of others, can help make the transition easier and more secure for the Soviet leadership. An America that once again slides into distracted complacency or continues to borrow rather than elevate productivity to sustain its amenities, could set in motion yet another cold-war cycle with potentially tragic results. The outcome might well be an extension of areas of chaos, including nuclear proliferation, beyond the capacity of either Moscow or Washington to control.

Be that as it may, the overriding lesson of the years since the Truman Doctrine and the Marshall Plan is that Soviet behavior cannot be predicted unless one answers the question: What is the Soviet view of the strength, unity and will of the United States?

AMERICA'S CHANCE[5]

Whatever success Mikhail Gorbachev has had in altering public attitudes within his own country, the new Soviet leader has had
an astounding impact in the West. A growing number of West European public-opinion polls show that Gorbachev has transformed the popular image of Soviet diplomacy. The British now
see the United States as a "greater threat to world peace" than the
Soviet Union by a margin of 37 per cent to 33 per cent. In spring
1987 slightly more West Germans believed that the head of the
Soviet Politburo was "really concerned about peace" than held
that view of the American president. Similar attitudes are developing in other key West European countries.

In the United States, suspicion of the Soviet Union is much
more deeply rooted than in other major Western countries; but
even here Gorbachev has made significant inroads. In 1986 the
Chicago Council on Foreign Relations conducted its quadrennial
survey of American attitudes on foreign policy. Its latest effort
revealed, not surprisingly, that Gorbachev is less popular than
leaders of countries allied with the United States. But the survey
also revealed that the average American now has almost as favorable an impression of the Soviet leader as of former President
Richard Nixon. And even such a pro-American alliance leader as
West German Chancellor Helmut Kohl was not too far ahead of
Gorbachev in American public esteem.

This Soviet success with Western publics has created a genuine problem for Western foreign-policy elites. Always before, the
impact in the West of Soviet peace initiatives had been limited to
the left side, indeed the far left side, of the political spectrum.
The popular appeal of such initiatives therefore was not wide
enough to affect policy in any significant way. But Gorbachev's
ability to attract support across the political spectrum in Western
countries opens a new chapter in East-West relations.

[5]Reprint of an article by Charles William Maynes, editor of *Foreign Policy* magazine. *Foreign Policy.* pp. 88–99. Fall '87. Copyright © 1987 by the Carnegie Endowment for International Peace.

Western governments are in danger of losing credibility with their own publics unless they stop being reactive and begin to develop an imaginative East-West program of their own to respond to the Gorbachev challenge. But attempts to develop such a program immediately pose a crucial question. Does the Gorbachev revolution represent a danger or an opportunity?

Already, attempts to answer that question are dividing the Atlantic alliance into two camps. Increasingly, the West European response, perhaps reflecting proximity or a longer historical view, is to suggest that the Gorbachev revolution represents an opportunity. Margaret Thatcher, the most conservative British prime minister of the century, has pronounced Gorbachev a man with whom she can work. Hans-Dietrich Genscher, the West German foreign minister, in a major public lecture urged that the West work with Gorbachev, who in Genscher's eyes presents the West with the possibility of a historic turning point in East-West relations. According to Genscher, "It would be a mistake of historic dimensions for the West to let this chance slip just because it cannot escape a way of thinking which invariably expects the worst from the Soviet Union." Lord Carrington, the secretary general of NATO, has suggested that Gorbachev is a reformer "opening up the Soviet Union to the outside world" and that this development "offers a greater hope of positively influencing developments within the Soviet Union where such a possibility barely existed in the past."

The American reaction to Gorbachev, reflecting perhaps a national tendency to expect the worst from the Soviet Union, is much more skeptical. President Ronald Reagan has challenged the Soviets to prove their sincerity by agreeing to a spectacular gesture: tearing down the Berlin wall. Senator Robert Dole (R.-Kansas), the Senate minority leader and a likely candidate for the Republican presidential nomination, speaks for many American observers when he warns that Gorbachev "is more dangerous and threatening to our country and to our ideals than all the brashness and bluster of a Khrushchev; all the stolid determination of a Brezhnev." The American fear is that if Gorbachev succeeds, the United States will face a foe with more resources for foreign expansion and ideological challenge. Thus former Secretary of State Henry Kissinger has argued that Gorbachev and his associates have the "intellectual equipment for a far more dynamic foreign policy than their predecessors."

It cannot be entirely an accident that virtually identical differences between European and American officials surfaced in the early 1950s when the alliance debated the significance for East-West relations of the reformist leadership that took control in Moscow after the death of Joseph Stalin. Then British Prime Minister Winston Churchill argued that Stalin's death represented a unique turning point in history. His successor as chairman of the Communist party of the Soviet Union, Georgi Malenkov, had begun to stress the categorical need for the world to avoid global war and had hinted at a major shift in Soviet economic priorities toward light industry. And President Dwight Eisenhower himself had declared Malenkov's statements "startling departures."

Churchill pressed for an early summit with the new Soviet leaders. But then Secretary of State John Foster Dulles argued that Malenkov's moves were purely tactical and, in a move startlingly similar to Reagan's challenge to Gorbachev to tear down the Berlin wall, began setting standards of performance with regard to Soviet policy in East Germany that the Soviets would have to meet before the West could judge the new Soviet approach serious. Churchill complained that "it would be a mistake [with Soviet Russia] to think that nothing can be settled with Soviet Russia unless or until everything is settled." But Dulles prevailed and Eisenhower delayed agreement to a summit.

Meanwhile, the Soviets were moving on a number of previously intractable issues: They accepted the Swedish statesman Dag Hammarskjöld as secretary general of the United Nations. They agreed to the Austrian peace treaty, which led to a complete withdrawal of Soviet occupation forces. They encouraged the armistice negotiations in Korea. And they renounced territorial claims on Turkey and established diplomatic relations with Greece, Israel, West Germany, and Yugoslavia.

America won the debate with Western Europe in the early 1950s with little cost to the Western alliance (even if there may have been a very high cost in terms of lost opportunities for East-West relations). The United States was then so dominant that Western Europe had little alternative but to follow. But alliance disagreements over East-West policy in the Gorbachev era could prove more damaging. Alliance fissures are greater now than in the 1950s. Economic and trade disputes over the size of the U.S. budget and trade deficits are widening them. And the Soviets are much more resourceful now than they were then in exploiting transatlantic disagreements. So it is especially important to examine the Gorbachev record carefully and dispassionately. To what degree do the foreign-policy changes thus far initiated by Gorbachev justify a conclusion that his arrival at the pinnacle of power in the Soviet Union represents an opportunity for the West and not a danger? The question cannot be answered without a brief review of his international record: What in effect has Gorbachev done?

He has altered the way Soviet leaders describe the world to the Soviet people, who can no longer look forward to yet another period of "further growth for the might, activeness and prestige of the Soviet Union and the other countries of the socialist commonwealth," in the words of the late Soviet leader Leonid Brezhnev. Now the Soviets face difficulties and implicitly cannot always get their way. The Soviet Union has reached a "turning point" both domestically and internationally. Continuity in foreign policy has "nothing in common with the simple repetition of what has already been covered, especially in approaching problems which have mounted up." In other words, Soviet citizens are being prepared for dramatic shifts in Soviet foreign policy.

Gorbachev for the first time has spoken to the Soviet people of the need for common security, recognizing that the outside world has legitimate concerns about Soviet power. He has permitted Western statesmen to express those concerns over Soviet television. He has informed his people that they should not expect the Western alliance to break up, given the West's strong economic, military, and political ties. Also, he has introduced to the Soviet foreign-policy agenda such global problems as the environment.

As part of what appears to be a new policy of becoming a more normal participant in the international community, the Soviet Union under Gorbachev has expressed interest in joining, as either an observer or a member, the General Agreement on Tariffs and Trade, the International Monetary Fund, and the World Bank. It has raised the issue of direct ties between the European Community and its communist counterpart, the Council for Mutual Economic Assistance, and has begun buying into the United Nations precisely at the time that the United States is buying out—making unprecedented contributions to U.N. peacekeeping operations it previously had refused to support.

In the highly sensitive field of arms control, Gorbachev has recast Soviet positions on intermediate-range nuclear forces, deep reductions of strategic forces, verification, and testing. To allay Western fears about Soviet conventional superiority, he has accepted a wider negotiating zone that would include the European part of the Soviet Union and has agreed in principle to on-site inspection for the first time in Soviet history.

Gorbachev also has taken important initiatives on a number of bilateral and regional issues. He has offered to reduce troops on the Chinese border, accepted the Chinese position on the location of the riverine border, proposed reducing to zero the number of medium- and short-range nuclear missiles deployed in the Far East, permitted Soviet envoys at least to discuss such sensitive issues as the Vietnamese occupation of Cambodia and the Soviet seizure of Japan's northern territories (the small islands above Hokkaido), and intensified negotiation efforts that might lead to a Soviet withdrawal from Afghanistan.

In regard to the Middle East, Gorbachev's diplomacy has persuaded at least some key officials in the Israeli Labor party that the Soviet Union would play a responsible role in an international conference designed to bring a peaceful settlement to the Arab-Israeli problem. To this end the Soviet Union has permitted Poland to establish an interests section in Tel Aviv, and Gorbachev himself has described the lack of relations between Israel and the Soviet Union as "abnormal." Several subsequent Soviet initiatives seemed designed to pave the way for a resumption of diplomatic relations between Israel and the Soviet Union. With respect to other regional hot spots like southern Africa and Central America, Gorbachev does not seem to have changed Soviet policy, but he also does not appear to have moved to exploit American vulnerability or to increase American embarrassment.

American Qualms

At first blush, there appears to be enough here for Americans to conclude that the West Europeans are right and that East-West relations face a historic turning point that the West should not allow to pass without a major attempt to forge a better relationship with the Soviet Union. Yet the Americans do have some important reasons for hesitating that should be discussed more openly than they are.

First, the record so far rests more on promise than on performance. In the 1950s, although the West did not follow Churchill's advice, the Soviet Union took many more concrete steps of conciliation than it has taken under Gorbachev. Soviet troops actually left Austria. They have not left Afghanistan. The Soviet Union actually recognized Israel then. It does not now. It actually facilitated an armistice agreement in Korea. It has yet to demonstrate a similar sense of urgency about the ongoing conflict in Cambodia. Under Gorbachev the Soviet Union has advanced sweeping arms control proposals. Under Nikita Khrushchev it actually reduced the size of the Soviet army by 1 million men.

Second, with regard to any Soviet leader there is the issue of possible rhetorical deception or policy reversibility. What guarantee is there that the Soviet Union will not say one thing today and do another tomorrow or simply change its policy abruptly from accommodation to confrontation? This possibility is especially troubling because the West knows so little about Soviet political life. Indeed, at times U.S. Sovietologists seem to resemble paleontologists more than other specialists in international relations. They collect a few helpful bones of evidence and from them claim that they understand the Soviet Union. But even those with the greatest erudition will, if pressed, concede how little they really know.

The problem of rhetorical deception or policy reversibility is, of course, not unique to the Soviet system of government. Leaders of democratic countries are not unknown to dissemble or change their minds. Reagan stated categorically to a joint session of Congress on April 27, 1983, that he did not seek the overthrow of the Sandinista government in Nicaragua. It is clear from subsequent events, however, that this statement, despite its solemn and categorical nature, was not true. As the elections of 1976 and 1980 approached, the presidential incumbents Gerald Ford and Jimmy Carter abruptly reversed their policies toward the Soviet Union. Ford banned the word "détente" from the U.S. government vocabulary and Carter embarked on a rearmament program that the Reagan administration only accelerated.

But there is a special problem with communist regimes. In the words of the late Soviet dissident Andrei Amalrik, "So long as questions of war and peace are decided by 10 men who are not accountable to anyone, no accords, however favorable on paper, will allow the Americans and Europeans a good night's sleep." In the United States, domestic and alliance pressures exercise restraint on a head of government who attempts to make a sharp change in policy. If these pressures exist in the Soviet Union, their strength is unknown, and that fact gives rise to uncertainty and concern abroad.

Because the Soviet system of government bestows on its top leader such extraordinary power over the country's fate, the West understandably fears that a clever leader may manipulate short-term policies of accommodation to serve a longer-term goal of confrontation. By contrast, for the United States to reverse course, several important centers of power must cooperate. Consider the difficulties the Reagan administration has encountered in Congress and with its allies as it has tried to change the U.S. interpretation of the Antiballistic Missile Treaty of 1972. Were a Soviet government to alter its interpretation, the Soviet position would be settled. It is still not clear that the Reagan administration will prevail in its new interpretation, even after several years of trying. Still another example of the inherent stability of the American system once a commitment is made is the perennial debate about the withdrawal of U.S. troops from Western Europe. The pressure for some withdrawals has been mounting steadily for nearly 20 years. But nothing has yet happened because every president has defended the status quo.

Ironically, then, a feature of the U.S. system that most presidents cite as a major weakness—the separation of powers and the proliferation of power centers in the formulation of foreign policy—is, from the standpoint of stable East-West relations, a potential source of strength. For under this system agreements are hard to reach but also hard to unravel. It is no accident that the arms control achievements of the period of détente have in their essence survived repeated assaults whereas other policy achievements of the period, such as the improved political relationship, quickly succumbed to criticism. The former were the result of a hard-fought agreement between the Nixon administration and Congress. The latter were often part of a public relations strategy designed to gain temporary political advantage for an unpopular president. The true promise of *glasnost*—Gorbachev's new policy of "openness"—is precisely that, over time, the Soviet system, although it is not likely to be democratized, at least will be opened up enough that foreigners can develop greater reassurance through greater knowledge. No single step by the Soviet leadership would do more to make possible steady improvement in East-West relations than continued development of *glasnost*.

So the West faces a dilemma. There seems little doubt that Gorbachev has launched a number of significant initiatives. From this standpoint the West European position is correct. But there also are legitimate reasons to hesitate. From that perspective, there is some merit to the high degree of American caution. What would be a sensible approach toward the Soviet Union in light of these conflicting considerations? Several steps seem advisable.

• The West should recognize its ignorance and state it openly so that the Soviets begin to comprehend a source of Western hesitation: No one understands the Soviet system well enough to know whether the Gorbachev era represents a danger or an opportunity. In short, Soviet secrecy deprives Western analysts of enough bones to construct the full skeleton. Moreover, even if the West did know more than it does about the domestic pressures that Gorbachev is trying to manage and concluded that it was in Western interests to see him succeed, it does not understand the Soviet system well enough to know how to go about that task effectively. The West should encourage more *glasnost* by constructive comments about new steps the Soviet Union might take.

• Recognizing its ignorance, the West also should not rush to negative conclusions. Western politicians do not know if Gorbachev is "more dangerous" than Khrushchev, just as they do not know if he is more benign. Indeed, there is a contradiction in the thinking of many Western observers who warn that the Soviet Union only wants reform at home in order to be more aggressive abroad later. Those who issue such warnings most vehemently are often the same individuals who believe most passionately that the Soviet system is bankrupt and beyond the point of reform. Western leaders must have enough confidence in their own system to believe that if the East and the West both concentrate on domestic matters for the foreseeable future, the gains in the West will outstrip or at least equal those in the East. Were Western leaders to lack this confidence, it could only mean that there were elements of the Soviet economic system that deserved more careful study in the West.

• Western leaders should recognize that there is a growing risk of losing support among their own citizens if they fail to be as bold as the Soviets themselves. It may well be that Gorbachev will prove to be not serious or to lack control if negotiations move beyond the current agenda to deal with some of the critical issues of the cold war—the overmilitarization of central Europe, the unpopular social order in Eastern Europe, a superpower competition in the Third World driven more by ideology than interest, and even the fate of Germany. But if Gorbachev is hypocritically bold while the West is disappointingly cautious, the Soviet Union will gain a cheap victory according to the old rules of the great-power game, and the West will never find out if it is possible to develop new rules for a new game.

• The West therefore needs to develop a policy of pragmatic but vigorous cooperation with the Soviet Union that will rest on the concept that each deal or agreement must stand on its own in terms of the advantages it brings to each side. But with that as the benchmark, the United States should begin to think the unthinkable politically, economically, and militarily.

Politically, Gorbachev seems to be trying to develop a less ideologically driven Soviet policy toward the Third World; hence the opening to such groups of states as the Association of Southeast Asian Nations. The United States should try to encourage this trend by resuming efforts to work out rules of the road, explicit or informal, concerning the superpower presence in the Third World—perhaps starting with Africa, where the strategic stakes for the two sides are not high. It probably will be easier for the United States and the Soviet Union to agree to cease and desist from certain areas of the world, such as certain regions of Africa, than it will be to discipline the activities of each according to some agreed rules. Each side needs to begin thinking rigorously about which actions of the other side it finds totally unacceptable in Third World states. In the case of the United States, what is it about communist or leftist Third World states, such as the regime in Nicaragua, that it cannot accept and that it can accept? Is it the very character of communism or is it primarily the tie to the Soviet Union, and what aspects of that tie are most offensive?

In the Middle East, U.S. policy has repeated by rote for nearly four decades that it was essential for the United States to keep the Soviet Union out of the area. But that is no longer in America's power, and continued U.S. efforts to achieve the impossible may now be retarding the peace process rather than accelerating it. The Soviet Union steadily is increasing its diplomatic presence in the area. It has major influence over the Palestinian movement, whose participation is essential in any settlement of the Arab-Israeli issue. Therefore, a more reasonable goal than total Soviet exclusion from the Middle East is arranging with the Soviet Union to manage the nature of the superpower presence in the area so that the presence is seen decreasingly as a security threat by either side. It is particularly important that the United States and the Soviet Union reach agreement on their policies during any political transition in Iran.

Economically, the United States should begin examining steps that can integrate the Soviet Union into the family of international economic institutions that also serve U.S. interests. It is becoming increasingly difficult to maintain the fiction that the Soviet Union and other communist countries play no significant role in the international economy. These countries now represent 25 per cent of the world's economic product and contribute 13 per cent of world trade. As these states continue their quest for development, they are bound to be more tied to the world market, which they already regularly influence or disrupt through involvement in Western financial markets and grain purchases. It makes sense to prepare for the day of their more complete integration and to begin developing a list of compliance steps the United States believes it is reasonable to ask the Soviet Union to undertake if it is to become a full standing member of the international economic community.

A good model for the United States to consider in developing a policy would be the European approach to the Helsinki process, a series of annual multilateral conferences, beginning in 1973, that aimed at fostering cooperation in a politically divided Europe. Then the United States was hostile to the very idea of a security conference in Europe. The Europeans developed an agenda of their own and opened up the human rights issue as their quid pro quo for an agreement in the trade and security areas. The result was a victory for both sides. Instead of simply rejecting the Soviet desire to join the international economic organizations as the United States and some of its allies have, the United States should develop a specific list of constructive steps, perhaps concerning the role of market forces or foreign investment, that the Soviet Union must take. These should be steps that the Soviet Union would find painful to reverse.

Militarily, the Soviet Union has put the United States on the defensive on arms control issues. The United States needs to come up with a list of steps that each side could take to defuse the situation in central Europe. Increasingly, it appears that America will withdraw some of its troops from Western Europe during the term of the next president. The United States should capitalize on the likely or the inevitable by packaging its decision as a constructive challenge to the Soviet Union. The lack of a Soviet response to a partial U.S. withdrawal might reduce pressures within the United States to carry out further cuts. Conversely, a constructive Soviet response might open the way for new steps by both sides that would tamp down tensions in central Europe. The United States also should develop proposals designed to press both sides to reconfigure their forces to reflect a defensive strategy. The suggestion of a tank-free or chemical-free zone in central Europe should be developed and pursued. At the same time, the United States should begin developing with the Soviet Union an informal code of conduct for European security to reassure each side that if military barriers did come down, neither side would exploit the situation through steps detrimental to the security of the other. Reliable verification would be essential not only to reduce the likelihood of cheating but also to compensate for the lack of transparency in the Soviet political system.

Before an opportunity can be exploited, it must be established that one exists. It is clear from numerous statements and actions that Gorbachev believes that the Soviet civilian economy is doing badly and that the USSR needs a respite internationally. It is not yet clear whether this development presents the West with a major opportunity. But if the West is ever to find out, NATO countries, particularly the United States, must have the courage and the self-discipline to develop a constructive policy that will test Soviet intentions. The time for boldness is now—certainly in thinking and perhaps even on occasion in action.

BIBLIOGRAPHY

An asterisk (*) preceding a reference indicates that the article or part of it has been reprinted in this book.

Books and Pamphlets

Afghanistan: torture of political prisoners. Amnesty Int. '86.

Alekseeva, Liudmila. Soviet dissent: contemporary movements for national, religious, and human rights (tr. by Carol Pearce and John Glad). Wesleyan Univ. Press. '85.

*Anzovin, Steven and Podell, Janet (eds.) The evil empire (speech). Reagan, Ronald. From Speeches of the American Presidents. H. W. Wilson. '88.

Bialer, Seweryn. The Soviet paradox: external expansion, internal decline. Knopf. '86.

Bialer, Seweryn. Stalin's successors. Cambridge Univ. Press. '80.

Cohen, Stephen F. Sovieticus: American perceptions and Soviet realities. W. W. Norton. '85.

Duffy, Gloria. Ever vigilant: the role of the military in Soviet society. Transaction Books. '87.

Dyker, David A., ed. The Soviet Union under Gorbachev: prospects for reform. Methuen. '87.

Frankland, Mark. The sixth continent: Mikhail Gorbachev and the Soviet Union. Harper & Row. '87.

Gilbert, Martin. Shcharansky, hero of our time. Viking. '86.

Gorbachev, Mikhail. Peace has no alternative: speeches, articles and interviews. Patriot Press. '86.

Gorbachev, Mikhail. Perestroika. Harper & Row. '87.

Gorbachev, Mikhail. A time for peace. Richardson & Steirman. '85.

Hewett, Ed A. Energy, economics, and foreign policy in the Soviet Union. Brookings Instn. '80.

Hill, R. J. and Frank, P. The Soviet Communist party. Allen & Unwin. '83.

Hough, Jerry F. The struggle for the third world: Soviet debates and American options. Brookings Instn. '86.

Kahan, Stuart. The wolf of the Kremlin. William Morrow. '87.

Laird, Roy D. and Laird, Betty A. A Soviet lexicon: important concepts, terms and phrases. Lexington Books. '87.

McCauley, Martin, ed. The Soviet Union after Brezhnev. Holmes and Meier. '83.

McCauley, Martin and Waldron, Peter. The emergence of the modern Russian state. Barnes & Noble Imports. '87.

Medvedev, Zhores. Gorbachev. W. W. Norton. '86.

Millar, James R., Jr. Politics, work, and daily life in the U.S.S.R.: a survey of former Soviet citizens. Cambridge Univ. Press. '88.

Nye, Joseph S., Jr. The making of America's Soviet policy. Yale Univ. Press. '84.

Oberg, James E. Uncovering Soviet disasters. Random House. '88.

Pipes, Richard. Survival is not enough: Soviet realities and America's future. Simon & Schuster. '84.

Reed, John. Ten days that shook the world. Bantam. '87.

Saivetz, Carol R. and Woodby, Sylvia. Soviet–third-world relations. Westview Press. '85.

Shevchenko, A. N. Breaking with Moscow. Knopf. '85.

The Soviet Union, 2d ed. Congressional Quarterly. '86.

Thubron, Colin. Where nights are longest: travels by car through western Russia. Atlantic Monthly. '87.

Yanov, Alexander. The Russian challenge. Basil Blackwell. '88.

Zinoviev, Aleksandr. Homo Sovieticus (translated by Charles Janson). Gollancz. '85.

PERIODICALS

GORBACHEV'S GAMBLE

Gorbachev's policy innovations. Brown, Archie. The Bulletin of the Atomic Scientists. 41:18-22. N. '85.

A Soviet turning point. Cracraft, James. The Bulletin of the Atomic Scientists. 42:8-12. F. '86.

Signs of a Soviet shift. Sigal, Leon V. Bulletin of the Atomic Scientists. 43:16+. D. '87.

*Will Gorbachev reform the Soviet Union? Bukovsky, Vladimir. Commentary. 82:19-24. S. '86.

The legacy of Stalin. Minard, Lawrence and Brimelow, Peter. Forbes. 138:156+. D. 1, '86.

Gorbachev and economic reform. Goldman, Marshall I. Foreign Affairs. 64:56-73. Fall '85.

Gorbachev and the third world. Fukuyama, Francis. Foreign Affairs. p. 715+. Spring '86.

*Gorbachev: a new foreign policy? Simes, Dimitri K. Foreign Affairs. 65. Sp Issue: 477-500. '87.

*Gorbachev's move. Bialer, Seweryn. Foreign Policy. pp. 59–87. Fall '87.

Gorbachev: the road to Reykjavik. Larrabee, F. Stephen and Lynch, Allen. Foreign Policy. 65:3–28. Wint. '86/'87.

Can the Russians reform? Galbraith, John Kenneth. Harper's. 274:52–5. Je. '87.

What Gorbachev wants. Sestanovich, Stephen. The New Republic. 196:20–3. My. 25, '87.

Gorbachev's bottom line. Peterson, Peter G. The New York Review of Books. 34:29–33. Je. 25, '87.

Orlov provides perspectives on Gorbachev's reforms (interview). Sweet, William. Physics Today. 40:79–82. My. '87.

Who really rules Russia. Barron, John. Reader's Digest. 127:113–17. Jl. '85.

How Gorbachev sees the outside world. Jones, Peter M. Scholastic Update (Teachers' edition). 118:18+. Mr. 7, '86.

*On Soviet history. Gorbachev, Mikhail. Tass. N. 2, '87.

*Can He Bring It Off? Sancton, Thomas A. Time. 130:30+. Jl. 27, '87.

The world according to Gorbachev. Duffy, Brian. U.S. News & World Report. 101:15–20. O. 20, '86.

U.S.S.R. foreign relations. Gorbachev, Mikhail. Vital Speeches of the Day. 54:130+. D. 15, '87.

Shifting Soviet diplomacy. Barthos, Gordon. World Press Review. 33:20–2. O. '86.

The new thinking. Malcolm, Neil. World Press Review. 33:17+. D. '86.

THE USSR IN TRANSITION

The ordeal of Afghanistan. Keegan, John. The Atlantic. 256:94–105. N. '85.

Reforming the Soviet economy. Galuszka, Peter and Javetski, Bill. Business Week. 76+. D. 7, '87.

Petropower and Soviet expansion. Epstein, Edward Jay. Commentary. 82:23–8. Jl. '86.

Economic problems in the Soviet Union. Goldman, Marshall I. Current History. 82:322–5+. O. '83.

Afghanistan at war. Rubinstein, Alvin Z. Current History. 85:117–20+. Mr. '86.

Soviet dissent since Brezhnev. Sharlet, Robert. Current History. 85:321–4+. O. '86.

The Soviet economy. Gorlin, Alice C. Current History. 85:325–8+. O. '86.

The continuing Soviet war in Afghanistan. Kamrany, Nake M. Current History. 85:333–6. O. '86.

Bits of life in a grey world: cultural life in the Soviet Union. Medvedev, Roy. Dissent. pp. 46+. Winter '87.

Glasnost (Soviet Union; special section). Film Comment. 23:33-8+. My./ Je. '87.

*Mad Russian. Batchan, Alexander. Film Comment. 23:48+. My./Je. '87.

The war in Afghanistan. Karp, Craig. Foreign Affairs. 64:1026-47. Summ. '86.

Reforming the Soviet economy. Steinberg, Bruce. Fortune. 112:90-2+. N. 25, '85.

Glasnost and the Russian revolution. Dukas, Paul. History Today. 37:11+. O. '87.

A face-to-face interview with Soviet atheist leaders. Edwards, Frederick. Humanist. 47:8+. Ja./F. '87.

Some reflections on religion in the USSR. Thrower, James. Humanist. 47:21+. Ja.-F. '87.

New thinking in foreign policy (Soviet initiatives). Evangelista, Matthew A. The Nation. 244:795-9. Je. 13, '87.

*The nationality question. Suny, Ronald Grigor. The Nation. 244:808-10. Je. 13, '87.

A poet's view of glasnost. Voznesenskii, Andrei. The Nation. 244:810-12. Je. 13, '87.

The émigrés speak out. The Nation. 244:812+. Je. 13, '87.

Reforming Soviet culture/Retrieving Soviet history. Condee, Nancy P. and Padunov, Vladimir. The Nation. 244:815-20. Je. 13, '87.

Can the Afghan rebels win? Strmecki, Marin. National Review. 38:32-4+. Jl. 4, '86.

The tenth year of the Watch (symposium on Moscow Helsinki Group). The New York Review of Books. 33:5-6. Je. 26, '86.

Russia: a people without heroes. Shipler, David K. The New York Times Magazine. 28-34+. O. 16, '83.

Where glasnost has its limits (trying to get published in Novy mir). Voinovich, Vladimir and Zalygin, Sergei (tr. by John Glad and Marie Arana-Ward). The New York Times Magazine. 30-1. Jl. 19, '87.

*Home from Afghanistan. Keller, Bill. New York Times Magazine. pp. 24+. F. 14, '88.

The catastrophe (visiting places related to the Afghan resistance). Lessing, Doris May. The New Yorker. 63:74-90+. Mr. 16, '87.

A hard bargain (freeing of A. Sakharov and E. Bonner; special section). Newsweek. 109:12-23. Ja. 5, '87.

*Yevtushenko feels a fresh wind blowing (interview). Vanden Heuvel, Katrina. The Progressive. 51:24-31. Ap. '87.

Different degrees of candor. Blake, Patricia. Time. 128:68-9. D. 15, '86.

*Surging ahead. Lemonick, Michael D. Time. 130:64+. O. 5, '87.

The Andropov era (symposium). World Press Review. 30:39-44. Ja. '83.

How We See Them

*Four decades of irrationality: U.S.-Soviet relations. Shulman, Marshall D. Bulletin of the Atomic Scientists. 43:15-25. N. '87.

Can the democracies survive? Revel, Jean-Francois. Commentary. 77:19-28. Je. '84.

The latest myths about the Soviet Union. Eberstadt, Nick. Commentary. 83:17-27. My. '87.

U.S.-Soviet quality of life: a comparison (address, May 22, 1985). Schifter, Richard. Department of State Bulletin. 85:70-5. S. '85.

Dealing with Gorbachev's Soviet Union (address, April 8, 1986). Armacost, Michael H. Department of State Bulletin. 86:63-6. Je. '86.

Human rights and Soviet-American relations (address, October 31, 1986). Shultz, George Pratt. Department of State Bulletin. 86:26-9. D. '86.

*The Soviet constitution: myth and reality. Schifter, Richard. Department of State Bulletin. 87:34+. O. '87.

The agenda of U.S.-Soviet relations. Reagan, Ronald. Department of State Bulletin. 87:4+. D. '87.

*On ending the cold war. Rostow, W. W. Foreign Affairs. 65:831+. No. 4. '87.

*America's chance. Maynes, Charles William. Foreign Policy. pp. 88+. Fall '87.

The perils of reporting from Moscow. Taubman, Philip. New York Times Magazine. pp. 60+. S. 21, '86.

A visit to Russia. Galbraith, John Kenneth. The New Yorker. 60:54-65. S. 3, '84.

Both continuity and vitality. Talbott, Strobe. Time. 125:22-3+. Mr. 25, '85.

The Soviet Union (address, November 29, 1984). Audigier, Pierre. Vital Speeches of the Day. 51:246-8. F. 1, '85.

Glasnost (address, March 13, 1987). Wick, Charles Z. Vital Speeches of the Day. 53:418-20. My. 1, '87.

Glasnost (address, March 11, 1987). Bukovsky, Vladimir. Vital Speeches of the Day. 53:596-600. Jl. 15, '87.

The Soviet challenge to democracy. Courter, Jim. World & I. pp. 137+. Ag. '87.

Should the West help? Tatu, Michel. World Press Review. 34:12+. Ap. '87.